Maternal Identity
and the
Maternal Experience

Reva Rubin was Professor and Director of Graduate Programs in Maternity Nursing at the University of Pittsburgh when this book was being written. Prior to this, she was on the faculties of the University of Chicago, Bridgeport University, Yale University, and the Frontier Nursing Service, and served as area supervisory nurse to the American Joint Distribution Committee in the American Zone, Austria.

Ms. Rubin's other positions have included: program consultant for the American Red Cross, the National Foundation (March of Dimes), the Office of Economic Opportunity, and the World Federation for Planned Parenthood; research consultant for the Children's Bureau and several universities and hospitals; curriculum consultant on graduate programs at many university schools of nursing; member of the steering committees and executive committees of the National League for Nursing and the American Nurses' Association in the Divisions of Maternal-Child Nursing. Author of some 20 to 25 articles and books, she has also been co-editor of the *Journal of Maternal-Child Nursing*. She is now retired.

Ms. Rubin holds a BA from Hunter College (Sociology), an MN from Yale University (Nursing), a CM from the Frontier Nursing Service (Midwifery), and an MS from Yale University (Mental Health Nursing). She has been admitted to candidacy for the Ph.D. at the University of Chicago (Human Development). In addition, Ms. Rubin has been awarded fellowships by the World Health Organization and the Rockefeller Foundation.

Maternal Identity
and the
Maternal Experience

Reva Rubin

Springer Publishing Company
New York

No part of this publication may be reproduced, stored in a
retrieval system, or transmitted in any form or by any means,
electronic, mechanical, photocopying, recording, or otherwise,
without the prior permission of Springer Publishing Company, Inc.

Springer Publishing Company, Inc.
200 Park Avenue South
New York, New York 10003

84 85 86 87 88 / 10 9 8 7 6 5 4 3 2 1

Library of Congress Cataloging in Publication Data

Rubin, Reva.
　Maternal identity and the maternal experience.
　Bibliography: p. Includes index.
　1. Pregnancy—Psychological aspects.　2. Identity (Psychology)　I. Title.
[DNLM: 1. Maternal behavior – Nursing texts. 2. Self concept – In pregnancy – Nursing
texts. 3. Body image – In pregnancy – Nursing texts. 4. Pregnancy – Nursing texts.
WY 157 R896m]
RG560.R83　1984　　618.2′001′9　　83-20375
ISBN 0-8261-4100-5

Printed in the United States of America

Contents

Preface

This book is written for nurses and other health and helping professionals addressing the needs and care of women in the maternity experience. The judgments that make for the art in professional practice are based in good measure on how much is understood of the woman's subjective experience of a situation at a given time. Recognizing the subjective situations, experience, and objectives of the childbearing woman enriches the effectiveness of the skills brought to bear in the practice of a science motivated by compassion.

Helping, whether instrumental or expressive, is an interactive process between giver and receiver that enhances both—a complementary partnership in a humane symbiosis, transitory but significant in situational time. The aim of this small volume is to promote the helping process by a systematic descriptive analysis of the subjective maternal experience.

More than six thousand women as patients provided the subjective experience data in a program of advanced training and research in maternity nursing leading to the Master of Nursing and Doctor of Philosophy degrees at the University of Pittsburgh. The programs of study were supported over a period of twenty years by the Children's Bureau, the Maternal-Child Health Services, and the Research Training Division of the United States Public Health Service. Magee-Women's Hospital with its rich variety of clinical services and personnel for the delivery of eight thousand women annually was the major clinical facility.

The method of data collection was modeled on that of the naturalist in the field. While giving nursing care in nursing uniform, we listened and observed. There were no interview or observation schedules. The primary question was: How does this woman feel about herself in this situation at this time? Extensive population sampling was done weekly or daily from the first missed menstrual period through pregnancy, delivery, and the sixth week postpartally. Patient selection was deliberately made to include the normative and deviations from the norm in age, parity, obstetrical history, complications of pregnancy and delivery, and the condition of the newborn as well as in marital status, race, nationality, education, and social class. Beyond these criteria for selection, each woman defined her situation behaviorally or verbally at the given time and experience in childbearing. In addition to the cross-sectional study patients, one hundred women served as tracers or longitudinal subjects through the entire childbearing, childbirth, and neomaternal childbearing experience. In addition to the regularly scheduled antepartal visits and hospitalization, nurses were on call for labor, for referral visits, for emergencies, for home visits and care, and for telephone contact.

A subsidiary question we asked was, "How do women use nursing help in each stage of the childbearing experience if nursing is available and accessible?" The normal services to the medical profession and to the hospital were assumed by faculty and staff to permit the availability and accessibility of the nurse to the patient without interruption for an identified period of time (two, three, or four hours) or for an identified experiential segment (antepartal visit, labor and delivery, or a morning or evening postpartally). This led to a much more extensive use of nursing by the women in their orientation to and their coping styles with the physical, social, and perceptual problem situations as these occurred.

Again on the model of the naturalist, the content of the data-collecting session was recorded at the completion of each session. The experiences of the patient and her behavior, verbally and nonverbally, were recorded in the sequence of occurrence and verbatim for expressive and communicative speech.

The protocols averaged ten typed pages for each observation hour except in labors of eight to twelve hours, where behavioral change in time spans is infrequent and observer fatigue is a real factor. For a situation such as labor, an observation schedule is necessary for reliability of nonverbal behavior recording.

Content analysis was done on the recordings. The unit of analysis was a complete behavioral unit of Subject (the woman), the object or referrant, and the action. By establishing a unit, measurements of change within and between sessions and within and between individuals at a particular stage or situation of childbearing could be made.

The analysis of the women's behavior, attitudes, and concerns has benefited from the work of others. These workers are cited in the bibliography. But we have to cite the particularly useful and insightful work of Helene Deutsch, Theresa Benedek, and Erik Erikson, of Paul Schilder and Karl Pribram, of Heinz Werner and Kurt Lewin, of Jean Piaget and Jerome Bruner, and of Talcott Parsons. Their work has influenced the conceptual style of analysis. The analysis has also benefited from testing and feedback from the women themselves in the continuing process of practice and data collection.

The presentation that follows is descriptive of the women's subjective experience in childbearing. The language is sometimes a direct quote or a paraphrasing of a collective representation. The organization by chapter headings is derived from content analysis of the central themes relevant in the subjective experience of childbearing. The organization by central themes relevant to the women themselves through the entire childbearing experience is, I believe, illuminating and useful. The reader accustomed to an organization by the situational sequence of pregnancy, labor, delivery, and postpartum may find repetitiousness as the thematic approach is carried through longitudinally and in progressive interaction, one theme with another, for a more complete description of the facets and factors in the holistic and purposeful subjective experience of childbearing.

I wish to express here my appreciation and gratitude to the women who as patients taught me most about wisdom, courage, and the creative process; to the students and faculty who shared the excitement and pleasure in learning; to my colleagues in this country and abroad who tested the findings as they were published or presented against their own observations and experience; to Dr. Florence Erickson and Dr. Judith Dunbar for their support and assistance in the drafting, editing, and preparation of the manuscript for publication.

Maternal Identity
and the
Maternal Experience

1

Introduction

There are two generally held beliefs about the origins of maternal behavior and its significant qualitative characteristics. One is that maternal behavior is "instinctive" and the other is that maternal behavior is formed in early childhood in doll play or in practice with siblings, in direct copy of the mother's behaviors. The original source, cause, or force which is set in motion genetically or in the early formative years is presumed to be inexplicably dormant for a period of twenty years, more or less, and then arises, epigenetically, in full flowering with the birth of a baby. The event of childbirth is assumed to be the releasor mechanism for the endowed or programmed maternal behaviors, attitudes, and character. Once these maternal behaviors and qualities arise, they continue as an irresistible force unchanged, except perhaps in velocity, for all subsequent children.

These concepts of the origins of motherhood are an amalgam of nineteenth-century thought and theory. Epigenesis was also the explanatory concept of the genesis of the child: the child stood in the uterus as a full blown but miniaturized adult awaiting birth. Even casual observation should have invalidated this theory. But paintings of children during this period portrayed a miniaturized adult. Child-rearing was based on the premise of the adult in miniature and made child labor rational and acceptable.

Today we recognize a series of nested and articulated stages of childhood in a progressive development toward adulthood: fetal, neonatal, infant, toddler, preschool, and school-age child, preadolescent, and adolescent. This differentiation makes for better understanding, a considerably less harsh environment, and a much more effective utilization of people power in a society.

Early childhood behavior is no longer considered to have such an overdetermined formative effect. In the nineteenth century the adage about childhood was, "as a twig is bent, so grows the tree," and there seems to have been a lot of twig-bending. Doll play is now recognized as no more relevant than the equally explorative role play of a child playing house, store, school, or baseball, in all of which the child also prefers the dominant position.

The "instinctual" or "inherent" explanation perseveres for a class of behavior which is not understood and for which an explanation is not available. Maternal behavior in general is often subsumed as instinctive, in the explanatory category of "don't know." There is nothing particularly mysterious or exotically sex-linked in the activities of feeding, bathing, protecting, or teaching the young. Enduring love, altruistic self-denial, and empathy are not exclusive to the maternal woman or to the mother–child relationship. And yet, together, these actions within the matrix of affinal bonds comprise the characteristics of maternal behavior which are seen as the bottom line. It is this sum total of maternal behavior that is explained away in attribution to instinct.

Attribution of "instinct" to a class of behavior connotes the normal, the natural, and the expected. Being normal or natural are desirable attributes. But being programmed for expected maternal behavior, at a level of function such as breathing and elimination, denies the volitional effort, the creative interplay of resources, and the consummate control of action in time and space required in the execution of maternal behaviors. When the instinct bias is confirmed in selective animal or primitive tribal behaviors as evidence, or as a model, for "natural" or expected maternal behaviors, the reductionism becomes an outrageous denial of the persona of the woman as mother.

There is nothing preprogrammed or prepackaged in maternal behavior. Maternal attitudes and behaviors change in relation to the age, condition, and situation of the child. Nurturant behavior for the six-week-old child may take the form of feeding, bathing, and dressing but for the sixteen-year-old child it may take the form of paid employment for the child's college education. The amount and kinds of proximal contact with the child are very different when the child is a baby, a schoolchild, or an adolescent. The content and mode of communication change with the developing, changing child: the cooing, sing-song, and higher pitched voice that is so enchanting to the baby is replaced by the crisp, concrete, and message-filled sentences for the schoolchild, and by the abstract level discourse with the adolescent. The infant is carried into the environment, but the environmental resources are brought to the older child who is immobilized in illness.

The mother of two or more children relates her behavior to each child according to its age, sex, condition, and situation at the time. Concurrent childrearing requires a variety of styles and forms of maternal behavior. There is a versatility in mothering a pair or several children, each on a separate and individual axis, simultaneously. It is only with identical twins of the same mental and physical condition that maternal behaviors can be the same for two children. This may be a contributing factor in the very similar behaviors or personalities of identical twins. All other children of the same mother share a family resemblance, but each child is uniquely different from his siblings in personality and style of interpersonal transactions. The individuated axis of each mother–child relationship is also manifest in the child's awareness of an exclusive relationship with his mother, one separate and independent from the shared experience with siblings of the same mother.

The adaptability and innovativeness of maternal behaviors in relation to the developmental capacities and limitations of the child as well as the versatility in maternal behavior appropriate and relevant for each and all children in the same time-space frame, signify a high order of intelligence. The maternal intelligence is derived from a deep and extensive knowledge base of each child, continually refreshed and refurbished in perceptive experience and in feedback from the child. This is an open intellectual system and not a prepackaged bundle of traits, instinctive or otherwise, superimposed mechanistically for built-in obsolescence or entropy.

All behavior, manifest or latent, originates in the mind, in the cognitive processing of subjective experience. The most striking characteristic of maternal behavior is the openness to new and additional learnings, the silent organization in thought, and the high value placed on knowing.

It would seem more relevant and more serviceable to look for the origins of maternal behavior in the phenomenological and subjective experience of a woman becoming a mother. The ideal theory or theories should explain the phenomenological and subjective experience of women becoming mothers in validatable terms and in a way sufficient to provide testable hypotheses for the variations in the human experience of mothering. This would include the child who is premature, or stillborn, who fails to thrive or is congenitally handicapped or deformed, is a twin, or is battered. This would also include the woman who herself is a young teenager or an "elderly" primipara or multipara, who is delivered by caesarean section or after a difficult and prolonged labor, who is physically handicapped, or who chooses not to be a mother. The ideal theory would distinguish between the genotypically or universally maternal and the phenotypical expression by social class and cultural style.

Helene Deutsch's (1944) work on the psychology of women is the singular achievement of this ideal goal to date. Her approach is developmental. Cognitive, biological, and social development of the feminine person are traced in their relationship, in their interface and interaction, from early childhood through puberty, adolescence, childbearing, and the menopause. Deutsch's concept of development is not of linear increment or of steps over time. Like George Santayana (1942) and Jean Piaget (1973, 1977), she conceives mental development to progress as a spiraling, a widening in scope of capacities and experience at advancing points of the life stream for increased hierarchical forms in mentation and behavior. The spiral stages are effected by a confluence of novel biological and social developments. Elements of the previous stage are regrouped to accommodate the novel elements in experience: there is articulation, transformation, and consolidation into the personality structure and then progression to the next stage.

At the beginning of each novel stage, the capacities available for accommodation and regrouping are those of an earlier stage. There are essays, trials and errors, explorations, and searches for further elements to incorporate and to transform the available resources to meet the new situation of the self. In childhood these essays and explorations are acted out, usually in play. In adulthood these are as often carried out silently, in thought, as in action. When there is cessation of these essays and explorations before articulation and consolidation occur, there is an arrest in developmental progression.

Following puberty, for example, there may be a surge of sympathy for those who suffer or who are deprived. The sympathy is not an identification with such persons but is a sense of noblesse oblige, as the protector and defender. Both identification and protector elements were present in prepubertal stages, but with a more highly developed capacity for identification than for protection. But in puberty the protector elements surface and are developed in practice essays. When this new development is articulated, incorporated, and consolidated into the personality structure, it often progresses into the next stage of development as a career choice or in the adoption of social causes. During the preceding trial and error essays there is a somewhat romanticized seeking of an object-person who is socially dispossessed, rejected, misunderstood, or unappreciated. The surge in sympathy in search of an object-person usually occurs in a series of short adoption essays. From the parental perspective, these object-persons and the nature of an adolescent girl's generosity are seen as excessive, bizarre, or hazardous. From the adolescent's point of view the parents are without understanding or misanthropic.

In the female's early adolescent stage, about thirteen to fifteen years of age, there is a period of essays in what Deutsch terms "mother's helper" and a parallel course of sexual arousal and experimentation. If there is a pregnancy as a result of heterosexual experimentation, the girl's intent is to give the baby to her mother and the concept of her relationship to the baby is as to a younger sibling. At this age-stage, the acts of caring for her biological child are perfunctory and begrudging, rarely self-initiated, and performed with neglect, indifference, or antipathy. The biological mother at this age-stage wants to become an adolescent, not a mother. A few years later when the same girl becomes a mother, she is clearly maternal in behavior relative to her child and very unlike an older sibling "stuck" with the baby.

Theresa Benedek's (1949, 1959) formulations focus in greater depth on the experience of being pregnant and on the nurturance of the newborn. Both Benedek and Deutsch address the unity of mother and child in childbearing and its uniqueness in the human experience. Deutsch uses the model of the living cell and carries the analogy of reproduction of the daughter cell from union to polarization to form two distinct living entities. Benedek uses the model of symbiosis with each member, mother and child, complementarily contributing to the wholeness of the functional unit.

Deutsch's analogy is more dynamic and illuminates the phenomena of separating out, first from the pregnancy for delivery and then in the puerperium from the unity as one to the union as two. Deutsch also explores the motivational wishes that promote the incorporation and sustain the unity during pregnancy. Since these are the most critical periods in childbearing, Deutsch's contributions have considerable significance.

Benedek's model is more richly descriptive though less dynamic. But she pushes the analogy of symbiosis too hard and ignores phenomena not supportive of the thesis. Symbiosis with discontinuities as violent as childbirth could not endure. A symbiotic relationship beyond pregnancy would be a disaster to the woman, the child, and the family. There is more substantive evidence of separating-out and individuation than of preservation of the unity postpartally. Nevertheless, Benedek cites lactation and breast-feeding as the exchange maintaining the symbiotic unit. A mother provides the milk; the child in his sucking effects the let-down and maintains the supply of milk; the suckling at breast promotes uterine contractions to prevent hemorrhage and ensure involution; antibodies in maternal milk provide the baby with higher resistance against infection and there is less risk of food contamination. Both mother and baby thrive in the complementarity of needs and reciprocity of actions.

It is in the explicit recognition of the child as a significant and contributing partner in the shared experiences of childbearing, childbirth, and childrearing that Theresa Benedek makes a unique and highly useful contribution. The maternal–child relationship, like all relationships, is anchored in the complementary mutuality of two partners. There is no maternal behavior unrelated to a child.

Each maternal–child relationship is uniquely different. Each pregnancy, each delivery, and each childbearing experience is different for the same woman with more than one child. There is a different child, unique and independent of any other child. There is a woman who herself is different in age, historical experience, and life situation in the birth order of her children. The woman who has a stillborn child cannot replace that child or that relationship with another child. Another child, like another husband or another parent, involves another relationship, separate and independent of the previous relationship.

The simultaneous coexistence of two or more ongoing maternal–child relationships, each with its own independent axis, is unique among human relationships. Polygamous or polyandrous relationships are seriated in time and place. Animals empty the nest of all previous offspring before the arrival of a newborn or a new litter. The human mother is so bound in by the mutual and reciprocal experiences over time with her older child(ren) that there is no replacing and no discarding for another child. On the contrary, there is a drive to maintain the equivalence of each separate relationship in immediate time and space. In the secundigravida, particularly, there is a sense of guilt in relation to the first child with the arrival of another child, as though in infidelity or in bigamy. There is a deliberate effort to maintain and to promote the well-established ties with the first child with time, companionship, and interest. The urging of children to share and to take turns is not only instruction in ethical conduct but a necessity for one mother maintaining co-equal relationships with two or more different children.

The contributions of one partner to another are asymmetrical in the maternal–child relationship. When the child matures to the point of symmetrical equivalence in contributive power with the mother, the relationship changes. The affiliative bonds loosen in their complementarity and reciprocity as the child matures, but they endure in sentiment. The bonds result from the qualitative context of shared experience and form the basis of further shared experiences. For the child, the qualitative experiences and bonds lie in the origins of the self and the lendings of maternal ego to supplement the self in survival, enhancement, and potentiation. For the woman, the bonds are more complex and derive from the qualitative bonds with her husband, particularly, and with her society generally, as well as with the child itself.

Without the functionally supportive system of affiliative bonds with husband, family, and relevant social groups, the early bond formation with a child tends to be thin, tenuous, and friable. Through babyhood, particularly, the child is too weak a partner to support the reciprocity required in bond formation. A woman binding-in, becoming a mother in the qualitative and affiliative context, actively recruits the functionally supportive behaviors of persons with whom there are strong affiliative bonds: husband and mother, family and friends. There is a direct relationship between the strength and function of the intrafamilial bonds of a woman and the quality and strength of her binding-in to the child.

The asymmetrical relationship and affiliative ties place the child predominantly in the role of recipient and the woman predominantly in the role of maker and giver. No act of giving is completed unless and until it is received. So, even in the action and context of the act of giving, a receptive and responsive partner is necessary for completion of the act and the intent of giving. In giving food to an infant, for example, it is the infant as partner in the transitive act who must suck, swallow, and retain what is offered for the act of giving to be completed.

It is pleasurable to be able to give, but this pleasure is produced only if there is a receptive and appreciative partner in the act. The mutually gratifying experience of feeding/eating, giving/receiving is a reciprocal exchange, a tie in the relatedness of two persons. In pregnancy a woman nurtures her baby and then seeks signs or evidence that what she has given has been well received: a child thriving on her giving. There is no maternal behavior or action that is a solo performance, independent of the child. There are behaviors in behalf of the child in which the child does not participate immediately or directly, but these are still "gifts," hopefully or predictably to be received by the child.

Without feedback from the child as partner, maternal behaviors are uncertain, oscillating in direction, and subject to entropy in the dissolution of relatedness. The firmer the bond of relatedness, the more resistance there is to dissolution. A woman will seek third-person interpretive inputs, evaluative feedback, and alternative behavioral intiatives to maintain an open and viable relationship. It is in the ties of other relationships and in the openness to their inputs relative to the child or to her own maternal behavior that a woman maintains the mother–child subsystem as an open system.

At the onset of the childbearing experience, however, there is no object of attachment, no relationship with another with whom to form affiliative ties. There is only the idea of a child, as abstraction, as possibility. There can be romantic ideas about a child. But the idea of having a child is only half of the equation. The other half of the equation is the subjective experience of becoming and being a mother. The prospect of becoming the bearer and giver in pregnancy, in labor, and in delivery is a costly and hazardous prospect. This giving involves giving up or giving away of the physical, mental, and social self. The more intellectually and experientially mature the woman, the more the subjective side of the equation predominates to increase the costliness of having a child.

The more significant the idea of a child is to the self and the woman's family, the more balanced the equation. It is the family of persons, their aspirations and their sharing in the giving processes, that lends weight and helps balance the equation during childbearing, childbirth, and the neomaternal stress periods. Abortion, prematurity, toxemia, placement in adoption, battering, and infanticide always have a deficiency or negative weighting by the family support system in the equation: "To have a child = to be a mother."

The supportive sharing by significant persons is not so much a matter of dependence but a necessary condition for the giving of self in the totality required for childbearing. A woman is quintessentially social and the transaction modality is in mutual and reciprocal giving and receiving (not give and *take;* a woman has trouble with *demanding* and *taking*.) Unlike members of the animal kingdom, a woman does not retreat into isolation for childbirth or for exclusive possessivity in childrearing. On the contrary, a woman moves closer to family, and to society, during the intense experience of childbearing and childrearing. There is neither a biological urge nor a biological necessity for a woman to reproduce. There is a volitional act of lending oneself, one's life space and life course, for the very significant giving to another. The wish to give a child to her husband, primarily, to her parents and/or children, secondarily, and by extension to society generally, is the primary motivation for childbearing. It is irrelevant whether the wish occurs before or after conception: her husband gives her a child and she makes and gives him a child. The mutual and reciprocal sharing in self-deprivation, in order to give or to receive a child, supports the pregnancy and the nascent maternal–child relationship.

Within the context of the supportive relationship a new and enduring relationship with an unknown and unknowable individual is begun. There is an incorporation and elaboration of the idea of a child and of an idea of a self as mother of this child into the woman's self system and self-concept. The psychological incorporation is interdependent and symmetrically parallel with the biological development of the fetus and the pregnancy. The incorporation is a progressive binding-in, a progressive investment of self in ideation and behavior, in active adaptation and accommodation, to both sides of the equation of having a child and of becoming a mother.

There is a cognitive mapping of the "I" and the "you" and a constant reformulation of the "I" in relation to the concept of "you." This mapping is the predominant behavior during pregnancy and continues through the neomaternal/neonatal period until the identity of this child and the reciprocal maternal identity are fully constructed. The conceptual interweaving of the reciprocal and instrumental self in relation to the stage of identification of the child binds the woman into this unique relationship mentally as well as biologically.

It is the child itself who actualizes the relationship. Beginning early in the fourth month of pregnancy, the sporadic fetal movements, the visible prominence, and the impact of his presence on the woman's bodily appearance, function, and activity convert the impersonal abstraction, *a* child, into a specific *this* child. The baby in utero communicates, surprises, responds, and makes a woman feel good about herself. There is some mutuality, some reciprocity, and there is a sense of unity in wholeness and oneness. The unity is such that it is difficult to distinguish what is self and what is baby; what happens to self happens to baby; what happens to baby happens to self. Delineation of what is self and what is baby is begun after childbirth in a process of individuation and boundary formation. The separating out of polarization into two discrete individuals to form a union of two is more complex and more difficult than the binding-in process of pregnancy. The unity of identification (what happens to the child happens to self) perseveres beyond pregnancy and beyond the individuation process to become the special empathy of mother with child that is characteristic of the maternal identity.

Maternal behavior, behavior in relation to or in behalf of the child, begins in the fourth month of pregnancy in direct interface with the condition of the child. There is a style in dressing, eating, activities, and socializing that recognizes and considers the child and the unity of the relationship. There is quickening of interest in learning more about the "you" and an elaboration of the scope and meaning of maternal protection and nurturance.

The attributes and meaning of protectiveness and nurturance are elaborated, squared really, as a product of interaction with the cognitive mapping of the substantive "I" and "you" to become four articulated and interdependent maternal tasks. The objectives of the woman's efforts during pregnancy are (1) to ensure safe passage for herself and the baby through pregnancy and childbirth, (2) to ensure social acceptance for herself and her child, (3) to increase the affinal ties in the construction of the image and identity of the "I" and the "you," and (4) to explore in depth the meaning of the transitive act of giving/receiving. Each woman addresses these maternal tasks in relation to her existing situation and with the resources currently available to her so that there is a distinctively personal imprimatur in maternal behavior in relation to the tasks of childbearing.

It is the goal-oriented maternal tasks, the subjectively perceived conditions for the successful outcome of childbearing, that establish the qualitative matrix of the particular actions in maternal behavior. Although all four task areas are advanced progressively during pregnancy, the blocking of either of the first two tasks arrests the pursuit and furtherance of the remaining self-assigned tasks.

The geometric progression of the interaction process that sustains the pregnancy and promotes the maternal identity is severely stressed in childbirth. Until childbirth, the bonds with the child are those of the pregnancy experience, a fantasy of what the child will be. The experience of the child in labor and delivery is, however, very different. The affiliative support system, particularly husband and mother, has to be augmented by a knowledgeable and skilled support system to sustain the existence of the "I" and the "you," mother and child. But not as a unity: the separating-out from the psychological unity has already begun in the antipathy toward the restrictions of the situation and condition of pregnancy at term and progresses during the course of labor. Survival in intact wholeness is paramount for self and for child: for each and for both.

The loss of the child, in death or in placement for adoption, terminates the further development and extension of the relationship but does not eliminate the bonds and investment of self in the maternal identity already achieved. An overwhelmingly difficult labor or a debilitating illness following delivery temporarily arrests the progression in development of the maternal identity. An incomplete or handicapped baby disrupts and gives pause to the furtherance in development of the maternal identity.

When the delivery is successful and both mother and child are well, intact, and whole, there is a charge of energy to ascertain the precise nature of the "you" in the relationship. There is an identification and a thorough construction of the appearance, features, functioning, and personality of the child. There is a fine tuning of the reciprocal "I" in relation to the nature of the child, its sex, size, and condition as neonate. The identification of the child and of self in relation to the child marks the neomaternal phase. The security in knowing the child and knowing herself in attitude and behavior in relation to the child that characterizes the maternal identity is markedly different from the preceding neomaternal phase.

The biological experience of childbearing serves to promote or to inhibit the incorporation of a maternal identity in relation to this child into a woman's self system. The rising levels of estrogens, progesterone, and circulating blood volume not only sustain the pregnancy but sustain the wish for a child in the improved sense of well-being. The state of well-being promotes perceptivity and philosophic centration on the ideal and ethical conduct in interpersonal relationships. The withdrawal of this biological support system at the time of delivery leaves the same woman in oscillation between elation at achieving a successful outcome of pregnancy and depression because of her low levels of energy, of intactness, and of well-being in the stage following delivery.

The increasing size of the pregnancy, at first very welcome, becomes burdensome and restrictive to motor and social activity late in pregnancy. The thinning abdominal wall, the indeterminable body boundaries, and the restriction in freedom of movement induces a heightened sense of vulnerability. Coupled with the increased level of binding-in to the child, the vulnerability is one of double jeopardy. The restrictive limitations and vulnerability promote readiness to separate out from the pregnancy. However, the juxtaposition of the image of the size of the baby and the body image in the act of the delivery is inhibiting. There is a starting and a stopping of labor in a conflict between holding on and letting go for delivery.

The restriction in motor and social activity also serves to constrict personal and interpersonal space and subjective time. The constriction in time and space enables the woman as mother to interface in the extremely limited spatial and temporal spheres of an infant. This capacity is a major qualitative attribute of maternal behavior and a preeminent condition for childrearing.

The capacity of a woman to enter and occupy both the child's and the adult time-space frame interchangeably is a remarkable and important achievement. In this the family and social support systems are again significant factors.

It is in the self-image, however, that the biological experiences and the psychosocial aspirations and realities are intermediated to sustain and to promote the maternal identification and maternal bonds with the child.

2

The Self and the Body Image

Experience is mediated in the self. The self is really a system of selves in open communication and transaction with each of its parts as well as with persons and events in the surrounding world.

There are two dimensions in the personhood of the self: self as subject, "I," and self as object, "me," "myself." There is a human tendency to stand aside and conceptually observe self as object, to communicate and transact "I" and "myself" somewhat as with another person. The "I" as self can see, hear, and feel "myself." There is, however, a fluid interchange between self as subject and self as object: "I" can feel "myself" becoming angry, "I" am angry and "I" can berate "myself" for becoming angry.

There is dialogue between "I" and "me," sometimes friendly, approving, or supportive and sometimes accusatory, critical, or demanding. The dimensional bipolarity of the self and fluidity of exchange of self as subject or as object form the energy field for thought processes. Language is essential to the dialogue within self. When language is inadequate, ambiguous, or vague, the dialogue can be circularly repetitive, frustrating in its amorphousness and in its nonproductive consumption of energy. In such instances the supply of a word or term as article, as definition, or as relationship can be a relief. The opportunity to relate a problem to another person also provides relief from the circularly repetitious impasse in the ordering of phenomena and in the clarification of ambiguities for the linear and sequential properties of speech.

There are three spheres of the self in which the self as subject and as object operate: ideal self, the known or actual self, and the body self. These spheres are conceptual images of the self. Imagery does not require language. When images are converted into language for speaking purposes, they are transposed into similes or metaphors, into analogies. Images are reflections in the mind's eye, an encapsulatory summary of a felt experience of the self in action or interaction. Because images are generated in situational action, they tend to be fragmentary and as transitory as the action situation itself.

Ideal Self

The ideal self is a person's own creation, a composite of bits, elements, or images of attributes or qualities identified out there, outside self, that one aspires to as part of self. Once a desired element is acquired as part of the self or the body image, it no longer exists in the sphere of the ideal. The ideal keeps on renewing and restocking, raising and refining the levels of aspiration as earlier elements of aspiration are acquired and incorporated into self. Ideal images of the self generate wishes and hopes and bring the future self into the current, ongoing conceptions and transactions.

The sphere of the ideal self is dominant among spheres of the self in time situations or stages of becoming. Childhood, puberty, adolescence, young adulthood, and childbearing are characterized by wishes, hopes, and idealism. The distance or gap between the ideal and the actual self in action and in capacity, however, is a void that can generate depression and despair.

The self system is open to society as a human ecosystem. It is through the ideal self that language, customs, values, and mores of society or social subgroups are transmitted. The transmission is not a force superimposed by society on the individual. The individual as "I" searches out selected elements that appear or are modeled in the accessible social ecosystem and that are relevant to the ideal self. The relevant elements change with age-stage and with conditions and situations of the individual. There is a quick trying on of the element in imagery for goodness of fit with self and self-potentiation and then a subscription to or an adoption of the desirable attributes. As the life space enlarges developmentally, the ecosystem enlarges, becomes more varied, and provides a larger pool for selection and adoption of desirable attributes.

Self-image

The self-image is at a more accessible level of awareness, has language for its expression and transactions, and is usually what is meant in the concept of self as subject or object. The self-image is constituted out of the spheres of ideal and body selves but has its own additive features in the self system.

The self-image incorporates the aspirations of the ideal self as a guide or standard of behavior. There is a measurement of self against the standard of the current image of the ideal self. When elements of the ideal self are achieved, there is pleasure in the image of self, narcissism. There is an expansiveness of the self-image and self-esteem, a "can-do" effect, in narcissism. The pleasure is gratifying and bears repetition in telling or showing others and in repetition of the achievement. Beyond the novelty in acquisition of an element of the ideal, the pleasurable surprise and delight in self attenuates in habituation. The acquired element is no longer an ideal but a small element of the self. Children have more experiences in the surprise and delight in discovering that they can do or can be what previously was only a wish or an impossible dream and are more unabashed in their narcissism than adults. Adults are unimpressed with their non-novel achievement in something like standing up or being able to walk—unless, of course, the adult has lost the ability to stand up or walk and these attributes and skills are wished for, strived for again and again, and then achieved.

Attaining idealized elements is serious work consisting of trials, errors, and practice for effectiveness and competence. En route to achievement there are felt experiences of rebuff, frustration, rejection, and hostility. The self-image mirrors the self in action, not only in observation but in evaluation, too. As evaluator and judge, the self can be a remorseless and relentless critic. Feelings express the bottom line of self-assessment in a particular action or endeavor.

Frustration results when one is ready for, perhaps even capable of, desirable actions but external circumstances are not coordinated or brought into alignment for enactment. Organization and coordination of one's own actions in relation to external events and situations is a major goal. Whereas the social space around one becomes the source of attractive elements for one's ideal image, the self-image arises from action in and interaction with the physical and social world. For actualization, for survival, and for potentiation, one is dependent on the world in which one finds oneself. Experiences and awareness of the self arise from the actions, interactions, and responses of the social and physical world around one at all stages of life (Schilder, 1970).

In states of physical and mental wellness there is an embrace of the world and a joy in living in this world at this time. In depression and despair, feelings arising from severely critical self-evaluations, there is withdrawal from the outside world. In short depressions, withdrawal times are used for reevaluation and correction, a shaping-up in order to reengage in life in the world.

There is a need, a drive, to learn, to know, and to understand the reality of the physical and social world. This knowledge is essential to self. The need of the self to know generates most of the elements of the ideal image. The surprise in being knowledgeable and in discovery of a new fact, as element or as relationship, is very pleasurable and reason for very positive self-evaluation (Pribram, 1963). Knowing what, how, when, where, and why in information bits and establishing the relationship of one bit with another, as well as their relevance to a larger context of reality, are of major importance in the self-image. The capacity for this intricate and complex knowing and understanding of relationships characterizes the adult person.

Knowing permits recognition. Recognition is a valuable acquisition, serving to conserve and to maximize living time and living energy. Recognition seems to be even more pleasurable than discovery of knowledge. Humor, laughter, and smiles are evoked by recognition. The self is enhanced in good, satisfying equilibrium and continuance with the world. Failure in knowing or in recognition leads to self-depreciation—seeing oneself as "stupid." If the failure is manifest in action or interaction for the world to see, the resultant feelings are of embarrassment, shame, or humiliation.

The sphere of the self-image is the concept of self in action and in response to the physical and social world. Self-imagery functions as organizer and mediator, promoting or inhibiting productions of the spheres of ideal and body imagery in relation to the perceived exigencies of the world around us and in relation to the self-concept. The capacity for self-observation, evaluation, correction, and action makes the sphere of self-imagery the regulator, much like a homeostat or governor, of the self system.

Body Image

The sphere of body imagery plays a central and fundamental role in the structure and function of the self-image. It is body imagery that delineates and orients the self as an entity in a world (Schilder, 1970). Bodily sensations, postural tonus, mass, and movement provide the information for body imagery. In states of good health the informational inputs serve as feedback to action and are subliminal to awareness. Changes or disruptions in any facet of informational feedback command awareness. Sleepiness, hunger, an eyelid twitching, dizziness, fatigue, a leg falling asleep, and itching are disruptions in the normative subliminal background of informational inputs. The self-awareness in body imagery serves as an early-warning signal for self-preservation or survival by preempting all attention of the self and arresting, at least for the moment, all motor activities. The redirection and focus of attention inward and cessation of all other transactions permits identification and assessment of the change or disruption.

It is from the long axis of the body that one orients oneself in physical space. Up/down, right/left, anterior/posterior involve a location on the body and then a projection of this location outward into physical space (Schilder, 1970; Wapner and Werner, 1965). The two-step process of introjection to body-self and then projection outward is so facile and instantaneous that it goes unnoticed except in the developing child acquiring a sense of direction and in the adult orienting to a new space situation. In the recumbent position in a strange space setting the adult is more deliberate in locating a point in space by correcting the image of the body's long axis to the vertical, locating the point, and projecting the located point into space. Adults make fewer "mistakes" in correcting for the position of the long axis of the body than children.

In the same way, estimates of height and distance are made. Another person's height is introjected, or one's own height is projected against the other's, and height estimates are measured in terms of one's own body image. Distance is measured by the amount of energy available and the duration of time that energy has to be exerted. Distances are much longer and much farther to the child, the handicapped, and the convalescent than to the adult in a state of well-being. The adult is more capable of estimating distance by trial in imagery. The adult can "try on," through imagery of the body in action, energy demand, and duration in time to anticipatorily determine subjective distance. In fatigue or convalescence, this capacity is a conservational and preservational capacity, "foresight" (Pribram, 1963).

The same capacity to project the image of one's own body in action in physical space operates for anticipated events and situations. Conditions of another person can be tried on in body imagery as experience in body tonus and resultant subjective feelings. This results in empathy for another (Schilder, 1970). When imagery is elaborated in fantasy to include scenarios of situations with the given conditions, this can result in insight. The plasticity of the body image in introjecting and projecting itself into a possible condition or situation, with involvement in muscular tonus and assessment in feeling outcomes, promotes survival, potentiation, and humaneness.

There are postural images of the body-self in action (Schilder,

1970). These postural images of position and tonus are taken as models for enactment of activities such as sleeping, going, fighting, resting, visiting, waiting, listening, speaking, or being entertained. Positions and tonus of the body are changed to effect the postural model of self for a specific action. There is a readying of position and tonus of self for expected activities of confrontation, engagement, or passivity, a "righting" reflex. The posture of confrontation does not permit engagement or passivity and the posture of passivity does not permit confrontation or engagement.

Clothing or dressing the body is an extension of the postural model (Flugel, 1969; Schilder, 1970). There is an image of the self in an action setting or situation, and clothing is chosen on the basis of the anticipated self in action in the anticipated situation. There is clothing of the body for swimming, for housecleaning, for church, for work or school, for not going anywhere, for dining out, for being an executive, for being a bride, and for being pregnant. The wrong clothing inhibits or prevents participation in the action setting. There is a "righting" reflex, based on the postural model of self in action, to change clothing for a change in activity setting.

The body boundary is a vital phenomenological image of the body-self (Schilder, 1970). There is a boundary defining self, containing and demarcating self as an entity separate from the surroundings.

The body boundary comprises the integumentary system—skin, hair, and nails—plus a radius of at least two centimeters. The radius is increased at the body orifices: eyes, nostrils, mouth, ears, and rectum. The radius is still larger at the genitalia, the breasts, and the neck. The integumentary system serves to protect against invasive organisms and destructive blows that are inimical to survival. The integumentary system is also a supportive, encapsulating system that incorporates and contains the vital organs and systems and their contents. For sheer survival the intactness of the integumentary system is mandatory. There is a degree of tolerance in the intactness of the integumentary system for abrasions, lacerations, and first degree burns; for contusions and fractures; for hernias, prolapse, and rupture; and for bleeding, vomiting and diarrhea. But an extension in degree and irreparability is fatal. The body boundary image with its increased radius at the more vulnerable zones of the body serves as an additive protective and preservative layer of defense.

There is a reflexive, autonomic response to threatening or unwarranted intrusions into the body boundary. There is a movement of the threatened body zone away from the threatening object and a recruitment of the adjoining tissues by constriction or contraction to cover the threatened site. The hand is often also recruited as added coverage of the threatened site. The eyes are fastened on the threatening object whenever possible. Some body sites have additional protection: the eyelids and the sphincters of the rectum can be shut very tightly. The mouth can gate-out threatening objects at either the lips, the teeth, the tongue, or the pharynx in gagging or vomiting. Blows to the mouth, however, elicit the whole protective response: movement away, contraction of the mouth, and adjacent facial tissues, including the forehead, and recruitment of the hand to intervene and cover the mouth. A slow but threatening approach to the skin surface, as of the forearm or the nape of the neck, will elicit a contraction of the erectile hair follicles, "goose bumps." There will be a sensation as though the skin were crawling; there will be a pulling movement away and an impulse to cover the site with the free hand.

The child whose ear is to be examined shifts away from the speculum, contracts his shoulder up, and bends his head down simultaneously to cover the ear on that side. The person who is about to have a rectal catheter inserted contracts the rectal sphincter and the surrounding gluteal muscles to cover the rectum and moves away from the catheter. A woman responds to the approaching vaginal speculum by bringing her knees together to cover the vagina and moving her entire body up, away from the speculum. The protective response occurs before the approaching or threatening object touches or hurts. That is the purpose of the protective response.

The constrictions and contractions of the adjoining tissues and the threatened site produce muscular tension that is painful and tiring. The urge is to move away and to be free, but in many engagements with threats to intactness flight is unwarranted, counterproductive, or impossible. The pull to escape and the push to stay with the situation increase tension in the conflicting struggle between the protective response for body boundaries and the self-image of self-control.

Reflexes can be inhibited or controlled under the power of the developed self-image. The protective response is fortunately never obliterated. With experience, acceptance of the legitimacy and necessity of body boundary intrusions, such as in the medical examination, occurs and the tension is distributed in an effective "holding on." The person subject to expected intrusions into the body grasps some object tightly so that the hand does not move and intervene between the hypodermic needle, the speculum, or other penetrating object and the threatened site. The chair arm, the mattress, or a helping hand is grasped tightly, aggressively, to hold on. The urge to move away from the threatening object is also countered by pressing the body down hard on the bed, into the chair, or onto the floor. Usually the sight of the approaching threatening object is avoided by fixing the gaze on some neutral object, while holding on aggressively to a neutral, safe object. The breath is usually held, suspended, to hold on to immobility. Permitting intrusion into the body boundary takes work, concentration, and tension. There is fatigue from the body efforts and the self-controls to be passive, to endure, and to permit the breaking of the body boundaries.

The skilled nurse or doctor tries to reduce the defensive protective response by traversing the body boundary in a neutral, deliberately separate step. Before an intrusive procedure, the free hand is placed in open and full contact on a zone adjacent to the site of penetrating entry. The less threatening transgression of the body boundary with contact reduces anticipatory tensions. The laying on of hands in full palm is perceived as caring, not threatening. Manual contact can be augmented with verbal contact in a neutral, flat tone of voice. The tactile qualities of voice also enter the body and can be penetratingly sharp, and therefore threatening, or can be steadying and caring. Educational or diverting messages, however, are perceived to be demands superimposed as an added burden to tension and stress.

Once the body boundary of a given site is broken and the body is penetrated, the tension of the protective reflex disappears. The tension no longer has purpose; there is no longer a recruitment of body tissues, parts, or posture for protection of the self. A battery or a succession of intrusive procedures, however, puts high demands on the capacity for controls. Each threat to the body boundary is a painful signal for awareness in recruitment and mobilization of defenses.

The newborn baby has no body boundary image and no protective response. The eyelids and rectal sphincter of an infant do close on direct touch, but there is no protective zone at these two points. When a needle or lance is put through the skin of a newborn, there is a delay of a second or two before the newborn responds. The toddler also has more delayed responses and few protective responses. Until awareness of the boundary of body-self is developed, the child is highly vulnerable to risks to survival. The protective response is also evoked in temperature change, but the young child is not aware or protectively responsive to temperature threats such as burns or freezing.

The infant and baby, with no body boundary, respond reflexively when not in deep sleep to an object as small as a finger, a nipple, or a feather by turning toward the point of contact, a tropism followed by full responsive contact. The face is more fully developed for this response. When any object touches the cheek of a baby not asleep or satiated, he will turn his head and open his mouth. He will also then bring his hands and his feet up toward the object in his mouth so that his body is curled up around the object. He will turn his head toward the point of touch and bring his arms and legs up toward that point in responsive contact when his neck is washed, a shirt is pulled over his head, his pants are changed, he is held against a nice warm breast, or he is pushed forward by pressure on the back of the head. On a more microscopic scale, he will also curl his tongue around a nipple or finger in his mouth and move his jaw upward to encompass the object in his mouth more fully. This tropism and encirclement of the contacting object may be another kind of protective response for the newborn and the baby. It does enable him to grasp, within his limitations, succorance and nourishment. Its manifestation in cuddling, touching the nourishing breast, and curling his toes while eating is endearing. Babies who are ill or damaged have reduced muscular tonus for this response to contact.

Established body boundaries become diffuse in conditions of pain. A throbbing head or other body part presents an image of boundlessness—of no boundary containing and confining the head or the pain. A severe toothache aches through the head, the limbs, and the torso. The ache spreads, the boundaries dissipate, and there is no separation of body-self from the surrounding environment. There is an obliteration of awareness of events and situations around one, and an increased vulnerability to noxious stimuli such as loud noises that impinge as tactile or pressure stimulation on the body. The subjective response is to move the hands to the painful site, to contain by pressure if necessary; and to restore the boundary manually. As long as the body boundaries are diffuse, there is reduction in self-control and in localization of the pain. In the diffusion of the boundaries of the body-self there is a recognition that one is not one's self at the time. Body boundary and ego boundary become identical.

The inner contents of the body are an undifferentiated solid mass in the body image (Pribram, 1963). The undifferentiated mass is the substantive body-self. Height and weight are indices of the substantive body-self. The short and frail person has an image and feeling of being less substantial. The tall, well-developed adult male radiates the substantivity and self-confidence of the solid body mass. The obese person seems to need excessive substantivity for adequacy or presence. General attitudes and behaviors forming personality characteristics evolve from the body image of the substantive mass of the body. Personality characteristics will, therefore, change with physical growth and conditions of episodic or chronic illness. Personality characteristics have an inner consistency but also considerable flexibility. The body image orients and defines the self in relation to a world of people and events. Thus, a boy can feel of diminished substance in relation to his father one moment and of significant substance in relation to a younger, smaller child the next moment, with a change in self-confidence that is immediately apparent in his attitudes and behavior. Similarly, the substantive and self-confident father will have a change in attitudes and behaviors in relation to the burly policeman.

The inner contents of the body mass remain essentially unknown, amorphous, and indistinguishable. The sensory organs of sight, sound, touch, taste, and smell are located on the skin surface and are directed outward, not inward to the body. Information about the inner contents and functions of the body are therefore indirect, secondary, or inferential. In good health and well-being, good tonus and energy, skin turgor and color, appetite and assimilation, physical, mental, and motoric function—indirect indicators that all systems are functional—there is no awareness of the background informational feedback of the body-self.

Adequate functioning is the predominant qualification of the inner contents of the body mass. The substantive body-self is defined in functional terms. Adequacy, competence, and excellence in body function are the essential measure of self-worth and self-esteem. In this, there is no dichotomization of mind and body: the brain and nervous system are body structures whose adequacy in functioning is as essential to self-esteem, to survival, and to potentiation as any other structure and system of the body. Inadequacy, incompetence, or loss of function in any system—mental, reproductive, respiratory, circulatory, motoric, or vegetative—is a disaster. There is no system that is expendable in functioning as a whole person. Wholeness is dependent on the synchronized function of many parts; one system is not more valuable than others. The absence or loss of function in even a relatively small aspect of the variety of functions within a system— insomnia, inability to conceive or to bear weight on a foot, loss of vision or hearing—produces a bereavement for the self as a whole, integral person.

Whatever the cause, loss of a bodily function is subjectively experienced as a disintegration of the body-self. In the instance of not being able to stand up and bear weight, the fear of disintegration occurs whether the cause is a momentary circulatory disturbance, a postoperative or infectious debilitation, a fracture, or a stroke. The differential in diagnosis lies in the probability of reversibility and recovery of function. There are, however, many moments of doubt and despair about the ability to walk again, to recover function, in conditions of fracture or debilitation. There are also many moments of mourning for the formerly whole and functional self in self-pity and in hostility towards the inadequate and incompetent present self. Since orientation to time and space is from the current body image, immobility makes the present time seem like eternity and the future seem very bleak.

There is a spread-effect in the loss of function in one part of the body to the loss of many functions. The spread-effect of functional loss is strikingly similar to that of the spread-effect in pain. The person who cannot stand and bear weight cannot get into a sitting position, turn, or bathe or dress himself and cannot effect transactions in physical and social space without enabling help. The initial and sustained spread from a particular to a more general loss in functional capacity produces a sense of powerlessness and helplessness. Dependence is an improvement over helplessness in that functional capacities are augmented and strengthened into effectiveness by another. But dependence is not a desired state. Children hope to grow out of dependence and adults hope to be delivered from dependence in a miracle of recovery and reconstruction of the integrity and wholeness of the functional body-self. There is pleasure in function, whether enabled by the help of another or not. But there is no pleasure in the helplessly dependent state, only hostility, resentment, and death wishes.

The inner contents, the substantive mass of the body-self whose functional capacities are necessary for self in action in a world, are only partially distinguishable anatomically. The schematas of the internal organs are those of still life drawings: two-dimensional diagrams demonstrating one system unrelated to any other system. Converting the diagram out there into the subjective inner spaces presents problems in goodness of fit. Because of the characteristic of pain to radiate or to be referred, pain also does not adequately serve in the location of inner structures.

The consequent vagueness in discrimination of the source of hemorrhage, pain, or infection induces anxiety or fear, painful alerting emotions. Localization of the source by touch or visualization and identification of the structure or syndrome by name serve to reduce the painful alerting emotions. Localization has a containment effect. A diagnosis defines, contains, and places the organic attack under control. The underlying image of the body in bleeding, pain, infection, or tumors is of progressively invasive and destructive degeneration or consumption throughout the amorphous mass of inner contents. Even the loss of memory or inattentiveness for a small series of items evokes images of degeneration and loss in the brain and mind.

Some of the inner contents of the body appear on the body surface and are subject to visual, tactile, olfactory, and auditory investigation and familiarity. The exudates and productions of the inner body mass tend to be shapeless, sticky, slippery, and malodorous: sputum, nasal discharges, cerumen, urine, feces, discharges from pustules or blebs, perspiration, blood, halitosis, vomitus, semen, or vaginal discharges. Children, with their poorly developed olfaction and fewer body discharges, are relatively sanguine and nonaversive to these discharges. The adolescent has a sudden increase in bodily discharges and these become indicators, representative of the inner mass: amorphous, slippery, malodorous, hairy, and dark. The adolescent has a particularly hard time with his inner substantive self—"if you really knew me, inside, you wouldn't like me"—and oscillates between shame and a great need to be accepted, to be popular. The pregnant woman ready to give birth has images of what she is about to produce from her body as amorphous, without shape or skin, dark, hairy, slippery, and malodorous.

Blood is a special case of inner contents. Blood is contained in arteries and veins, but blood also bathes and perfuses all internal organs. Blood is the transmitter of nourishment and sustenance to the vital organs and the substantive self. Blood belongs inside and any seepage at the orifices or on the surface is accompanied by the apprehension—the panic-alerting response. Any excessive flow of inner contents outside the body, as in vomiting or diarrhea, is alarming. But the flow of blood in even small quantities is alarming. The fear is that the flow will not stop. The tension relief is marked when even slight bleeding is stopped or the open site is covered or packed to hold the blood back. But this does not prevent the removal of the Band-aid, the scab, or the bandage to make sure the blood is not coming out.

There is a difference between giving blood and having blood taken. Giving blood is a courageous and generous act and the transfusion is of one's substantive self to another. Having blood taken, however, is a preemptive incursion on the self to be endured, but not graciously or generously: "blood samples" are too many and too much.

In terms of the subjective experience with the inner contents of the body, the biological mother's intensity in proclaiming her child as her own flesh and blood cannot be taken just as a figure of speech but as an experience in body imagery. Like all verbal expressions of body imagery, this statement is not made during actual experience of pregnancy and childbirth but later. Nevertheless, the image does much to explain the universal fear of delivery, the holding on and holding back in labor, and the dread of the initial sight of the delivered baby.

Body images emanate from the inner spaces of the self in the service of self-preservation, survival, and potentiation in the world.

From this centered position, there is an orientation of self in action, mentally and physically, in the world. The sphere of the self-image originates in the body imagery but is centered on engagement in action and transaction in the surrounding world. The sphere of the ideal image adopts desirable elements (not persons) from the outside world for self-enrichment and potentiation. The self-image, in its origin in the body imagery sphere and its bias for competence in action in the world around us, mediates between the spheres of ideal self and body-self, monitors self performance in the discourse between the "I" and "me," and evaluates outcomes in performance in an expression of feeling.

The self system is part of the world and the world is an inseparable part of the self system (Schilder, 1970). The personal world of action and transaction in physical and social space changes over time so that the life-space in each stage or in each decade of a lifetime is progressively different in scope and demands on competence. The experiential world is not a Cultural, Social, or Class abstraction, but an encompassible microcosm of relatedness in mutuality and reciprocity.

Events and situations in the experiential world occur in the here and now. Self-reflective imagery and action, in thought and in manifest behavior, occur in the here and now. Past events and situations become a part of the historical self. It is the historical self, cumulative and distilled for redundancies, that forms the formal and informal learnings and knowledge base and the inner sense of continuity and consistency of the self in a world of action.

3
The Developing
Feminine Identity

There is a knowing, a concept of self as feminine. A feminine identity exists as soon as there is an awareness of a self, as early as the second year of life. The feminine identity develops and changes in direct relationship to biological, cognitive, social, and environmental developments and changes. Maturation into adulthood is not the end point of the developing and growing feminine identity. As long as there is a life, as long as there is a self, there is a feminine identity.

The feminine identity is essential for orientation and definition of the self and of the outside world. The underlying stability and consistency of the feminine identity promotes accommodation and adaptation in an enlarging and changing interpersonal and physical space during the lifetime.

There are times of instability or diffusion of the sense of identity as a woman. Massive physical and physiological change, such as at puberty, childbirth, and the menopause, or following a mastectomy or hysterectomy, destabilizes the identity as feminine, the orientation to self, and the value or worth of self. Infertility, miscarriages, a stillborn or a defective child produce traumatic misgivings about the competence of self as a woman and as a person of worth. In such an experience, there is a marked reduction from active engagement in the prevailing physical and social world.

Feminine Identity in Preschool Ages

In the beginning, with only sporadic awareness of a self and in the absence of body boundaries, there is no evidence of an identity. There is a difference in motoric behavior of babies even while still in the uterus by gender: boy babies tend to be more angular and more rapid in the movements of their bodies and body parts; girl babies move about as much as boys do, but their movements are less angular, somewhat smoother. But these are objective and comparative observations and statements of general tendency by gender. Babies are more similar than dissimilar, but by the age of nine months, the personality is elaborated clearly as male or female. But personality is the obverse of identity. The subjective experience of being, of self, does not include comparisons or generalizations of central tendency at this age.

With development of the erect posture, increased movement in space, improved muscular tonus and control, speech, and intelligence, selfness develops rapidly. Self is more than gender, but gender is mandatory for a self-image, a self-concept. By the third year a little girl knows that she is a little girl so well that she can make comparisons, inquiries, and generalizations about gender.

By the age of five years, the little girl manifests typically feminine behaviors. Analysis, synthesis, and organization are strong cards in feminine behavior and in the feminine value system. The five year old is still weak in analysis and synthesis, but she is remarkably good at organization. She organizes games, the order of a meal, the household, her sibs, and her playmates. In some things, like an outfit of dress or a scene to be enacted, she has a clear idea of the necessary parts to form a complete whole and is not satisfied until she successfully secures the necessary components and organizes them into a complete, symmetrical whole.

At five, a little girl knows that she is a little girl. But her wish, her ideal, is to be big. If she can, she will arrange or persuade her siblings, her playmates, her pets, or a doll into a game where they are little and she is big. She will recruit adult clothes, tall and long, to dress up in, and up is where she wants so much to be. She has a patronizing disdain for someone younger, smaller, and less knowledgeable than herself, but she also needs them for this comparative value, the reciprocal of self as big, and she is loyal to them out of need and gratitude.

Intellectually, the five year old operates on a concrete level (Piaget, 1977). Relationships are the antithesis of two concretes. There are no degrees, no relativity, yet. She can be big one moment, in one situation, and little in another moment, in another situation, but these discontinuities are seen as disjunctions; the changes are perceived as inconsistencies, as antithetical. There is a simple dichotomy: she, persons, situations, and events are either good or bad and there is an absolutism in the dichotomization. Good is virtuous, bad is abhorrent; big is power of competence and knowledge, little is insignificant in competence and knowledge.

The most prominent model for the ideal images of the five-year-old is her mother. The little girl sees the knowledgeable attitudes, skillful behaviors, and awesome competencies of her mother as most attractive and desirable. This attraction to the mother as ideal model is the reciprocal of the mother's identification of her little girl as her self with all the potentials of the mother's ideal self. The reciprocal and complementary attraction creates a mother–daughter bond on the ideal-image level that produces a very special companionship. They shop together, walk together, sometimes even holding hands, making things together, consider things together. Both mother and daughter enjoy these times of companionship, but to the little girl the shared time and experience with an ideal is very special and reinforces the value of being big and of being good.

A mother, however, is not always one to adore, to emulate, or to love. A mother also punishes, withholds, deprives, restricts, plays the wrong favorite, and has many other grievous but powerful behaviors. This asymmetry in maternal behavior cannot be organized into a comprehensible whole for the five-year-old girl. So she dichotomizes the antithesis: there are two mothers, a good one and a bad one, a goddess and a witch.

Fairy tales hold a fascination and realism for the girl at the end of preschool age and into early school years. Literature illuminates the felt experience by articulating the situational problems and wishes and by having a happy ending when there seems to be no ending. At each age-stage of development there seems to be a literature relevant to the experience: rhymes in the nursery and preschool ages, fairy tales at this stage. Fairy tales are more complex than nursery rhymes and have a plot rather than a single scene. Most fairy tales have a heroine with whom a young girl can identify: the heroine is unappreciated, lost, or mistreated. At the end of the story the heroine is magically discovered and restored, not to her original status, but to her rightful, higher status, to the surprise of many people and to the chagrin of others. In addition to this problem-wish theme, the more interesting tales have two maternal figures, both very powerful, but the good maternal figure triumphs in the grand finale. The stepmother or the witch and the fairy queen or fairy godmother do not meet each other or share a scene together (Deutsch, 1944). The witch or stepmother is a mean old hag who deprives the heroine, even makes her work all day or stay in the house, and either favors the other siblings, ignores the heroine, or singles the heroine out for malevolent treatment. The fairy godmother or the fairy queen, on the other hand, is a person of radiant beauty and great power who, with a flick of a magic wand, creates order out of disaster and enthrones the heroine in her rightful place as princess. Fathers and charming princes appear as props to the story, but they have neither form nor character.

Sibling rivalry and envy are not peculiar to the feminine identity. It is characteristic of childhood to desire everything, to want more, to envy apparently special privileges granted an older or a younger sibling, and to envy curly hair, brown eyes, straight teeth, a penis, an attractive doll, a new pair of shoes, or a new toy. Childhood is a time of being given to by omniscient and omnipotent parents (Erikson, 1963). Gifts are pleasurable, whether the gift is material, a physical characteristic, or the time and interest of an adult. But when these gifts are given away to another, this is an unfair deprivation. Until the concepts of time and number are developed, the scorekeeping of who and how much is given is concrete, in the antithetical dichotomies of all or none and good or bad.

Feminine Identity at Early School Age

The feminine identity changes in the early school years by development of the earlier stage and by elaboration with new features of the enlarged life space that now includes school and community activities in addition to those of the family. The sphere of the ideal image enlarges. In addition to mother as ideal model there is a series and a pool of women, teachers, and aunts, for new elements for the feminine ideal image. These women are of the same generation as the girl's mother, but there is variety and novelty in elements of competence, skills, and behaviors of feminine ideal images. The variety and novelty are stimulating, enlarging possibilities for self-potentiation. Because most of these women are considerably less accessible than a mother, there is a romantic quality to the new attributes or behavior, a distance between self and ideal that generates a greater ascription to the desirable elements. There are some teachers who are "unfair," giving of their time, interest, and special privileges to someone else. If any of these exceptional women give the schoolgirl of their time, interest, special privilege, or material gifts, however, there is a welling of affection for the benefactor that endures for a day, a week, or a school term.

The new feature at school age is the girl friend or chum. The age-mate is not a model or source for ideal image, but a reflection of self. Not a generation ahead in attributes, behaviors, competencies, and knowledge, and not occupying such a large life space beyond that of a schoolgirl, friends are more accessible, more companionable. There is a special friend with whom one has an intimate and exclusive relationship that fortifies the spheres of the self and body image. Together, they know who they are, what merits knowing, and what deserves doing. This is a sharing experience, not a rivalrous one, and a supportive relationship where two consider themselves reinforced by the other, $1 \times 1 = 1$. There is sometimes an exchange of rings, vows of eternal friendship, or a designation of "best" friend. There is a long series of these exclusive friendships, each lasting approximately six months or for the duration of their common experience in learning and adjusting to a particular phase in living.

The major thrust in the school age is that of attaining competence, particularly that aspect of competence having to do with knowing: knowing what and knowing how. Being knowledgeable is part of the status of being a schoolgirl, as distinguished from a child, and the schoolgirl tends to do well, even to excel, in school and related activities. It fits with her self-image to be and to be recognized as knowledgeable or skilled. It gives her narcissistic pleasure whenever she is superior or unique in her competence.

Her mother is less the model for knowledgeability in situations where these attributes are no longer just an ideal, but becoming part of the self-image. The mother and persons of the mother's generation are overwhelmingly superior in competence and knowledge. On the mother–daughter axis the girl's self-image is often deflated or infantilized. With age-mates and peers in situational experience there is a less assymmetrical power axis for achievement, discovery, and self-confidence.

There is a need to know things no one else, neither peers nor parents, know. This starts with the riddle, "guess what." Riddles are collected, brought home, and posed to parents and sibs. If the question is fouled, or the adult knows the answer, there is deflation in self-image. But if the adult does not know the answer, or cannot even guess the answer, there is elation and a gratification that cannot be delayed, in being able to tell the answer.

Then there is the secret, something she knows but no one else does (Deutsch, 1944). Early in the school years the girl wants everyone to be aware that she knows a secret. She then divulges her secret so that they know that she has a secret. The secrets tend to be neither secrets nor discoveries. But it is not the item as such that is significant, it is the self-image possessing the power of knowing more than the general or childish currency of knowledge. This is further elaborated in a secret language system, usually by attaching the same syllable on every word, pig latin, used to communicate only with best friends, a select knowledgeable group of peers.

Secrets are elaborated and given further structure in the school-age, sex segregated, social group of secret clubs. Nothing much secretive goes on, but there is an exclusiveness about who belongs and who cannot belong, and the proceedings are not divulged to anyone. The group fortifies the self image, a re-echo of self through multiplication of equals, $1 \times 1^n = 1$. For added resonance, the status in belonging is made known by some article of clothing emblazoned with the secret name of the club. Self-organized clubs are more satisfying than the adult-made structures. The organization of the social microcosm of the club—the officers, rules, and rituals—is the major order of business. Since all members of the club are good organizers, the process is endless. And because the club is not a social microcosm but a collectivity of peers in age, experience, and capacity, the group dissolves in a short time.

The need to know and the quest for secrets, the unknown, is given a hormonal assist with puberty. The drive to learn, to know, extends outward beyond the family and school communities into a larger, less known world.

Secrets are replaced by mysteries which are more complex, more intricate, and more exciting. Mysteries require a greater capacity to use information, to recombine and reorganize information bits for analysis, synthesis, and solution. Women's literature is rich in mystery and suspense. Suspense requires a capacity to delay gratification, to tolerate ambiguity and complexity. These capacities are strong features and values of the feminine identity.

Toward the end of the grade school years a girl is an eager consumer of mysteries: houses or persons which are uniquely different because they have seven gables, or are haunted, or have a hidden secret, or are isolated by the burden of their secrets. The heroine happens on the situation and in a generous, resourceful, and highly competent manner solves the problem. The schoolage girl identifies with the heroine, follows the heroine through a series of adventures, each volume a separate mystery, until the series is exhausted, when another heroine and another series is started. There is an informal exchange library among age-mates to make the volumes of the series available. The models for the ideal feminine image are now quite removed from direct proximity of the home, school, or community.

Craftsmanship is another aspect of the schoolgirl's self-image development as competent and knowledgeable. Here there is even less reliance on a direct model, though there are generalized models, but more reliance on a pattern to follow for a successful outcome. In music, art, or crafts, the patterns are followed in analysis, synthesis, and resolution for a series of complex maneuvers with sustained attention and self-discipline until completed. When one work is completed, she takes on another one to effect a series of works in the same medium, and then begins to work in another medium for another series of works.

The body image of the schoolgirl is amorphous and indeterminate. She is neither little nor big, and although she still aspires to being big, she does not play at being big. Her shape tends to be chunky and uninteresting to others and to herself. Sports and crafts give her a more satisfying body image as functionally adequate, if she is good at these activities. The corrective eyeglasses, dental work, and surgeries highlight the inadequacies of her body image. The future is very promising, but very far away, and in the omnipresent meanwhile, the body image is a girl but not a woman.

Changes in Feminine Identity at Puberty

Prepuberty and puberty, with their gradual but massive physical changes, initiate changes in body image, self-image, and ideal image (Deutsch, 1944). The increase in hormones affects her with an increase in confidence or self-worth and with the sense of potential for something great and very different.

Hours are spent in privacy with a mirror, studying the features of her face at rest and in action. No matter how attractive she is, the girl finds nothing just right or acceptable. Each feature is too small, or too big, or asymmetrical, a poor fit in relation to its paired feature or the total configuration. One eye is smaller; the nose is too large; the eyebrows are too close, too high, or too low; the forehead is too large or too small; the lips are too thick or too thin; the smile is asymmetrical; the teeth are too gappy, or too short, or too big, or too yellow. The self-criticality is a consequence of the rise in admiration for perfection, an increase of idealism that is focused on symmetry in appearance and control in action.

It is the age of renovation. All things are possible, especially improvements. The renovations begin with experimentation before the mirror and are then carried into debuts in public: the smile that does not show the unsightly teeth or asymmetry, the eyebrows that are held together or up or down, the hand and facial movements and tone of voice that are more sophisticated. The self-control and control over body movements is quite impressive and affords pleasure to her self-image. The essays in control impress girl friends and younger children, dismay adults, and provoke brothers and mothers. But then, mothers, brothers, and the like simply do not understand. Indeed, control of body movement and expression is a valued characteristic of the feminine identity that requires practice for development.

There is also a renovation in fantasy of her family: her family is not really her family of origin at all, and when this is discovered and her real family is found then it will be evident that she really belongs to a noble and genteel family, possessing grace and wealth (Deutsch, 1944).

Diaries supplement the mirror image. As the mirror is the tool for the body image, the diary serves as record of the self-image and the self system. Observations of the stream of events, thoughts, and feeling have to be recorded, contained. The diaries replace the best friend as confidant and as alter ego. There is a movement toward wholeness of self, a self with discrete ego boundaries. Diaries are secret, but secrecy is beginning to change in meaning to privacy.

Diaries and picture albums reflect the awareness of the historical self. Self as child is gone, preserved by parents in mementos and anecdotes. The current self, the big girl, is felt to be impermanent. The diary and the photo albums hold the experience of the self for posterity. Impermanence and awareness of mortality are a part of the integrated self's experience at the ending of a stage in the life stream. This will happen again many times in the future, but right now the future is a void and the identification is of self in a child's world. She vows never to forget what it is like to be a child and to be the kind of adult and mother who understands children, to be companionable and helpful to children, and, above all, to be fair. She generates her ideal images for a future self. This vow will be kept in mothering and will be expressed in guilt when she feels she has failed in being fair, helpful, companionable, or understanding to her child.

The physical changes at puberty raise essential questions and misgivings about self. The insidious growths, eruptions, and discharges from within oneself are unwanted and experienced as freakish. Hair appearing anywhere on the body is perceived as male or animal-like, and there is anxiety about her femininity. Deposits of adipose tissue, even at the breast, are disparaged as fat. Pimples, acne, or increased perspiration are foul exudates arising from within, as though that which is bad or evil within is extruding. Conversely, the exudates represent what is essentially and substantively inside. There is an increase in feelings of anxiety, self-disparagement, and shame.

Menses are also an exudate possessing malodorous and sticky qualities, but are more impacting at first in that menses are experienced as an exsanguination, a loss of blood, the life substance and sustenance. The experience of near tragedy orients the girl at puberty to tragedy, so that even a minor disappointment can have intense, tragic overtones at this stage. The orientation to tragedy enlarges to an identification and empathy with persons who through no fault of their own suffer pain, sickness, or poverty (Deutsch, 1944). Arising from the unspoken tragedy and the surprising gift of survival in good health, compassion for the victimized, the dependent, and the handicapped is established as an essential component of the feminine identity. Aggressivity becomes incompatible with the self-concept and immoral in the feminine value system.

There is also anger that in being feminine one is burdened with a messy discharge, exsanguination to the degree of flooding, or painful contractions at the onset of menstruation. The synonyms for the menstrual period at this stage, including "the curse," are good-natured expressions of the anger. But the feeling is that this is an unfair burden, that men have it easier. There is enough evidence to substantiate the double standard; an easy, free, and unburdened standard of behavior for men and a hard, restricted, burdensome standard of behavior for women. The anger makes for an assertiveness in thought and action and for an increased involvement in justice, ethics, and morality.

The other physical changes of puberty, the growths and eruptions of the body, are handled differently. They do affect the self-concept and the personality. Unwanted hair is aggressively removed or hidden by bleaching or clothing. Unwanted height is reduced by contracting the head and shoulders downward. The skin is scrubbed and foods are avoided to eliminate pustules or acne. The breasts are covered by a bra that is hardly necessary or by the contraction of the shoulder line.

What helps most is learning that the eruptions and growths have external or normal origins and are not necessarily a manifestation of inner being. Talking about the physical manifestations of puberty with a mother or girl friend helps abort the elaboration of images of the body into depressing fantasies of the body and the self. Talking requires putting a name on images and feelings. This articulation and naming objectifies the images and feelings, stabilizes them, and establishes a good measure of controlled boundaries to the otherwise fluid imagery and fantasy of thought. Models or suggestions of actions, behaviors, or attitudes provide welcome alternatives to hopelessness or despair.

Equally helpful in coping is the learning that one is not alone or unique in a freakish way. Within the family, the subjective experience of puberty occurs in an isolation by sex and by age to produce a sense of alienation from the family members and to intensify the turbulent feelings of self-rejection. Maternal counsel or guidance is often experienced as implacable reinforcement of a system that is essentially unfair. With peers in age and sex, however, the subjective experience of puberty is reflected as shared and therefore normal and acceptable. There is a thrust into more social activities with peers. To be accepted, to be liked, and to be popular among peers becomes an increasingly important validation of self-worth. To be accepted or liked by someone two or three years older than herself is even more gratifying.

With a stronger self-image, advertisements and articles are also helpful in coping with the various enigmas posed by body changes in the postpubertal development. Here the experience of others, detached and removed to form a generalized other (Mead, 1934), reflects the normalcy of self in a wider, more general sense, and opens up alternatives or reinforces already chosen attitudes and behaviors for assimilation, adaptation, and accommodation in being a woman. The advantage of the neutral, distant advertisements and articles is their accessibility without having to be asked. Asking about one's self is doubly painful. It exposes self as unknowing at a time in her life when knowing and being knowledgeable are very important. Questions about her own feminine identity are particularly difficult. And the answers seem to be patronizing, condescending, or demeaning so that one is in a childlike position when answered. To avoid derision and exposure, questions are often formulated as depersonalized generalizations or as belonging to someone else's situation. Frequently, personal questions are referred to a respected stranger who will not be met again.

There is an increasing amount of daydreaming with self cast in the leading ideal-image role (Deutsch, 1944). In puberty, the role essay tends to be enacted, much as in the games played earlier in childhood. Later, however, role enactment is in fantasy, a silent process that goes beyond the stimulus model and the stimulus script in originality of the story. The stimulus elements originate in a movie, novel, or biography for an elaboration in fantasy of self in action in an adult situation or career. There is a hunger and search for models in action situations of adult living, and the adolescent girl is an avid movie goer and an even more avid reader. These sources provide the material for elaboration in fantasy. One common fantasy is self on stage being acclaimed by a large audience of total strangers, the world itself. The stage can be a courtroom, a theater, an athletic field, or newsprint. Another fantasy is the discovery and acclaim of her manuscript. More women are writers than is generally recognized:

diaries, long letters, poetry, novels of adventure, romance, mystery and journalism reports, articles or feature columns.

The fantasies stimulate research on the current situation or career of interest, and there is a hunger for learning more about the action-situation. There is a learning spirit, self-initiated and self-assigned, extending beyond formal education.

Fantasies are future oriented. In the consequence of puberty and the expiration of childhood, there are fantasies of death, mostly of her own suicide. A typical fantasy is self on stage, dead, and the audience of discovery is her own family members or friends. Early in adolescence this can be acted out in some form of self-destruction. Peers sharing the same experiential stage accentuate a daring behavior that is usually innocuous but sometimes irreversibly destructive. The richness of silent fantasy and the exploration of the series of possibilities of self-roles in an as yet unknown world opens the future as an appealingly attractive life-space. The richness and scope of fantasies increase in adolescence.

Feminine Identity during Adolescence

Adolescence is the culmination of childhood and an entering into adulthood, without yet having the capacities, resources, and life space of an adult. There is a fulfillment of some of the wishes of childhood. The prom or the big date is a chance to dress up like a princess, with great attention to the details, to act like and to be treated like royalty, and to be escorted by a charming prince. The prince is still little more than a necessary but disposable prop for the scene and the role. At midnight the whole scene reconverts to the mundane, like a pumpkin, so it is important to continue beyond the witching hour, all night to dawn, despite the fatigue, to preserve the status and the freedom from the restrictions of the guardians of childhood.

The transitional stage of adolescence requires validation that one is no longer a child in self-concept and in the perception of others. Childhood is repudiated, children and childishness are scorned as primitive and not to be affiliated with, except possibly as patron. Maternal solicitude, paternal support, and parental regulations provide a welcome security and stability but are perceived as threats to the self-concept, anchors to childhood. The struggle to be independent, an adult, goes on despite the lack of knowledge and capacity to actually be an independent adult. The knowledge and capacities of the parents are challenged as old fashioned or archaic, or are diminished in value to effect equality.

The protests and skirmishes against parents, particularly mothers, are a denial of the sense of inadequacy and uncertainty within. Essays into independent adult-like behaviors are daring adventures, like being an intruder into alien territory, always as part of a group of two or more peers for protection and reinforcement of the self. The daring adventures are not essayed in the family home but in the large, outer world, containing persons and spaces not accessible to children, a different world. At the end of each adventure there is a return home, to security and stability, to replenish the energy for the next adventure into adulthood.

It is most important to the adolescent self-image to be perceived as competent and knowledgeable, not childlike. Being a junior or senior in high school has status significance, but any lower grade is a blow to the self-image. Going to school is a child's occupation, but a trade school or college has status significance. The idiomatic language of adolescence is rich in metaphors for knowledgeability: "sophisticated," "cool," "with it." The metaphors are abandoned and replaced by newer metaphors periodically, but the significance and the high valuation are the same. Coining new terms or metaphors gives the adolescent peerage an advantage over parents and children in knowing what others do not, of being "in" while all others are "out" of the new age, the "current" and "modern" age of action and innovative potentials of the adolescent.

Neither of the older generation nor of the younger generation, the adolescent girl is a member of the now generation. The subjective experience of time is that of a closed system. There is no wish to move into an older, less active, and terribly serious generation and certainly no desire to return to a child's generation. The present is active, novel, and therefore pleasurable and exciting. Without strong bonds to anyone or anything the future looks dull and uninviting, prudence and care seem pointless, and death itself seems no more a terminal event than becoming and being an adult.

There is resistance to adulthood. After a lifetime of wishing and striving to become bigger and older, the adolescent has fear of becoming older, "old." There is a resistance to being "tied down" by the seemingly monotonous sameness of activity in adult work, responsibility, and style of living. The adolescent hiatus in now-time is depressive as a closed system without a future.

There is, however, a continuity in self, an inner consistency conceptually that is further developed in the stress of adolescence. The adolescent girl addresses herself to making a better world: a better home, a better family, a better adult occupation, a cause or several causes where man's inhumanity to man must be ended. Her pleasure in competent mental and physical activity and her feeling of unlimited potential give her the energy to take on several of these goals concurrently. The pleasure in novel experience is extended to the pleasure in differences, not just sameness, among friends and companions. Her capacities for analysis, synthesis, and organization are accepted and respected by others of any generation. She is moving into adulthood with the developed capacities to make her own contributions to a world she claims as her own and a commitment that binds her to the world and to life itself.

Adolescence is a human experience, so there is a strong similarity in male and female assimilative and adaptive behaviors at this developmental stage. Adolescence follows puberty and ends in young adulthood. It is a process in which psychosocial development progresses to a level of maturation compatible with the biological maturation to equip the individual for adult activities in a society.

Male puberty occurs at a later chronological age so that adolescence is late in onset. When a boy of fifteen or sixteen is still coping with the body image of growth spurts and facial hair, a girl of the same age is well past puberty, well into adolescence. Male and female puberty result in uncertainty, the disorientation that results from the new and strange body/self in an otherwise unchanged world status and situation.

The concentration, intensity, and acuteness of the feminine puberty produce an accelerated thrust to the cognitive processing of the experience and of the meaning of life itself. Adolescence is a period of silent organization as well as of active exploration of the maturing feminine identity. With puberty at the age of eleven to thirteen, a girl is coping with her body image in early adolescence, age thirteen to fifteen. In the second phase of adolescence, age fifteen to seventeen, she is bringing her body image and self-image into alignment. In late adolescence, age seventeen to twenty-five, the alignment of self and the world is made: not just the world of one's parents, but one's own world. Late adolescence in the feminine person is more correctly attributable to young adulthood. Physically, cognitively, and socially, the young woman demonstrates the capacities and behaviors of an adult by the age of seventeen.

4
Maternal Identity

With each childbearing experience there is an incorporation into a woman's self system of a new personality dimension. The incorporation is by way of successive and progressively refined ideal images of the self as womanly mother. The incorporation is a volitional process, motivated by aspirations in becoming and achieving the desired attributes and performance of the ideal. The incorporation is sustained, fostered, or inhibited in the intimate and continuous involvement in the imagery of bodily experiences of childbearing and their congruence with the woman's self-image at this stage of her life. The outcome is more than a sentimental attachment and more than a role that is stepped into and out of again. There is a belonging as a part to the whole personality, bound-in and inseparable, a maternal identity.

Just as the biological structures and processes of childbearing start anew and continue essentially independent of previous childbearing and childbirth, the psychological incorporation of a maternal identity starts anew and develops independently in relation to the cognitive processing of the social and physical experience with this child (Rubin, 1967a). There is no carry-over and no transference of a maternal identity from one child to another. A woman occupies a different life space and a different self system at each childbearing experience. It is into this current and real self system and life space, rather than the archaic and no longer relevant self system and life space, that a woman originates and binds-in to a maternal identity for this child and under these circumstances.

The incorporation of a maternal identity relative to *this* child is the implicit reciprocal of having a child. Pregnancy is a period of preparation for becoming the psychosocial mother, for receiving a child into the woman's self system and into her life space. The motivational energy is the wish for a child. The development of a maternal identity for this child is effected in a progressive series of cognitive operations that are manifest in conceptual and behavioral modes. The progression in cognitive operations and their respective conceptual and behavioral modes parallels the development of the pregnancy and the child. The formation of a maternal identity that binds the woman in to this child and to becoming the mother of this child is gradual, systematic, and extensive. The progression in development is in replication by close adherence to models and by essays of role play, to exploration in fantasy of the nature of this child and her experience with it, to loosening established bonds to accommodate the new bond and the new personage, to the final stage before identity is achieved by dedifferentiation from models (Rubin, 1967a).

Incorporation of the maternal identity into the self system is by way of the idealized image of self as mother of this child. There is an orientation toward the ideal and a searching of the environment and of memory for models of new and desirable attitudes and abilities, ideal elements, to replicate and to incorporate as one's own. The orientation, searching, and openness to ideal elements, to the better or the best attributes, enhances the attractiveness of the woman's personality during pregnancy and becomes a characteristic of maternal behavior.

Replication

Replication of separate valued elements in behavior and attitude "like" those modeled or socially esteemed is the primary and predominant mode of incorporation or binding-in. It is a beginning or entry mode in becoming that is cycled and recyled to admit new dimensions and new phases in becoming pregnant, in going into labor, and in identifying and caring for the newborn. Replication is self-initiated, an active searching out of new, desirable elements to be replicated, to be taken on by self. Most replicative behavior is not taken in, integrated into the personality, but serves as a bridge, a linkage, an intent to bind-in, with each specific phase of childbearing.

At the beginning of pregnancy, early in labor, and in the early neomaternal stage, there is a direct, literal copying of the practice and customs of other women going through the same situation, or of women who have successfully achieved these situations, or of the recommendations of experts, "they," "the doctor," "the nurse." Wearing maternity clothes can be symbolic, "like" a pregnant woman, as often as it is adaptive. The election of the nature and extent of prenatal, intrapartal, and postpartal regimens is based on models in the environment. The woman at home with her newborn will feed her baby the same formula in the same amount and way, bathe her baby with the same kind of soap and in the same procedure, and dress the baby with the same kind and amount of clothing as "they" did in the hospital.

The literal copying or mimicry of the behaviorial elements of the expert or successful model provides a probabilistic certainty in a stage of great uncertainty. The probability of certainty increases as the sample population of models is increased. The childbearing woman continues sampling, searching out relevant populations of true masters of the situation she is encountering, until there is redundancy or resonating consistency. Based on the sampling, the conclusion is the hypothetico-deductive: if this is what and how the successful, the expert, or the best do this, then. . . . Sampling is weighted in favor of those with direct and subjective experience in a situation like her own at the given time. So the election of prenatal preparation, delivery with or without anesthesia, feeding by breast or bottle, or the use of contraceptives has more certainty based on even a small sample of an experienced population—peers, mothers, or self.

The environment is searched for models (Rubin, 1967a). Suddenly the world seems filled with women who are or have been in some situation of childbearing, a factor not so much as serendipity as of selective searching. Newspaper items, magazine articles, books, television programs, the grocery and shopping mall, the waiting room and coffee shop near the doctor's office, as well as reminiscent anecdotes in family and social group gatherings add to the sample population. Both the favorable and unfavorable experiences become situation-specific models for adoption if favorable, for avoidance if unfavorable. A news item or secondary report of a woman's experience with the teratogenic effects of a drug may well cause the avoidance of all medications in the desire not to emulate that woman's experience. If the medication cannot be avoided, there is an alertive apprehension about the probability of having an irreversibly damaged child, "like" the other childbearing woman.

The population of models also serves as a guide for expectations in the probabilistic course of the childbearing experience. There is a sense of control, of order, in knowing what to expect. Surprise tends to be unpleasant in its chaotic disorder and in the absence of preparation time to cope anticipatorily with the situation. Going into labor at term can be pleasurable in its meeting of expectations in the order of events, but the same situation occurring in the first or second trimester is startling, and harder to cope with, if there are no models.

A woman tends to be pragmatic in her search for expectations in the experience pattern of childbearing, focusing on the current and next stages of experience. In early and midpregnancy the overly anticipatory anecdotes or overzealous preparation for childbirth are received as noisy communication or as malevolent overdosage. In the second and third trimesters there is pleasure in seeing babies, but communications about bathing or feeding are screened out as irrelevant or shelved in memory as disjunctive imagery. But when labor is imminent or the baby is born, there is a rush of interest and a searching for models and patterns for expectation in childbirth and in child care. "One step at a time" is a learned value that becomes a maternal injunction in childrearing.

The primigravida expects to have morning sickness and to have her pregnancy show abdominally. When in the first trimester these expectations do not materialize, there can be self-doubt or a destabilizing dissonance between expectations and reality. The secundigravida, using her own experience as model, expects to carry the pregnancy high, have an appetite for grapefruit, have a long labor, and care for the baby when it is born "like" she did the first time. As each of these elements fails to materialize, there is dissonance: this is "not-like" or "different-from" the previous experience. Dissonance destabilizes, and the secundigravida enlarges the population sample base to specialize in multigravidas, to correct the expectation hypothesis.

In the puerperium, when the expectation of a happy, thriving baby as an outcome of feeding the exact amount and kind of food in the same way as they did in the hospital does not materialize, there is again dissonance, but in the fatigue and lack of intactness postpartally, there is also a sense of rejection and failure. If the baby is born with an extra digit, webbing of the toes, or a hare lip, "like" the woman or members of her family have or had, there is less dissonance and dismay than if the anomaly is a total surprise and a rejection of all her efforts to ensure a good baby. After the shock of surprise, the woman re-searches the environment for the specific population of experts and women with experience of the same situation. The object of the research is not to lay blame or to assuage guilt—there is usually no intentional act that warrants guilt feelings—but to gain control, to reestablish order, and to find a model and pattern for becoming the mother of a child with a handicap.

The woman's own mother is the strongest model by virtue of the self-evident expertise (Rubin, 1967a). The loosened bonds between mother and daughter during adolescence are realigned and tightened on a new basis as the woman searches for models for becoming a mother. Contacts between mother and daughter are increased during pregnancy. Visits and telephone calls increase in frequency and duration. The childbearing woman in a foreign country is sorely deprived and seeks out women who speak the mother language for even a small measure of contact. The incidence of hyperemesis and toxemia is high in women who are deprived of even symbolic contact with their mothers during pregnancy. The effector of childhood happiness and character traits—such as honesty, despite relative or actual poverty—takes on greater significance as source and model for a woman wanting to become a mother.

In expectations, particularly, the woman's own mother is the dominant model. If her mother had twins, this possibility is high in each pregnancy. If her mother had only girls, or had a son first then a daughter, whatever the birth order by sex, then the probability and expectation of birth order by sex is "like" that of her mother. If her mother had varicose veins, loss of teeth, long or premature labors, then the woman expects the same. The expectation results in a mix of sanguinity and anxiety; the sanguinity is from the long-range perspective of the model, the anxiety is from the expected development. The woman whose mother died in childbirth expects each of her pregnancies to be the last one for her. If she knows that the cause of her mother's death was hemorrhage, then even the smallest amount of spotting has significance to her that is not apparent to the objective observer. If the expected date of delivery falls on or near her own birthdate, this has a double promise of pleasure: as a birthday gift and as a replication of her mother's successful experience.

In the logical inference of the hypothetic-deductive expectations of replication, numbers have representative significance. Her mother's chronological age when she had her first or last child, the date or the month her own or her mother's children were born, the date or chronological age of her pregnancy that miscarried or her child that died take on significance for expected replication. Some numbers have a symmetrical value of wholeness, like two or four as the desirable number of children in a family. But in adverse situations, such as two deaths in the extended family during the current year, there is an expectation of a third death, hers or her baby's, as a property of whole numbers.

Another form of replication is role play. Role play is a trying-on of the maternal role. Role play is more sporadic and less frequent (Rubin, 1967a). Instead of a model, there is a partner, an alter whose responsive behavior in enactment of the isolated essay is very important. The primigravidous woman, particularly, offers to baby-sit, or engages a child in the immediate environment in a short interaction situation "as if" she were the mother and the child were hers. For the woman this usually involves giving food, care, interest, relief, or companionship. A small pet is often substituted for a child. The secundigravida explores maternal role behaviors in having two children, with her child and his playmate of the moment, or, as opportunity presents, with a child of a different sex than her own child.

The response of alter, the partner and object of the maternal role essay, is closely observed. If the response is positive this is rewarding, and the woman feels this augurs well for her competence as mother. If what the woman gives is rejected by alter, however, there is a loss of confidence, a feeling of rejection or failure of self as mother. Since primigravidas are not too discriminate about the age of the child in this trying-on essay, alter may well be an eight-month-old child who rejects all strangers, but the primigravida nevertheless experiences this rejection as her own failure. The first neomaternal feedings, bathing, or dressing are also role play with close adherence to a script. If the baby does not suck or burp, or if the baby flails or cries in response to the offered bathing or dressing, this is perceived as a rejection of self as mother by her baby. If the baby then accepts the feeding, dressing, or bathing by a third person, then the rejection of self by the baby is confirmed. The next episode of giving and receiving is approached defensively and with the expectation of rejection.

Multiparas do less role play during pregnancy, but there are sporadic situations in which they expect their children or their husbands to behave "as if" the baby were born and present. Many of the episodic role try outs are shared experiences with the husband, but most role play is a private and silent essay. Husbands of primigravidas and secundigravidas seem to do as much role play "as if" they were fathers as their wives do of the maternal role. In fantasy and role play a man has an image of or chooses an older boy as alter. Primigravidous husbands buy a big dog to train and discipline, take a neighbor or related child to a baseball game, help him fix a broken bicycle, or give him a candy bar. Since both the primigravidous woman and her husband have previously been more distinguished for their indifference than their interest and concern for children, the changeover is apparent and indicates the beginning of binding-in to becoming a parent in the as-if stage.

Replication in mimicry and role play serves as a bridge to becoming a mother, and, as volitional acts, are a preliminary binding-in to a maternal identity. In the implicit or explicit use of models, there is conservation in replication of the best social attributes and values. There is a conservatism and social belongingness that increase with the formation of a maternal identity to become characteristic of maternal behavior.

The search and collection of instances of other persons' experiences and situations continues beyond the childbearing episode, with less intensity but with interest. There is a storage in memory of living experiences and situations for a "knowing" of probabilistic outcomes based on sample populations which evolves into the maternal prescience, the fairly accurate prediction of outcome before an experience or situation is engaged in actively.

Replication serves as a guide through the course and sequence of situations in pregnancy, in childbirth, and in the puerperium. There is considerably more stress and turbulent confusion when a woman is isolated and deprived of cohort and expert models. This sometimes occurs during a pregnancy, but is almost typical of the puerperium and neomaternal period in the nuclear household. Without parameters that can be viewed at a distance in anticipation or expectation and with time for preparation, orientation and organization are diminished.

Replicative behavior and expectations are stage-specific and are of no use once the anticipation and entry into the stage are completed. The woman preparing to enter the stage of labor and delivery is indifferent to models of pregnancy, and the woman entering the neomaternal stage has no need of expectations for labor. Observing another woman in a stage she has already passed, a woman uses herself as model and her own experience as referent for assessment of where the other woman is, what she feels, and what lies in store for her.

Novel or desirable elements of the experience in becoming a mother are taken on by replication. A silent organization and reorganization of cognitive elements is generated out of the experience of mimicry and role play. The elements are centralized to an inner consistency and continuity with the self and with the body image. Selected elements are then taken in, assimilated into the self system, by loosening and reorganizing the previous context of the personality to accommodate the new elements into an orderly and continuous whole, an integrated personality.

Fantasy

Internalization is transacted in fantasy, which is the projection in imagery of mother and her child into the future: "how it will be." Although the stimulus for fantasy often originates in the models and situations of replication, there are no third persons in fantasy. Fantasy is the cognitive exploration of possibilities in situation and experience of the self and the child. There are fleeting images and scenes of situations of how it will be. Because anticipation and preparation for becoming a mother and having a child are so important, fantasies of how it will be occur in dream work as well as during the day. Pleasurable fantasies generate hope. Unpleasant fantasies generate anxiety.

The preponderance of fantasies during pregnancy are of the child (Rubin, 1967b). In the initial replicative stage, models of children are probabilistic; it could be "like" this child, it could be "like" that child. In fantasy, it is the wished-for child: her own. In the second trimester, under novel and continued inputs and stimuli from the child within, the fantasies tend toward the idyllic. A typical fantasied image of this period is of a light-haired, light-complexioned child, regardless of parental coloring, of about six-months in size, floating peacefully in space, very much like Michelangelo's pure cherubs. A woman's creative image of her wished-for child is that of an angel.

Fantasies are instrumental in the binding-in to the child and to self as mother. Depending on the age-stage of the fantasied child during pregnancy, there is a "giving" of food treats to the child—pies, pastries, cupcakes, potato chips—foods she herself received and enjoyed as a child. There is a yearning for foods that her mother made and gave her in her childhood home, for the smells and the atmosphere in which the food was given. The woman usually does not make the foods herself, but receives them either by purchase or as gifts. The food is then partaken in a communion, in a receiving and giving with her child. The act of giving food-treats to the child tends to be exclusive: the two cupcakes, or the whole eight-inch pie are consumed ceremoniously in the giving of food to baby and to the self, in a unity.

Although feeding food to the fantasied child is the major action modality of binding-in to the child, clothing is also used. The observation of a clothing outfit stimulates the fantasy of what she can "wear" on the child: play clothes, a cute outfit, ruffles. Gifts of clothing for herself in pregnancy or for her child reinforce the binding-in and generate more fantasies about what the child "will be" in appearance. Clothing gifts in pink or blue are symbolic of the gender of the child and represent the wish of the giver or the giver's approval of the mother's own wish. It is not uncommon for a woman to dream of a departed parent or friend appearing and encouraging her to have a child, a son or a daughter. Signs and clues to the gender of the child are sought: it is impossible to be a mother of an either/or child. It is also impossible to be a mother of a child of indeterminate size, shape, and appearance. Dressing a child in fantasy is a series of exploratory locations of the child in size, shape, and gender.

The acts of feeding and dressing the child in fantasy are pleasurable. There is a playfulness, stimulated and reinforced by the growing size and movement of the baby within. A woman grasps a protruding leg, "spanks" the baby on the bottom, talks to it, and finds that the baby provides a comfortable ledge to support her folded hands or arms. A sudden appetite for a particular food during pregnancy is seen by multiparas, particularly, as originating with the child inside. In the same way, changes in her bodily shape and pigmentation are ascribed to the sex and size of the child: boys are more vigorous, are darker in pigment, and protrude sharply in front.

Where there is such a strong set of wishes, there is fear that the wishes will be thwarted or mocked. In the context of the woman's increased sense of vulnerability in the third trimester, there is an increase of fear-fantasies of how it will be for the child and for the self. The image of the child as angel is replaced by the typical image of the feared child: darkly colored, covered with hair, and screaming—an animal. The growing size and vigorous action of the infant within conjures up considerably less sanguine fantasies. There is a decrease in generous feeding, a marked deadline to the pleasure of dressing the pregnancy, an avoidance of dream-work and dream imagery, and a wish to be shed of the pregnancy state. Fantasies of the child become subordinated by fantasies of "how it will be" in labor and delivery.

The man becoming a father also has fantasies of how it will be when his wife goes into labor, when he and his son go fishing, or how he will teach his son to be a man, get him a good education, set him up in business. The fantasies mobilize and direct his energies and the long-term goals give meaning to his efforts. He buys a new car to accommodate his plans and hopes, works harder to get a raise or promotion, or takes a second job to provide the means for his wishes.

But the man becoming father does not have the abundant stimuli, the immediacy of involvement, and the felt experience of the fantasies of a woman becoming a mother. The activity, size, weight, and pressure of the baby against the woman's diaphragm, against her moveable ribs, on her spine, on her bladder, in the pelvic inlet, against her sacrum, distending the coccyx and the vagina are a progressive variety of immediate and continuing experiences. These stimuli generate more than a response at a tissue-pressure level: they generate the conceptual image of how it will be *next*, not someday, sometime in the distant future. Time and space contract during the last trimester and in delivery to the point where the future is now, and fantasies of "how it will be" pertain not to years ahead, but to weeks, days, minutes, and seconds.

The fantasies of a woman in late pregnancy do not have the

daydream quality usually associated with fantasy. The images of the mind's eye are not the pictorial image of ocular vision, but a percept, with meaning. Some images are repeated, some are so vivid that their meaning requires no repetition, and some images recur naggingly in different forms. The perceptual qualities of the fantasies are as felt experiences, with participatory affect, feeling, and resultant emotions. Pleasant experiences and feelings are easy to share. But unpleasant experiences and feelings are worrisome and tend to be rebutted or denied by reassurance when they are shared.

The woman at term is reality bound and distinguishes between real and fantasied experience. Therefore, she tends to censor communications about fantasies and busies herself to "occupy her mind" and "to get her thoughts off" the unpleasant images and feelings. This becomes a somewhat characteristic maternal behavior.

Nevertheless, the felt experience is a real experience to her, a part of childbearing and as real as the living presence within her that everyone else considers not present until it is born. So a woman has another lock put on the doors, works at not being left alone, washes all the curtains, and cleans all the cupboards so that everything is in dying order or ready for a very welcome arrival. The multipara quietly writes a will and arranges for her child(ren) to be cared for when she is in the hospital by persons who could substitute as mother, if necessary.

There is fear, there is dread of delivery, but there is also hope and the wish for the child and for relief from the burdensome pregnancy. The fear and dread are for her baby as well as for herself. There would be no fear for the baby's welfare and wholeness if there were no affiliative bonds of physical and fantasied experience with the child.

It is in fantasy that a woman makes the child uniquely her own (Rubin, 1970). Because the child is an unknown entity, there is fluidity in fantasy imagery. But there is a growing unconditional involvement and commitment, a binding-in of affiliative bonds to the child and to self as mother of this child.

As a woman binds-in in fantasy, there is a loosening and realigning of affiliative bonds to other persons (Rubin, 1967a). Tentative reorganization of relationships, particularly with husband and children, are introduced in pregnancy and firmed in the trimester following delivery. There is distancing; a toddler is not picked up or held as frequently, there are plans for and arrangements with spouse and children to reduce the amount of exclusive interpersonal time and space to accommodate the fantasied baby and the fantasied context of the family unit. Loosening strong bonds is resisted by the woman as much as by each of her partners in a close relationship, but there is no alternative. There is an ingenious "making up" and enrichment of the reduced time and space with husband and child. There is frustration when her own resistance to loosening and reorganizing to accommodate another, and still preserve the ongoing ties, is in turn resisted. The multipara has a particularly rich feeling of gratitude and appreciation toward the oldest child and her husband, the ones who have had successive loosenings and displacements in shared interpersonal time and space.

There is also a loosening of facets of her own personality, her own identity in aspiration and in action in the life style and in the life space of her world. The resistance to giving up or distancing from the achieved and recognizable self in a world is acute in the first trimester when fantasies of the child are minimal and the contributive inputs from the child inside are not yet present. Binding-in to the child in fantasies of how it will be to have a child and to be a mother of this child promotes the loosening and distancing from other roles, other commitments, aspirations, and involvements. The disengagement is felt by the woman as gradual and tentative, as a brief interruption in the continuity of self in action. The expectation is that many of the activities of self in a world will be resumed after childbirth, another fantasy of how it will be. When these activities are not resumed, as they are not for several months after delivery, there is identity diffusion. The fantasy that she will resume sports, social and creative work, and that there will be time later, makes it possible, with the help of the growing fetus and increasing hormonal levels, to forgo the activities by which she identifies herself.

There is also a preparatory releasing of former historical self-concepts. There is a review of a past stage of the life stream, a recognition that this aspect in life space is irreversibly finished, a possession of memory, not action, and a turn in fantasy toward the future. There are reviews of the pleasures, successes, or failures of student life, of dating and courtship, of the exclusive and special companionship with an only child. Snapshots, photo albums, and conversations with family members promote the review of past selves, but such reviews are not dependent on these aids. There is an awareness of career wishes—a nurse, teacher, beautician—a course and direction not taken in the possible junctions of a life stream, and an awareness of the junction and course now taken in becoming a mother.

The review in memory of who and what she has been is a self-initiated process of disengagement from the self and from ideal imagery which is no longer relevant or compatible with becoming a mother. During pregnancy, the process, a form of grief work (Lindemann, 1944), is tentative and is expressed in the past imperfect tense:

"I used to . . . ," "I always thought . . . ," "I was . . . ." In the pragmatic and conservational style of the pregnant woman, actual disengagement and release from an earlier identity is contingent on a successful delivery. Following a successful delivery, the work of disengagement accelerates and there is an increase in reviewing and releasing of ties to the former self-images. The completed past is recognized in the conceptual tense of speech: "When I was younger, I had . . . or I did." "Before we were married . . . ." "When I had my first baby . . . ," "Before the baby came . . . ."

There is a distancing of self, the present and the future self from the historical self, in time and space. Disappointments and frustrations of the past are reviewed and resolved as bygones. There is a release and an acceptance of self that has a therapeutic effect: the recognition of self in continuity and progressivity is pleasurable. The reviews are short, dealing with single elements or patterns, and, on completion, always end with an embrace of the present self in a life space, "but now . . . ," and of the future self, "but when . . . ," in acceptance and anticipation of the new self and the new life space. Disengagement accommodates and promotes binding-in in fantasy, in planning, and in action.

Review in disengagement from the bonds of a former identity and life space requires a partner, a listener. Women tend to be receptive listeners since this adds to their sample populations of anecdotes of situational possibilities and probabilities. But there is also a parallelism in conversation, with both partners waiting a turn and each disrupting the other. Nevertheless, marshaling images into speech for communication to another crystallizes experience into discrete units with a beginning and an ending. The control and containment of experience within boundaries of beginning and ending in time and space separates the experience out from the ongoing experiences and feelings.

Much of this review is done silently, in thought. But this tends to be circular and repetitious, without a beginning or endpoint, and, without boundaries in time and space, remains concurrent with interfacing experiences and situations in the immediate present. The more significant the past situational experience, the more thought is centered on it for purpose of containment and control. Conversations with the self in the I-me duality, however, suffer from a lack of structural language, and the result is a progressively circular entanglement, undefined and unlimited. In relative or absolute isolation from a receptive and permissive listener as structural agent, imagery in memory and in fantasy can agglutinate rather than sort out in sequential and orderly time and space.

Dedifferentiation

The accommodations made in the wish for replication, the felt experiences in fantasy, and the preparatory relinquishment and reorganization of bonds to self and to others form the subtantive core of a maternal identity. With this substantive core, a woman continues to be open and receptive to elements for replicability of the ideal. But now there is no longer a taking-on in the ready adoption of mimicry. Instead, there is a dedifferentiation, an examination and evaluation for goodness of fit with the current self-image. There is a trying-on, an introjection of a new modeled element, then a projection of the mental image of herself with that element in action or in appearance, and a decision to accept or to reject the new element as a congruent part of self.

There is no alteration or revision of the earlier expectations of replication in dedifferentiation. What is new is that additional inputs are now screened against the substantive maternal core, in a test of goodness of fit that can be rejected as often as accepted. In beginning stages an element is adapted as a modeled abstraction, a desirable or necessary element in order to become a mother. A woman will snap the soles of the baby's feet to arouse him for feeding, or wrap the baby in a blanket bottom section first, then each side, just as they do in the hospital. At the advanced stage of maternal identity formation there is a substantive core to test against, and some degree of freedom for choice and criticality. Snapping the soles of the baby's feet is essayed mentally now, not carried out in action, and eschewed as undesirable. With a complete maternal identity, the woman will judge the baby as too warm for a blanket or use alternate ways of covering or tucking the blanket around the baby.

The full sense of maternal identity involves a shift in focus from third-person models of a child or of an expert mothering person to this child and to self in relation to this child. This requires an identification of her child in reality and a stabilization of the image of the child to the point where she knows the child and what to expect of him. This occurs at the end of the neomaternal–neonatal stage, about a month following delivery. There is then an operational location of the "you," the "I" in relation to the "you," and the "you" in relation to the "me." She can "read" the child's appearance and behavior with recognition; she knows when he is hungry, sleepy, too warm, or not feeling right. She knows how, what, when, and why she does something for or with him as his mother, as her child. She gives him solids before his milk, or mixes the solids into the milk, or adds milk to the solids because that is "the way he takes it best," and that is "the way I do it." There is security and confidence in knowing self and child in the we-ness of two complementary individuals.

Binding-in in affiliative attachment to the child and the formation of a maternal identity are interdependent coordinates of the same process. Without the wish for a child there is no investment in the active accommodations of replication and no readying in expectation for the childbearing experience. The wish is strengthened with fetal movement, and strengthened again with a successful delivery, to produce a surge of active adaptation and accommodation in the wish for replication of the best, the ideal maternal behaviors.

In response to the experience of the child within, there is a further binding-in and involvement in the hopes and fears of fantasy. The fear fantasies marshal the protective maternal resources.

If the newborn is not the wished-for child in sex or in condition, but particularly in condition, the motivation for accommodation is depressed. There is a resistance to disengaging from the wished-for child and from the wished-for self as mother. The resistance marshals the woman's resources for restoration of the perfect child.

Fantasies are predominantly of the child during pregnancy, of the self and the child as a unity during labor and delivery, and predominantly about the self postpartally (Rubin, 1967a). Postpartal fantasies are generated in wishes about the abundance of help she will have when she returns home, of the smooth organization of household activities, of the fine lawn and picket fence that will surround the house, of the enhanced reunion with her husband, and of the resumption of favorite and satisfying activities beyond the home that she had to set aside for the childbearing interlude. Postpartal fantasies do not have the intensity or vividness of felt experience as in pregnancy and, therefore, do not carry the same ominous and urgent qualities of warning.

There is little dedifferentiation from models antepartally, but a great deal with healing and restoration of body boundaries postpartally. The dedifferentiation of self from models, without closure to further replicable ideal attributes, immediately precedes the establishment of a maternal identity.

5
Maternal Tasks

At the onset of the childbearing experience there is a functional equilibrium in the interpersonal relationships of family, work, and social interests. The functional equilibrium of self in a dynamic system provides the sense of identity of who one is and what one is about. At the completion of the childbearing experience, the life space and the life style will be radically altered. Primary relationships will be altered significantly; some secondary relationships may be discontinued. A new, major relationship will be established with a person, the child, who did not exist at the onset of childbearing. Moreover, the self, the ideal self, and the body self will be irreversibly altered from the point of onset to the point of completion of the childbearing experience.

A woman does contemplate the outcome of the childbearing in its meaning to her and to her world. Having a child is perceived not only as an act of acquisition. Becoming a mother is unlike taking a role where self and relationships with others remain constant, unchanged. From onset to destination, childbearing requires an exchange of a known self in a known world for an unknown self in an unknown world.

This is an act of courage, but no woman sees herself as courageous in childbearing and childbirth. There are fears and misgivings that she does not possess the strength or knowledge to cope with the procession of situations involved in childbearing, childbirth, and child-rearing. But a woman perseveres pragmatically in the here and now, one step at a time, doing what has to be done in the situational context, recruiting resources within herself, her family, and her social systems.

A woman defines her tasks in childbearing as twofold: to conserve the intactness of the self and of the family as ongoing, open systems and to orchestrate the assimilation and accommodation of this child into the self and family systems. The modality is conservational and incorporative. Some of this work is done in material ways, but most of it is done in the realm of human behavior, human attachments, and human values. There is an analysis of the rights and privileges, the capacities and limitations of each member of the family as well as of the coming child, and a balancing of what each person's relationship with this child could or should be.

During pregnancy there is an idea of a child but not an identifiable child. The existence and presence of the child is known indirectly by its mass, gravitational pull, and movement. The identity of the child can be ascertained only after childbirth. Until then there are hypotheses of this child based on images and fantasies evoked by other models of childhood.

The idea of a child, child in the abstract sense, fosters in the mother an idealized conceptualization of what a child could be and of what the relationships, particularly hers, with a child could or should be. Conceptions of the ideal lead to considerations of the morally good, the ethically right. Pregnancy holds pleasure as an experience in its preoccupation with concerns at an elevated level, in reinforcing the belief in human perfectability, and in clarifying the meaning of a good society in a limited but attainable sphere. The neomaternal period can be a letdown from pregnancy in its disjunction of the real from the ideal, but this is a temporary disappointment: the ideal is a pursuit, not a reality.

The focus and elaboration of elements comprising the ideal of a child, and the ideal of the contextual relationship of self and others to a child, generate the motivation, direction, and orientation to the future. The formational and operational maternal identity arises from and functions in *ethos*—the ideal, the moral good, the ethical principle.

More of a woman's efforts go into assessing, exploring, reviewing, and studying qualities of relationships than into determining possible or probable situations that can occur in childbearing. The interpersonal exchanges in her environment serve as data for distilling the essence and significance of human interpersonal relationships. She becomes more aware of the intent or meaning of behavior in the nonverbal as well as the verbal modes of expression. The microscopic examination of the details of personal and interpersonal behavior promotes a developmental thrust that serves her well in mothering later. The interest, tolerance, and patience for minute details of action and inaction, in verbal and nonverbal expression, are necessary in rearing a young child successfully.

The pregnant woman addresses her self-assumed tasks of conserving the self and family systems while assimilating and accommodating a new, indeterminate person into these systems in four interdependent task areas. There is a seeking of safe passage, physically, through the increasingly complex course of childbearing and childbirth. There is the seeking of acceptance by the significant members of the family of this child, her child. And, conversely, there is the seeking of acceptance, involvement, and commitment of self as mother of this child, the special case of binding-in to this child. And with binding-in, there is a searching and exploration of the meaning of giving, particularly the giving of self in behalf of another.

The tasks are addressed by means of the taking-on, taking-in, and letting-go operations of replication, fantasy, disengagement, and dedifferentiation. With supportive inputs from family and other significant persons on the one hand, and with encouraging feedback from this child on the other hand, the fabric of a maternal identity is actively woven in the themes of the maternal tasks. It is the involvement in the continuous and increasingly more complex maternal tasks, with the commitment for effectance in these tasks, that makes for the binding-in to the maternal identity in relation to this child. In these self-designated maternal tasks, the wish or motivation is not only for a child, but also for competence for self and for preservation of the family. Maternal tasks address three interpenetrating systems: the self system, the maternal–child subsystem, and the larger family system.

Safe Passage

Seeking and ensuring safe passage through pregnancy and childbirth involves more than obstetrical and prenatal services, though these are of great importance to the pregnant woman. In the first trimester the concern for safety is more related to herself, not to the baby, since there is no way—tactile, visual, or kinesthetic—that there can be an awareness of the embryo or fetus. All a woman has in the first trimester is an event, or rather a nonevent, amenorrhea. Besides pregnancy, amenorrhea can signify cancer or some other serious disease or dysfunction. It would be better to be pregnant, under any circumstances, than some of the alternatives.

By the end of the second trimester, the pregnant woman becomes so aware of the child within her and attaches so much value to him that she possesses something very dear, very important to her, something that gives her considerable pleasure and pride. Others, if they are aware at all, are aware of her pregnant state, not of her child. She begins to be protective of her unseen child. It is during the second trimester that a woman seeks prenatal care in order to make a good baby and in order to protect the child from being marked or damaged.

In the third trimester, the concern is for both self and baby. There is no separation: what endangers one endangers the other. Labor and delivery are seen as a double jeopardy to self and child: there is a danger of not surviving or of surviving impaired by loss of function, of body parts, or of body intactness.

Ensurance of safe passage is done primarily by a loading of knowledge of what to expect, the probable and the possible, and of how to cope with the manifest phenomena. The data-gathering process is continuous and cumulative.

Women are avid readers: books, magazines, newspaper articles, pamphlets. During pregnancy the literature is selected for its relevance to childbearing and childbirth, and there is a literature search, a reading up on the subjects. A woman in childbearing is well-informed on the Rh factor, the teratogenic effects of drugs, nutritional deficiencies, and genetic defects, particularly mongolism. This knowledge base is not evident at the onset of pregnancy. There is a personal, intense, and extensive review of the literature in order to take preventive or avoidance measures to ensure safe passage.

The literature is supplemented and then replaced by case histories, the personal experience of other women in pregnancy and in childbirth: what happened to them, how they coped, and what they did or did not do that helped or that made the situation worse. There is a searching out of women who can provide firsthand information of what can be expected experientially. The supermarket, shopping center, and theater are used for observations. The waiting rooms and hallways of clinical institutions provide a rich concentration for observation and for confidential interviews of other women in childbearing.

The multipara has a good store of information, but she makes many more observations and initiates or permits many more interviews than she did in her first pregnancy. The very young teenager is constricted in searching for models, makes fewer observations, and rarely participates in conversations with women older than herself. The constriction seems to be a factor of the stage of cognitive development with its limited concept of future time, an isolating sense of uniqueness—neither child nor adult—that promotes alienation rather than identification, and a defensive barrier of sophistication, of appearing to know. The young teenager does have less capacity to cope with body intrusions and threats to body intactness and is more susceptible to the constrictive or hypertensive complications of pregnancy and to premature delivery. A pregnant woman in a foreign country, where language is a barrier to access to other women as models or preceptors, is also less prepared to cope with the stresses and threats to intactness or survival.

Because the subject is of the dangers and threats to the integrity of the body and to the survival of self and a child, the literature, the observations, and the personal reports of other women can and do raise the anxiety level. It is not a pleasant subject at best, and overdose can be overwhelming. However, women regulate the level of anxiety by reducing further input when overdose occurs. They stop reading "those books," avoid seeing films of delivery, and avoid the superwomen who birthed twins or triplets, all of whom weighed eight or nine pounds. They also ignore or avoid information about the postdelivery stage when they have yet to cope with delivery. In the isolation of the post-delivery lying-in period, the primipara is unprepared for the actual loss of intactness and loss of function. She suffers the sense of abnormality and disorientation resulting from an inadequate schema of expectations. The woman whose child's body is not whole or intact, as in cleft lip, or whose child has a loss in function, such as the cardiac or premature baby, and who herself does not have a schema of expectations for the situation, suffers a sense of uniqueness. She searches for women who have a child with the same condition, to learn what to expect, how to cope, what to do, and what not to do.

The vigilant, knowledgeable, and competent doctor is the major source of help in ensuring safe passage for herself and her child. She needs to know if there is anything wrong or going wrong within her— "Is everything all right?"—and whether the symptomatological aches and functional changes are normal. Before the first medical examination there is a sleepless night, hours of preparation or travel, and a need for someone to accompany her to take care of the ordinary but necessary details, because her attention is riveted on what the doctor might find. The waiting period before the medical examination is marked by increasing tension. The more thorough the examination and the more thorough the laboratory tests, even though these can be painful or difficult to endure, the more secure she feels. She pretests the phrasing of her symptoms with the nurse, studies the doctor's face for nonverbal expressions during the examination, and needs to review what was said or what was found with someone after the examination.

The hospital is a haven in the stress and danger of labor and delivery and, after delivery, in the care of the newborn. The concentration of knowledgeable and competent personnel, who know her, her situation and condition, and what they are supposed to be doing, provides a sense of order and control. The later it is in the course of pregnancy, the more reluctant a woman is to change doctors: a new doctor does not "know" her. When the professional staff does not know her, her situation or condition, or what they are supposed to be doing, the threats to survival and to intactness are increased.

There are dangers within and dangers external to her body. The sense of danger from both sources is heightened in the seventh month of pregnancy when the size of the pregnancy becomes burdensome, the abdominal wall is so much thinner that there seems to be less of a protective boundary, and the freedom of movement is sharply reduced. Fetal growth and strengthening fetal movements become less pleasurable, more threatening. She is less sanguine than others about the striae or stretch marks on her abdomen and about the baby's "kicking": the body image is one of abdominal rupture.

The awkward distribution of the sudden weight and body mass, with its postural shift to support the weight and mass, makes movement slow and ponderous. The slowed movements, insecure posture, and thinned-out abdominal boundary reduce her response time, alacrity, and capacities to cope in the hitherto simple protective safeguards. Suddenly the loose board on the staircase, revolving doors, moving escalators, rapidly moving crowds or traffic become hazardous. Unable to move away quickly from onrushing forces, careless drivers, or impulsive actions of children, a woman rapidly develops an acute awareness of hazards in the ordinary environment in sufficient time to avoid accidents. This special awareness not only protects a woman and her pregnancy but serves her as an invaluable maternal skill in the protection of the young child from the hazards to him in an ordinary environment.

One's own experience and the experiences of others in childbearing and in childbirth demonstrate that will, plans, and careful control are not always sufficient and that there is indeed an element of luck, good or bad, that is operational. The early miscarriage is often referred to as "bad luck." Childbirth that was relatively easy or occurred at an appropriately good time is explained as "lucky." Having an intact, whole, and functionally normal child is attributed to being "lucky."

The disappointments of pregnancy can be massive, and there are many examples. There is the woman who missed one or two menstrual periods and in her pleasure and excitement told everyone that she was pregnant and then miscarried. There are women who prepared a lot of baby clothing, furniture, and caretaking equipment for a baby and then had a stillborn child. There is the woman who trimmed the layette, the bassinet and the room in blue and then gave birth to a girl; or had names picked out for a girl and then had a boy.

A woman who wishes very much to have a child, or a child of a particular gender, learns to avoid the capriciousness of luck and the consequences in disappointment by modifying her behavior. There is reluctance or an avoidance of expressing her wishes aloud to too many people. By the end of pregnancy, a woman will reply to a question that she "does not care" whether it is a boy or girl, or evades the question by answering that her husband wants a child of a particular sex. Although she enjoys looking at baby clothing and the fantasies of the dressed child, she avoids buying or making any until late in pregnancy, and the articles of clothing are few or of any pleasant color other than pink or blue. There is an avoidance of more than the absolutely necessary planning with others for the period after the baby is born.

The less control a woman has in protecting herself from sudden, forceful, or rapidly moving objects, from accidents, and the vicissitudes of fate, the more vulnerable she feels.

External threats are more pervasive than the internal threats. There is a hypertension manifest on the mercury of the blood pressure apparatus and in the cognitive and overt behavior. Fires, thefts, and rapes in the neighborhood are too close. Additional locks are put on the doors. Silences become ominous, hearing becomes acute for sounds, and the radio or television is turned on to fill the silences. She hates to be alone, entreats her husband to stay home more, even if that means giving up one of his jobs, and spends more time at her mother's or girlfriend's house, or on the phone, just to have contact in the presence of another for reinforcement of self. Nights are the hardest and longest part of the day. Sleep patterns are not good in the last trimester, and when the dreams fill with the dreaded fantasies of this child or of the subjective meaning of delivery, sleep is disrupted and shortened. The sleep deprivation decreases control so that her feelings are expressed more and in ways not too endearing to herself or to others. There is a sense of entrapment in a body and in a situation. She yearns for deliverance.

A woman starts and stops in labor frequently. The uterus is as tense and as irritable as she is. But the image of an incompletely formed baby, the hazards awaiting such a baby, and the dangers to the intactness and wholeness of her own body in childbirth help her to "hold on" to the baby and the pregnancy. She cannot bear to invoke danger to her baby or to herself through her own actions, so she focuses on the expected date of confinement, when she is supposed to deliver. She starts correcting the date of delivery, moving it forward, by two weeks, three weeks, or a month. Any rationalization is possible; the wish for permission, sanction to "let go," is there. The multipara is more aware of holding on and letting go than she was as a primigravida. It usually takes anger at the baby and at the entrapment of pregnancy to let go, to get out of the misery of pregnancy, and to go into progressive labor, with all its attendant threats, to delivery. Deliverance becomes a promise, not just a threat, and there is relief and excitement in going into labor if the other maternal tasks are brought to a point of readiness.

Acceptance by Others

Childbearing stresses the social fabric of a woman's established relationships in the primary social group of the family and in the secondary affiliative and instrumental groups of the school, the work place, and the community. The stress is incremental with the progress of the pregnancy, in the primacy of the maternal tasks, and in the formation of a maternal identity.

The secondary social groups, which with primary family group constitute the woman's "world" at the onset of pregnancy, are structurally and functionally incapable of accepting a child. There is a mutual dissolution and a final breaking of secondary group relationships before arrival of the child.

During the first trimester of pregnancy, the prospect of the dissolution and loss of even part of the woman's world is overwhelming. It is in relation to and in interaction with others that one defines one's self, one's meaning and significance, and one's identity in a world. But the cataclysmic prospect does not materialize. In a stable family relationship, there is a transition from one set of social groupings to another, less demanding set of social groups, equally tentative, who share her current interests and goals in childbearing and childrearing.

The family is made for the intimate care, protection, and supportive nurturance that is necessary for the baby and the growing child. It is the family also that provides the motivational wish, the supportive strength, and the context of the confidence, resourcefulness, and creativity of the woman in childbearing. The woman's husband is the key contributor. The course of the pregnancy, the formation of a maternal identity, and the execution of the maternal tasks are profoundly influenced by the qualitative relationship of husband and wife.

The family of the thirteen to fifteen-year-old biological mother is neither structurally nor functionally equipped to rear a child as a mother. Sexual play and reproductive capacities at a child's level of mental, moral, and social development are a preposterous claim for maternal capability. A girl expects parental anger but in her naivete thinks the anger is because of her sexual activity. She avoids eliciting the anger by not telling about the pregnancy, letting them discover it for themselves. She then works for parental acceptance, as father and mother, not as grandparents. The only basis for acceptance and accommodation of the child into the family by the parents is indeed as mother and father of the child, a particularly difficult burden and enormous change in a small family. The young biological mother's task is centered on being a good, acceptable daughter, not a mother. There is no formation of a maternal identity in relation to this child and no assumption of other maternal tasks.

The single woman has a complex problem in social acceptance to having a child and becoming a mother. There is no one who wants or needs her child and no one who cares particularly about the sacrifices she must make in childbearing, childbirth, and childrearing. Her efforts during pregnancy are addressed to correcting this situation. If she has not already done so, the woman moves into her own residence, a separate household from that of her family of origin. As long as she hopes that the partner in conception can or will accept the child, the woman pursues all maternal tasks. If the partner in conception is unacceptable to her, or is rejecting of her and the child, the woman cannot support and pursue the maternal tasks of pregnancy. She tends particularly to avoid binding-in to the child. Despite popular myths, abortion as a solution is most difficult; the experience of a child, even in the abstract sense and even without the pleasures of pregnancy, changes the woman's self. Abortion and placing the child in adoption are traumatizing events, not easily undertaken, and never forgotten. When the woman has another child under more favorable conditions, the earlier, painful experience is revived as a model to be avoided.

Although the divorced woman has an experience similar to the single woman, the widowed woman treasures the pregnancy and the child as a gift from her bereaved husband. Her bereavement is more acute in childbearing, childbirth, and childrearing but the affinal bonds to the child are more intense.

A married couple usually has plans and commitment—his, hers, and theirs—for finishing school, buying furniture or a house, or taking an important, long trip. Plans of the young couple for the first child seem to be for "someday, but not now" (Rubin, 1970). There are many goals and attainments that have precedence over "having a family and settling down." The event of pregnancy and its inherent commitment to a child involves sacrifice by both partners in the pleasure of goal achievements or in the accommodations necessary to pursue an important goal, such as finishing school or a degree, and becoming parents. In the already established family with children, a pregnancy signaling the arrival of another child can be even more destabilizing, requiring sacrifice from each family member to accommodate another unknown and unknowable child. Everything done or not done in behalf of an as yet unborn child is essentially in the abstract concept of a child and of the present and future self in relation to a child.

Acceptance of the coming of a child requires an awareness of the personal sacrifices and the willingness to let go of some ego-satisfying pleasures. The awareness is progressively less schematic and more concrete and particular as the pregnancy progresses to childbirth and into childrearing. There is always resistance to letting go of ego-gratifying pleasures; willingness is a factor of superordination of another, more gratifying objective. What is most important in acceptance by each member of the family is the awareness of the other's acceptance of sacrifice in behalf of a child. A man who is aware of his wife's acceptance of the self-deprivations and dangers in childbearing and in childbirth in order to give him and their union a child has a profound experience in joy and humility. He works harder to provide for and to protect his wife and coming child. A woman who is aware of her husband's appreciation, reordering of priorities, and efforts in husbanding readily forgoes the pursuit of the now trivial pleasures and objectives and binds in with greater love for her husband in the maternal tasks of pregnancy.

Children in the family are not aware of the deprivations and delayed gratifications inherent in the enlarging family. It becomes the woman's task to ensure acceptance of the coming child by her other children. This is usually begun late in pregnancy, when safe passage through pregnancy seems assured. The child's awareness is directed toward what to expect in relinquishing some pleasures and privileges and in the anticipation of other pleasures and privileges with the coming of a brother or sister. When a woman hears her child proudly tell a playmate that his family is going to have a baby, there is a welling of love for the accepting child. A child's resistance to letting go or giving up any pleasure or privilege, however, is profound. The real maternal task of ensuring the acceptance of deprivation by her children begins in earnestness when the baby is born. It is only when a child becomes an adult that there is an awareness of some of the maternal and paternal self-deprivations in behalf of self and other siblings. The awareness heightens the love for the parents, and it is this adult love of the parents that endures for the lifetime of the child now an adult. But in the limitations of the developing child's intellectual and social awareness and capacities, the weak and unresilient ego's resistance is manifest in jealousy, envy, and rivalry.

The letting go of some of the time for the intimate caring and attentive interest between any two members of the family in order to accommodate the new child is harder than relinquishing an antici-pated event or acquisition. There is resistance to loosening the amount of time for the exclusive relationship between husband and wife for the first child. With the coming of the second child, there is more stress. The woman's resistance to loosening the bonds with her first child for the time, attentive interest, and caring for a second child is a felt experience, confusing and disarming. Her own problem in adult resistance to letting go of some of the intimate pleasures on the exclusive-relationship axis with the first child gives her the em-pathy and understanding for her child's resistance. She works at giv-ing her first child exclusive mothering time, interest, and caring when the second child arrives.

Binding-in to the Child

Acceptance of the pregnancy and a child is a necessary but not suffi-cient condition for childbearing, childbirth, and childrearing. As long as the child is but a theoretical model, motivation for becoming a mother is low, a detached and remote possibility unanchored in reality. It is in direct experience between mother and child, in its communica-tive initiatives and responses to the woman, that the child is trans-formed from a remote theoretical model to personhood, an object-being that gives purpose and significance to becoming a mother of this child and assuming the maternal tasks in behalf of the child.

It is the fetal movements that begin to transform the theoretical child to a real, living child. The awareness of a child, not just a pregnancy, adds a new direction and a new dimension of affinal bonds and reciprocal relatedness to the woman's experience. Fetal move-ments are felt by the primigravidous woman in the twentieth week of pregnancy and by the multigravidous woman in the eighteenth week, a difference explainable only by the factor of recognition of the sensa-tion. Early fetal movement is pleasant, gentle, and of short duration, "like the fluttering of a bird."

Before fetal movement, in the first trimester of pregnancy, it is the pregnancy itself that preempts attention. The pregnant condition focuses attention on the body-self: amenorrhea, a despiriting fatigue, the dry or foul taste in the mouth, welling nausea with movement, more frequent urination, and perhaps even vaginal bleeding that threatens the woman's ability to carry the pregnancy. Pregnancy is a series of body-self deprivations, and if pregnancy were not a means toward a desired outcome, it would be intolerable. But a woman takes these losses in functional capacity and well-being, reads them as signs of the expected normal pregnancy, and feels good about herself as a functionally competent woman despite the feelings of irritability and self-disparagement (Rubin, 1970). A woman's capacity to observe absence or loss, such as amenorrhea or absense of well-being, like the scientist attentive to the empty cell, enables her to make valid inferences of presence when there is absence, to make "something out of nothing." This capacity serves a woman particularly well in child care as an early warning system promoting the preservation of the child.

The experience of pregnancy is an experience of the self, conceptually quite separable from the childbearing experience. In pregnancy there is a taking-over of the woman's body, its boundaries, functions, appearance, and intactness. The idea of pregnancy in its consummatory relentlessness is not easy to accept. Pregnancy is temporary, but it lasts "too long," goes "too far," and there is no guaranteed return of the usurped body. The cost of pregnancy is inordinately high and the benefit is moot. It is the tipping of the balance in favor of the benefits that a woman binds-in to the pregnancy to sustain, endure, and accommodate to term and through labor.

The acceptance of the pregnancy by others fortifies a woman's narcissistic pleasure in her body's functional capacity to make a child. Social acceptance of the pregnancy is increased in the second trimester of pregnancy, and there is an increase in the woman's taking on of modeled attitudes, behaviors, and expectations of being pregnant. Social acceptance of the pregnancy becomes very thin in the third trimester, however. There is mounting social pressure to finish, to terminate the pregnancy, and to give birth to the child: "Haven't you delivered yet?" "Are you still pregnant?" "When is the baby supposed to come?" The increasing irritability of the husband and other members of the household with the pregnant condition of the woman becomes burdensome. It takes a strong ego or, more correctly, a strongly formed maternal identity to withstand the pressures for an early termination of the pregnancy.

It is the child within who directly and indirectly contributes to the narcissistic pleasures of the pregnancy, to the benefits in the cost–benefit ratio of pregnancy, and, as alter with inputs and responses, to the formative maternal–child relationship. The level of development of a maternal identity is directly related to and dependent on the development of the child.

The child maintains a low profile in the first trimester, hidden in the recesses of the maternal pelvis. In the second trimester, however, the child rises above the pelvis, attains some prominence, and begins behaving. Fetal movement, the feeling of life, of another living being, is a "quickening" in the woman's experience and commitment. The perception alerts a woman and redirects her attention and awareness to the child, this child within her.

A woman cannot always identify the activities of the baby within because other sensory modalities than enteroceptive sensations are necessary for identification. But she is aware that he turns, stretches, somersaults, crosses his arms or legs, stands on one foot or the other against her diaphragm, arches his back, and spreads his fingers and toes. He likes some foods and does not care for others. He waits until she stops her activities and sits down to eat or rest or lies down to sleep, to attract her attention by increased movement. He's warm, cuddlesome to sleep with, and provides a nice shelf for her folded arms and hands. When he kicks too much, a spank on the fundus will cause him to desist kicking.

The experience of the child in action and in being is an intimately private experience in pregnancy. Others cannot share the pleasures or happenings, may even be alienated by descriptions of the exclusive mother–child experiences, and, lacking the enteroceptive sensations, ignore the existence of the child, as though he is not already present. This increases the maternal protectiveness for the child. The intimacy of sensory experience, the exclusive communication, and the hidden nature of the child promote a romantic love for this child. There is a communion with the child in giving and in sharing with him special treat foods. The romantic love promotes idealization of the child. There are fantasies of the ideal figure and form of the child and of what he will be when he grows up. And although romanticism is hardly characteristic of a maternal identity, the propensity to see the ideal in the real child persists and endures to become characteristic of the maternal woman. When a child is born with some defect, the maternal woman mourns the loss of her idealized child and then musters her energies, as though driven, to restore or to recreate the ideal.

Attendant on the child's presence is the increasing level of the hormones of pregnancy. Progesterone relaxes smooth muscles, suffuses the woman who is pregnant with an inner peace that promotes gracious acceptance, a philosophical perspective, and, through the facilitated circulation, improves body functions and the complexion of the skin. Estrogen increases energy, physical and psychological, giving tonus to mind, body, and the pleasure in living. A woman looks good and feels good in pregnancy. In the second trimester, particularly, a woman feels good, fulfilled, and quite benign about the vicis-situdes of the world around her. The attractiveness of a clear com-plexion, bright eyes, facial expressions of alert intelligence, and a congruent posture are recognized and appreciated socially. Social ap-preciation of her and her pregnancy serves to reinforce the woman's sense of well-being and good-fit with pregnancy. This feeling of good-ness of self in a world, reflected and amplified by the world around her, produces in a woman a love for this child who enriches her. When a woman loves, her attractiveness is increased, there are social rewards, and the love bond grows. This love for the child who en-riches her comes on strong in the second trimester, goes into abey-ance during the third and fourth trimesters, and then increases again as the child responds and thrives in her maternal care.

The sense of goodness of fit of self in the world and the growing evaluation of the child within her combine to generate a possessive love. She invests in making a good baby, and in providing a good home for him, in utero now and in her household later. Possessive love stimulates the maternal protectiveness to ensure safe passage for this child through the remaining course of pregnancy and delivery and to ensure acceptance by others in the household for the child after it is born. In the third trimester, when pregnancy itself becomes burdensome, when the woman becomes tired of being pregnant and of what the pregnancy does to her body image and her self-image, it is the possessive responsibility for protection of her child that keeps her from separating out prematurely from the pregnancy. The conflict between holding on to the child and letting go of the pregnancy mani-fests in starts and stops in labor in the eighth and ninth months. The wish to unburden from the pregnancy is tempered by the desire to make and to ensure a good, whole, and healthy baby.

When the child is born at term there is a patent manifestation of the woman's binding-in during pregnancy to the child as "you," not a theoretical model. The child is an experientially known being. The complementary "I" in relation to "you" is a maternal identity. The joyously accepted child enhances both the child's and the self's worth, strengthening the bonds between the woman and her child. The re-sponsibility for protecting and caring for the child as "my child," an especially valuable gift and possession, is given added surgence and significance. It is the possessive love that endures during the fourth, postpartum trimester when romantic love dissipates under the pres-sure of everyone's advocacy of the child and when the enhanced body-self image is replaced by the limited and confined puerperal body-self image. The baby's smile replaces the earlier fetal movement to signal the renewed and reinvigorated commitment in love.

Giving of Oneself

Giving of oneself is the most intricate and complex task of childbearing and childbirth. The progressively consummatory demands and deprivations of pregnancy, particularly on the woman's body-self but also psychologically and socially, cannot be passively endured as self-sacrifice without purpose. The multigravidous woman is more aware of the prospective demands and deprivations and has more to lose in another pregnancy.

There is a healthy resistance to passive submission to pregnancy as a happening. This resistance is high in the first trimester when the demands are high and the benefits are moot. As the benefits become more apparent, the demands are actively reduced by pursuit of the maternal tasks to ensure safe passage through pregnancy, to ensure the acceptance of others, and to permit the binding-in to the child. As these tasks are progressively attained, the woman works at the essential and substantive meaning of giving.

Childbearing is in itself an act and a climate of giving. Her husband gives her a child; a woman gives her husband a child and her children a sibling; the parents give their parents a grandchild and their church and society at large another member. It soon becomes apparent that it may be easier to give than to receive, that no act of giving is completed without being received, and that receiving is in itself an act of giving and not just passive acceptance.

A woman has an appreciative awareness of gifts during pregnancy. It is not the material worth of the gift that receives attention but the meaning of the transaction in giving and receiving between two persons. Emphasis is on the felt experiences of the receiver and the communication from the giver to the recipient through gift objects.

Each gift the woman receives during pregnancy is shown or described to others whenever possible not only to renew and prolong the pleasure in receiving and in being given to, but in a search for the essential ingredients of the pleasurable experience. Most of the gifts are small, even trivial: a new blouse, an item of food or a box of candy, an article of baby's clothing costing no more than a few dollars. But the maternity blouse, new or old, given her by her husband, mother, sister, friend, or neighbor becomes a communication of appreciative approval of who the woman is and of what she is doing. If the blouse fits her body, her wardrobe, and enhances her appearance, then the gift is even more pleasurable.

Gifts serve as narcissistic supplies (Caplan, 1955), charging the batteries of self-respect and self-esteem through the symbolic expression of another's objective respect for and esteem of oneself. Large or expensive gifts tend to overload, becoming a demand for performance rather than an expression of appreciation.

From the receiver's point of view a true gift is unexpected and has no contractual content of payment, compensation, or reimbursement. The art of giving lies in its unconditional, spontaneous, and free expression. A woman working at the art and meaning of the transitive act of giving avoids asking for or demanding a gift.

In the third trimester of pregnancy, when the woman's narcissistic stores of self-respect and self-esteem are low and are further depleted by the injuries and blows from others around her, a woman is highly receptive and aware of narcissistic supplies in the form of gifts. As delivery becomes more imminent, she feels she has little or nothing to give. Without asking or demanding she indirectly solicits the giving by others to her. The capacity of others, particularly her husband but also those who will be attendant on her during labor and delivery, for giving becomes highly relevant.

At first, the medium of the gift object serves to define the transaction in giving and receiving. When Valentine's Day, her birthday, or their anniversary comes around, a woman waits to see whether her husband cares enough to make the association and to act on the awareness with the representative communication of a gift. Indifference by a husband to signal occasions carries a very poignant message to the woman, especially during childbearing. The gift object itself owes its intrinsic value to caring, not cost in money. If the gift is of food, such as a box of candy, the pregnant woman usually eats all or most of it herself, sharing her gift with and giving to the child inside.

As an object in the transaction between two persons in giving and receiving, food is more than subsistence, nutriments, or foodstuff (Rubin, 1967c). Food represents the regard and caring for the receiver. When the food is one that her husband or the child within particularly enjoys, then the procuring, making, and giving of that food enhances the receiver and is representative of the caring of the giver. Pleasure giving treat foods for the child within tend to be of low nutritional but of high love value: candy, pastries, pies and cakes, Cokes and potato chips. A woman starts giving in intent and in action through the intermediary of food to her unborn child in the second trimester of pregnancy. In the increased longing for the security, acceptance, and care that she experienced in childhood, foods made and given by the woman's own mother take on special significance: a gift of love, warmth, and reaffirmation. Her mother's food, given and received, will be indigenous to the economy and geographical location of the family of origin: spaghetti and pastas from southern Italy; papattas and beans from Mexico; Argo cornstarch or clay from the Carolinas; grits, biscuits with gravy and shoo fly pie from the South— "home" cooking, a message of love known and reaffirmed.

It becomes apparent that in giving there is caring involvement and a self-deprivation of the giver in behalf of the receiver. The extent of involvement and deprivation is represented in the gift object and gives it its intrinsic value. It also becomes apparent to the woman exploring the experiential meaning of giving and receiving that there are transaction experiences of giving and receiving without an intermediary object. The husband, doctor, or nurse who takes time from a busy schedule for her says something about her worth. The doctor who gives generously of his time and the doctor who is too busy to waste time communicate the extent of caring involvement and regard for the woman in present and future interpersonal transactions. Interest, attention, and caring concern for the woman are also experienced as gifts that enhance the receiver as a person of respect and worth. When the interest, attention, and caring concern are centered on the "giver" in the exchange, this is not perceived as a gift but as a demand to be given to in time and attention. In a relationship of equality, there is an exchange of roles in giving and receiving, and this is the most satisfying of relationships. But in situations of stress and uncertainty or in a dependency relationship, demands and role reversals are burdensome.

Companionship is also experienced as a gift. Companionship and attendance involve another's time, interest, and caring for the recipient. The attendance of another, particularly in situations of uncertainty and stress, is perceived as a gift. A woman seeks companionship of someone who knows her and cares about her in going to the doctor's office and in awaiting labor or delivery. There is a reinforcement of her capacities to cope with stress as well as a resonance in her capacities for pleasure in companionship. The companionship given generously without request or solicitation is received as a gift, unexpected and pleasurable.

Relief from uncertainty, anxiety, pain, and the entrapment of frustration is also experienced as a gift. The knowledge and skill of another given spontaneously, without solicitation, is experienced as an unexpected and pleasurable relief, a gift. A woman expects to muddle through or to cope with painful situations or conditions on her own. When the situation becomes too painful to cope with, as in labor, she avoids asking for help as long as possible. When she has to request or to demand that "somebody do something" or "give me something," she finds this demeaning, a source of shame later. The knowledgeably successful, spontaneously given, and appropriate relief measures are experienced, as one woman phrased it, "as a gift from home."

It is this distillation of what is involved in the complete transaction of giving and receiving that becomes the hallmark of maternal behavior: the giving of one's time; of caring attention, interest, or concern; of companionship in stress and in pleasure; and of relief from degradation.

There are qualitative changes in the personality of a woman in the course of childbearing in her mastery of the dilemma between self-deprivation and giving of herself. The narcissistic pleasures and supplies during pregnancy make the deprivations "worth every bit of it." The narcissism is extended and transferred to the baby after his birth. There is pleasure in his appearance, good health, thriving, and attainments. The compliments, material gifts, and attention given to her child are experienced as though given directly to herself.

As a multigravida, the woman develops giving to a higher state, a state Helene Deutsch (1944) defined as moral masochism. There is a great capacity for self-denial, for depriving oneself of immediate gratification and pleasure, and for enduring unpleasantness in behalf of another. Moral masochism is akin to altruism and different from masochism, the pleasure in suffering, in its ethical principle underlying action. A woman deliberately "makes" time to give to her child or to her husband, even though she has less time to give and no time for herself. Appreciation of her capacities for self-denial is sufficient to recharge her capacities and abilities in giving (Rubin, 1964).

There is still a higher state, one clearly definable as a state of grace. This is manifest in women who have had three or four children or who have reared children with love for several years. There seems to be no awareness of self-denials, deprivation, or personal suffering. There is, however, profound pleasure in the child, his life style and life space, as if he is and has become what he is without the creative maternal sacrifices on his behalf.

6
Body Image in Childbearing

With the extensive physical changes of childbearing, there is a concomitant production of images of the body. Images are the tentative cognitive constructions or impressions that originate out of bodily sensations, out of sensory stimulation in all sensory modalities, and out of the mirrored reflection of self in the attitudes and responses of other persons. Body images function as an early cueing or alerting system for survival, adaptation, and accommodation in living. In childbearing, the woman's images of her body are inextricably interwoven with impressions of the child.

Body images in the childbearing experience center on structure and function of the body, its parts, and its contents. There is an orientation toward the wish-expectation of growth in structure and function of the body. Growth, however, presumes wholeness, completeness, and intactness in structure and in function. Structural or functional loss in the body is incompatible with growth or survival. Structure and function of the body are intertwined. There are some unique structural changes in the childbearing experience of size, body boundary, and postural model.

Growth in Size

Growth in size of the woman's body represents growth of the child within her. Growth of the baby has a positive connotation, but growth for self tends to be unacceptable. Even the woman who needs the added weight and roundness distributed along the long axis of her body feels that any such growth in size is related to the childbearing function only. Once childbirth occurs, a woman fully expects that all the growth in size and weight added to her body during pregnancy will be shed with delivery. Any residual weight or size after childbirth is rejected as fat, flabby, or useless. The woman who feels that her breasts were underdeveloped, however, finds the fuller development of her breasts a welcome manifestation of her structural maturity. Otherwise, all growth in size and weight is the baby's or pertains to the baby, while she remains unchanged in the constancy and continuity of her body and self-image that existed before the pregnancy experience.

Since there is no manifest growth in the first trimester, there is no baby or representation of a baby. A positive test for pregnancy represents the woman's situation, not the baby's. If there is a loss of weight or of appetite instead of a gain, there are doubts and misgivings about the existence of a baby and about her own functional capacity to have a baby. She needs a growing, thriving baby during pregnancy for a sense of adequacy in her feminine identity just as the childrearing woman needs a growing, thriving child for a sense of adequacy in her maternal identity. Getting pregnant and being pregnant with a child are different feminine functions and activities. For some women getting pregnant is a functional impossibility and this is a painful disturbance in identity as a woman. For some women being pregnant, carrying a pregnancy without losing it, is difficult or impossible, and this is an equally painful disturbance in identity as a woman.

The second trimester of pregnancy is more gratifying and more stabilizing. The child arises out of the bony pelvis, moves, and grows in size in a gratifyingly manifest and comfortable position in the abdomen. It is not a pot-belly, which she abhors, but a delightful prominence of baby. The mirror, other people's responses, and the scales are searched for reflections of the growing size of the child. Each pound in her weight gain represents to her the growth in size of the baby. She eats to nourish and to promote the growth of the baby within.

There is a minute inspection of the surface and shape of her own body. Her changing body profile, the more prominent veining of the breasts and the erecting nipples, the striae on the abdomen and thighs, and the increased pigmentation of the areola and linea nigra are observed with interest. She searches for other bodily changes that can be expected in pregnancy (Rubin, 1970). There is a sanguinity in noting the bodily changes of the second trimester that is generated by the expectations of normal pregnancy and fortified by the attractive skin coloration and general well-being produced hormonally.

In the third trimester, as the growing child's prominence rises above the umbilicus and the accrued weight gain becomes measurably significant, there is a progressive decrease in tolerance of growth. The child pushes against her ribs and diaphragm, weighs heavily on her spine and pelvis, and no longer stays contained in the long axis of her body but rides forward when she stoops or turns. In the seventh month there is awareness, tolerance, and even pleasure in the baby's activities. But in the eighth and ninth months, the growing size and vigor in activity produce an almost continuous aching. The aching becomes tiresome.

As the baby's activities increase, the woman's motoric activities decrease. Lying on her abdomen or on her back becomes impossible and turning from one side to another becomes difficult. Frequent turning and positional change is part of restful sleep, but this is denied a woman approaching term, and she rises from sleep still tired. Each movement of positional change during the waking hours is deliberate and guarded for the flotation. Bending at the waist becomes impossible. The ponderous movements become less amusing and more tiresome. Pregnancy itself becomes tiresome. There is a growing wish to be rid of the pregnancy, but not of the child. The reduction in activity affects the experience of time; the present seems endless and pregnancy seems forever.

The growing size of the child in the third trimester of pregnancy also interferes with the woman's functional competence in breathing, eating, digestion, and elimination. She copes with small, frequent intakes and outputs, but the careful regarding of bodily function and bodily maintenance becomes tiresome and too consuming of attention.

The restrictions in motoric and functional activity lower self-respect (Rubin, 1968b). The sanguinity of the second trimester is replaced by irritability, and there is anxiety about how much more will be demanded of her in childbearing. Changes in the body surface, profile, and shape of the body are less interesting and more threatening in their progression. Striae, the stretch marks, are seen more as splitting. The growing size of the baby takes on ominous undertones. The prospect of delivering a twenty to thirty-five pound baby vaginally is awesome. There is a decrease in appetite in the last three weeks of pregnancy. A loss of a pound in weight just before delivery does not elicit the anxiety it did earlier in pregnancy. The baby's kicking and the social teasing about the baby's trying to get out become less amusing.

Body Boundaries

With the growth in size of the woman's body during pregnancy there are changes in the boundaries. There is no change in the body boundary during the first trimester and only a slight but pleasurable change in the contained size and significant prominence of the abdomen in the second trimester. There is a remarkable change in the body boundary in the third and fourth trimesters of the childbearing experience.

In the third trimester, beginning at the seventh month of pregnancy, there is a remarkable thinning of the abdominal wall in all women except those who are obese. A thinner abdominal wall is in itself not too remarkable, but there is an increased protective response of the hands and arms to the abdomen at this time when there is close or rapid approach. A woman has to exert effort to resist the protective response even at a medical examination of her abdomen, which she very much wants to have done, by holding onto her own hands or onto some object.

Body boundaries serve to hold inner contents inside and outer contents outside. The thinner abdominal wall and the thinner uterine wall do not provide as efficient a sense of containment against the growing size and activity of the child within. Moreover, the thinness is not supple and elastic but taut and stretched. There is sometimes the eggshell image with chick about to emerge. There is a deliberately careful, slow, and restricted movement of the body with its contents. There is a sense of fragility of the body and of the self, and it is from this sense of fragility that a woman perceives the world around her at this time.

The image of the inner contents within the body boundary is that of an undifferentiated mass. The arms and legs are schematically different because of the amount of accessible visual and tactile information of the bony, vascular, and connective structures and because of the feedback in motoric and postural positions. The torso, however, is a solid, undifferentiated mass containing vital organs indistinguishable for size, shape, location, and relationship one to another. Awareness of inner organs is in terms of function, or rather dysfunction, but not structure. The vital organs do not have to be discerned as separate entities in the normal state and constitute in mass the vital core of the body-self.

The image and fantasies of the fetus within the body are confluent with the amorphous impressions of the vital organismic contents. The subjective imagery of the fetus is considerably less repulsive and more acceptable than scientific models. Like any other vital organ the fetus has no skin surface. This image of the fetus is so prevalent that many women avoid eating the nutritionally recommended organ meats as if in avoidance of cannibalism. The child within is not thought of as having its own body boundaries with skin, nails, and hair. A woman is delighted to find on delivery that her baby is covered with skin and has fingernails and hair.

The intellectual knowledge that the fetus is contained in the uterus and its own sac gets lost in her own changing size and shape and in the indiscernible mix of sensations. The fetus seems to occupy the gastrointestinal tract to produce heartburn, burping, and constipation. There are images of expelling the fetus in severe vomiting and in strained or uncontrolled defecation. Despite the fetal movement, there is no articulation in the image of the body parts of the fetus, particularly the extremities, into a whole structural form.

The image of the fetus within the woman's body is different from the woman's fantasies of the child, the wished for or dreaded fantasies of what the child will be when it is born. In the present, ongoing experience of being pregnant, the image of the fetus is of an inner organ, a part of the vital self, without separable physical boundaries but differentiated by its own movement and mass. There is no polarization of self and baby in this imagery, but an inclusion into a system unity. Just as what happens to her heart or lungs happens to her, so whatever happens to the baby happens to her. In the task of ensuring safe passage through pregnancy and delivery, there is no possible distinction between what is self and what is baby. Bleeding of internal origin of any magnitude is a threatening sign that alerts the anxiety-recruiting defense for both self and child simultaneously.

During labor the woman's body boundaries are diffused by the pressure of the contractions against the bony structures and by the increased peripheral circulation. By the end of labor there is a core of dry, hot pain radiating outward, without localization or limits of boundaries. Attention is concentrated on the inner core of pain. Without body boundaries to serve as protection or as a barrier, peripheral stimulation such as loud, sharp, and sudden noise or hard, sharp, or sudden touch on the skin is transmitted additively to the painful core. The eyes are usually closed and when open are unseeing, so that there is little or no visual stimulation, only tactile and sound conduction.

Soft, rhythmical sounds, coming from outside self, seem to provide an "outside" for the self, a containment by surrounding. Such sounds are heard intermittently, and only at the beginning or end of a contraction, not during the contraction or in the intervals between contractions in the last phase of labor. Cool intermittent contact, such as by washcloth or hand, renews the awareness of body boundaries, providing that the contact is gentle, firm, and with the full palm. Counterpressure on the sacrum, firm but not pushing, is supportive to the conservation of body boundaries at the acme of contractions.

The newborn is often in a similar situation of body boundary diffusion. A newborn baby has skin but no body boundary to separate what is self and what is outside self. With the peristaltic contractions of hunger or of defecation, pain radiates from the body core outward without bounds. The energies exerted in crying diffuse the blood supply to the periphery of the baby's body, causing him to redden and become sweaty. Gentle, rhythmical sounds and contact with another contains and encircles the infant's body for immediate relief. The relief is a body boundary containment and suggests further that the absence or diffusion of body boundaries exacerbates pain that is not contained. It is empathy, not instinct, that makes a mother respond to a child in pain. It is her own experience in receiving relief that makes her effective in providing relief from layered pain.

Postpartally, a woman's body boundaries are not wholly restored. There is a lack of intactness at the perineal or abdominal sutures and in the edema around the sutures. The lack of intactness in body boundary makes a woman feel as though everything inside is falling out on movement or is being extruded by the internal pressures of coughing, sneezing, laughing, forceful speech, or elimination. Healing of incisions and restoration of the body boundary takes two to three weeks for an episiotomy, longer for a laceration or extension, and six to eight weeks for a Caesarean section. Until body boundary intactness is restored, movement and postural support will be labored, painful, and limited. Compresses and contact with warm solutions promote healing more effectively than nature unaided.

There is a collection of minor postpartal aches, pains, and discomforts. These are minor in the sense of risks of fatality. It is a testament to modern obstetrics that the serious illnesses of the postpartum period—cardiac failure, eclampsia, septicemia, and hemorrhage—are very rare. But the subjective experience postpartally includes afterpains, hemorrhoids, abdominal distension especially following a Caesarean section, night sweats, headaches, and breast engorgement. These situations are responsive to simple treatments and soon run their course to extinction. But they are all pressures from within the body, quite painful and with a spread-effect of the pain to flood the body and diffuse the body boundaries.

The floppy uterus increases low back pain and adds a feeling of congestion and pressure in the lower pelvis. The vaginal discharge increases every time the woman gets into the upright position or increases motor activity. There is a feeling of gravitational drag in the pelvic area and a distressing feeling that the inner contents are draining out through the vagina. This image of the body is most disconcerting postpartally. A woman who has successfully delivered a well-formed and living baby feels like dancing or bouncing around energetically, full of life. Instead, she finds herself crawling back into bed, sinking into a chair, or walking heavily, slowly, and with a broad base to support the increased pelvic mass. Because there is no pain, just heaviness, and no reason for these sensations, feelings, and curtailed freedom in movement, this troubles a woman postpartally in terms of her self-concept and normality. She describes her body-self as lazy, fat, useless, a mess that should be pulled together for integrity. It takes at least three weeks for the placental site to heal and the uterus to involute, for the boundaries to heal into an intact and integral body-self.

The odors from her perspiration and vaginal discharge intensify a woman's disparagement of her self and her body image. The restoration of the sense of smell, after an apparent absence during the last phase of labor, is acute and, like the restoration in function of the externally oriented sensory modalities of vision and hearing, indicates the beginning reestablishment of body boundaries.

Postural Model

The experience in the model of a woman's own body position in relation to the world around her changes radically after the second trimester of pregnancy. The enlarging fetus lies fluidly above the maternal pelvis to occupy more of the abdominal cavity above the umbilicus. The abdominal cavity, lacking bony structures, permits the growing size of the fetus. But the lack of skeletal support enables the fetal mass to float forward or laterally with every change in position or motion. The fluid sac enveloping the fetus adds to the after-effect of maternal movement so that mother and baby do not move simultaneously. There is a continued duration of movement of a few seconds in the fetal mass after the mother has completed a change in position.

Each movement of the woman's body becomes an experience in awareness of the postural model. The image of skeletal position and muscular tonus precedes each movement to form a postural model for action. Cerebellar and cortical feedback corrects the postural model for position and tonus until the intent of motoric action in or on the environmental object is effected. The closer a woman comes to the end of pregnancy, the more consideration is given to the postural image for the position change that involves sufficient muscular tonus to move self and fetal mass in flotation.

Previously easy body movements like rising from the sitting position, walking up or down stairs, turning over from side to back in the lying position, and bending over become deliberate assessments of skeletal support and energy expenditure. Many changes in position and movements are decided against on the basis of costing more energy demand than warranted. Counteracting the gravitational pull when the midline of the body is indeterminate requires considerable muscular energy.

Loss of balance and falling should occur frequently during the third trimester but are, in fact, extremely rare. Although women are particularly aware of the risk in losing postural balance and of falling forward, they have no intention of allowing these situations to occur. The same woman in the nonpregnant state could take the tumbles expected in riding a bicycle, skiing, or mounting a step-ladder with moderate care not to fracture a leg or arm. When pregnant, the concern is not with the extremities but with the thin-walled and fragile abdomen. The vulnerability is more central than peripheral and, therefore, more vital.

The normal environment is perceived from the postural model of the third trimester as hazardous: the loose floor board that might not support a ponderous weight, the high step that requires a springy push to get the second foot up, the hand rail that causes lateral displacement of the body, escalators that require nimble footing to get on or off, revolving doors that may be safe on entry but whose speed of revolution can be increased markedly by the next entrant so that one cannot get out even if one could move with the rate of speed of the doors.

The world looks different from the orientation of the fully pregnant body image. Constricted space reduces the hazards of open but indeterminate or uncontrolled space. Time is a factor of action in space. With reduced body action and limited personal space, time does get longer.

Coping anew with gravitational pull in a body with a new distribution of weight, a woman compensatorily arches her spine, hyperextends her knees, and supports her weight in the upright position on her heels. The ability to spring quickly forward or to the side is curtailed. This severe reduction in movement leaves her vulnerable to attacks or mishaps in the external environment. The vulnerability promotes an anticipatory control of the environment by accommodative change or avoidance. She becomes dependent on others to provide a buffer of protection.

The broad-based stance and the leaning backward in order not to fall forward is not a particularly amusing experience. It is tiresome as well as restricting. But later when her own child is mastering gravity in learning to stand and to walk, his posture will be endearingly humorous to her. The smile or laughter is the pleasure response to an act of recognition. The sympathetic use of her own body to envelop and to buffer her child's vulnerable body and to lend him her motoric capacities for his postural changes is augmented by her own recent experiences in physical dependency in coping with gravity.

The image and fantasies a woman has of her child during her pregnancy are remarkable in that the child is conceptualized as two-dimensional and never takes on a sitting, standing, or walking position. The images and fantasies are transitory, appearing from nowhere and disappearing into nowhere, without background space. The only action of the child in image and fantasy, other than her own in relation to the child, is of her child floating in space.

There is compelling hunger after delivery for a woman to feel her baby as a solid three-dimensional mass with gravitational weight. A fingertip feel or a visual observation of her child is not sufficient. She must hold the child fully in her arms and against her breast, feeling the full weight of him in extensive contact with the sensitive surface of her own body. Holding a baby becomes a necessary part of having a baby. Holding a baby stabilizes the reality of the baby in real space rather than an image, a fantasy, or a dream that appears and disappears but never endures. The weight, the smell, and the warmth of the baby in contact with the surface of her body also help to redefine her own body boundaries. The movement of the baby's hands, feet, head, or mouth against the sensitive surface of her own body does even more for her healing (Benedek, 1949). The baby itself contributes to the well-being of the mother, to the binding-in process, and to the reception accorded him.

The postpartal postural model is continuous with the postural model at the end of pregnancy and is affected by labor and delivery. Balancing the body for weight distribution is still a problem postpartally. Pelvic congestion, tight sutures, and perineal edema require the broad-based stance and weight carried on the heels. Walking is as slow and as labored as in late pregnancy. Since lochial flow is increased in the upright position and in motion, walking is held to a minimum. There is back pain, a general dull ache, internally from the pressures of descent of the baby and externally from the position sustained for delivery added to the strain of postural maintenance in the last weeks of pregnancy. Maintaining the upright position in sitting, standing, or walking is stressful. Sitting without a pillow to pad the perineum puts all the body weight on the sutures.

But the most important change in the postural model postpartally is the fatigue. There is profoundly less energy available or recruitable postpartally than antepartally. There is also a marked decrease in body tonus. This is most marked in the position of the spinal column: antepartally the thoracic cage and cervical vertebrae are held up and back; postpartally the thoracic cage and cervical verte-brae fold forward and down. There is not enough energy to support the body upright or to support the additional weight of the baby's body for more than a few minutes. The energies mustered for any activity as simple as standing, sitting, or walking are soon exhausted.

The fatigue is a normal consequence of labor and delivery, of the protective tension to control both the hazards and the pain of labor. The sheer physical fatigue is magnified by a profound anemia. The anemia is a consequence of any blood loss at delivery, the blood loss in lochial discharge, and the changeover from the watered-down, hy-dremic, enlarged red corpuscles of pregnancy to the smaller red cor-puscles richer in protein, iron, and oxygen. It takes two to three weeks for the normal changeover in circulating blood structure and volume to occur, longer if there has been hemorrhage or heavy lochia. As long as the circulatory blood volume is deficient in amount and structure, there is not sufficient nutriment to repair tissue, supply vital organs, support body tonus, and sustain body activities. Faint-ing or feeling faint is not uncommon in the first two weeks.

There is no way the normal but profound anemia postpartally can maintain and repair body tissues and still supply sufficient nutri-ments and oxygen to meet the energy requirements for sustained or increased motor activities. Sleep hunger, sleep deprivation, and sleep disruption postpartally add to the fatigue and to the demands on limited circulating blood supplies. With sleep, lowered metabolism reduces demands on the circulating blood so that tissue repair is more efficient and organic function is restored.

The prolonged fatigue of the postpartal phase makes this phase one of the most difficult in the childbearing experience. The depressed postural model of the body pervades the concept of the self. On the one hand, there is the exhilaration and joy of deliverance and a successful delivery with its thrust toward active and creative giving to others, a readiness for potentiation. On the other hand, there is not enough energy to get up, get out of a tub, or push a vacuum cleaner. Between aspiration and reality there is a void filled with a self-estimate result-ing in depression, a despair of self, or in hostility, a self-hate.

As long as a woman cannot muster the energy to get up and get away from the entrapment of her own body, she is victimized and is dependent on others for change in postural perspective and outlook on life in the world. Dependence is an unpleasant status for a woman who feels she should be a mother, not a baby. The self-image and the body image share the same postural model instrumentally and ex-pressively. It is only the ideal image that is desynchronized for time and space in the postpartal healing and recovery period.

Pain

Pain is a particular experience in the body-self image. Pain can occur at any time during pregnancy or the postpartum experience but is concentrated in labor and delivery.

Pain is a subjective experience (Schilder, 1969; Szasz, 1957). Pain does not exist as an entity outside the sensory and cognitive experience. It is a recognizable subjective feeling, like happiness or misery, in its suffusive and expressive properties. Pain has as its sole function the arousal of awareness to destruction of body function or body intactness.

Pain is the essential and ultimate early warning signal for survival. The other sensory modalities can augment the attentive cueing for dangers but are not sufficiently reliable alerting mechanisms for recruiting protective defenses for survival. The sensory modes of seeing and hearing function outward from the body boundary into the surrounding environment and are made more effective by the positions and movements of the body in space. Taste and touch function at the body boundary. The sense of smell supplements the functions of vision and taste to reinforce the attractive and repulsive cues at the body boundaries to the immediately surrounding environment. None of these sensory modalities provide data on the inner status of the body boundaries nor do they have the properties of loud, arresting signals to initiate immediate attention and focus on a threat to survival.

Pain is transmitted neurologically as pressure overload for cortical arousal in milliseconds and yet is conducted through the reverberating circuits of the autonomic or sympathetic nervous system simultaneously (Magoun, 1958). When the car door slams shut on a fingertip, the abdominal muscles contract into painful knots, there is a feeling of nausea, and there is a headache of such pressure that it feels as though it is splitting or bursting. This is the consummatory spread-effect of pain (Schilder, 1970).

The first time a finger is caught in the car door, hit with a blow of the hammer, or whatever, the consummatory spread-effect makes it impossible to define and locate what hurts. It hurts all over. The carpenter inadvertently slams his finger with a hammer and simply stops, sucks his finger for a minute or two, and then resumes hammering. He is not insensate or habituated; he has the same sharp, penetrating pain and the same consummatory spread-effects that serve to stop and arrest activity. What is different is the experiential knowledge, the cortical control, that delineates the smashed finger as central and all other pain as peripheral background, and can place borders around the extent of damage by experiential knowledge of the course and endpoint of the trauma.

The function of pain is to signal, not to sort out or decide on the merits or relevance of the signal. The advantage of the consummatory spreading pain is that it arrests ongoing activity. The spread-effect of pain can produce fainting or shock, which also serve to arrest self-destructive activity. Pain spreads and pain immobilizes. It is meant to do just that, protectively, to prevent self-destruction. Because pain is so noxious, experiential cognitive engrams of the experience, particularly the cause-effect course, serve preventively to avoid repetition of the pain, so that the danger of pain itself extends the efficiency of the warning system.

The noxious emotions such as anxiety, fear, and panic are anticipatory signals of the danger of destruction or loss in wholeness and intactness. These emotions are painful, have a consummatory spread-effect through the body, and arrest ongoing activity for the same purpose of preventing self-destruction. The noxious emotions function as an additive layer to amplify the signal-alerting properties of physical pain. When physical pain fails, as it does in nonpainful bleeding or internal hemorrhage and in many altered physiological functions, then the emotions generated by the perception of these phenomenal occurrences serve as a fail-safe guarantee in signaling danger.

The noxious emotions are on a continuous gradient of intensity depending on the perceived extent of the threat, the subjective assessment of the self in coping control, and the time interval between awareness of impending danger and the actualization of destruction (Rubin, 1968b). In anxiety, the threat is in the future and coping capacity is problematical. In fear, the threat is immediate and control is inadequate. In panic, time and opportunity have run out. There is a fluidity between anxiety, fear, and panic. Panic has a duration-life of seconds, fear has a duration life of minutes, and anxiety can be endured with remissions for hours. Once the disaster has occurred and is past, there is no anxiety, fear, or panic. These emotions have only signaling and arousal functions. When disaster does occur it is too late for emotional arousal: there is subjective apathy, enormous fatigue, and resignation.

In the economy of the body design for function, the noxiously painful emotions serve as alerting signals for the preservation of the wholeness and intactness of significant social relationships as well as for physical preservation. The threat of destruction of a social relationship produces anxiety, fear, and even panic to arrest the present course of action and to recruit alternative resources for conservational actions. When destruction occurs, anxiety, fear, and panic are

replaced by shocked disbelief, anger or guilt, and sadness (Lindemann, 1944).

The elaborate mechanism for preservation and survival has one
more guarantee against failure in the system and that is the cry for
help when there is inadequate capacity for countering destruction. In
acute pain and in panic, the cry is short and loud. In severe pain and
in fear, the cry is sentence structured. In lower pain-pressure or anxiety, there is more time for exploration of the resources for help and
therefore no cry.

An effective response to any component of the signal system reduces the overlayment of pain. The cry, appeal, or solicitation of help
when answered reduces the level of pain: the toothache seems to
disappear when the dentist appears; many aches or pains are hardly
remembered when the doctor arrives. When a nurse or a mother
responds to a call for help, it becomes apparent that the overlayment
of the pain signals system is often more troublesome than the primary pain.

The presence of another person identified as willing to help and
capable of helping often restores the pain-dissipated body boundaries
by proximity alone. Direct and healing contact helps in reducing the
spread-effect to a concentrated local area and in restoring body boundaries. Pain under conditions of isolation has no limits, however: the
body, mind, and surroundings can be flooded with panic. Other persons in the environment who are indifferent to the pain-signal system
produce a sense of abandonment. Isolation and abandonment intensify pain in all components of the arousal system by adding the layer
of pain in uniqueness: "Why me?" The uniqueness, the selectivity for
destruction, is exacerbated by the indifference and rejection of others
to the worth of the self for preservation.

The knowledge and skill of the helping person also helps establish cognitive boundaries to the signaled warning. The spread-effect
of pain is eliminated by focusing on the original site, localizing the
pain by looking at its organic source, naming it, and touching it.
Where knowledgeable experience can be brought to bear, the course
from origin to endpoint is identified for cause, purpose, and time
duration. This defining of the course and meaning of the alerting
and resonating warning system turns off or turns down all pain
signals. The signals have been received, the message has been de-
coded, and appropriate action or inaction measures are put into effect for self-preservation.

The ability to contain and decode the message of pain is a factor of
experiential knowledge, one's own or borrowed from another, and of
intellectual development. The neonate and young child cannot compre-

hend the messages of pain signals, so they tend to be flooded in the consummatory spread of pain. The neonate particularly has the emotional capacity for fear and panic, highly urgent and painful signals. Apprehension and anxiety are developed out of experiential knowledge, repeated over time, to permit a schema of probabilistic expectations in the near or distant future that will be noxious. Considering the self-destructive situations a child can get into, the potency of pain signals early in life and the high frequency of distress cues are well designed, built-in safeguards for survival. The helpful adult has to lend the child the benefit of accumulated knowledge to define a danger, its antecedents, and its consequences and to contain and reduce the terror of pain.

It is the endpoint of pain-signaled danger that is not always determinate. As long as the end is not known or is actually or potentially dangerous, pain signals of tactile pressure or cognitive pressure continue. The cognitive pressure signals of apprehension and anxiety continue intermittently when there is no certainty that the damage is ended. For the carpenter who smashes his finger, the endpoint is either a blackened or lost fingernail. For the diabetic, however, the blackened or lost fingernail may well be only a stage in progressive danger.

To the woman in labor, the first phase of labor contractions is painful, but each pain signal is identifiable, has purpose, and has a beginning and endpoint. Pain is contained cognitively and there is even some pleasure in this ability to recognize and to cope with the signal system. There is also apprehension about the next contraction. As the contractions increase in intensity and frequency and the pressures mount, the intervals blur, and it becomes harder to discern beginning and ending. Boundaries between contractions are harder to identify when body boundaries are diffused with pain. The difficulty in perceiving intervals makes time in pain interminable. The intensifying pain signals and their perseverance heighten the feelings and awareness of disaster. The feelings move from the leisurely noxiousness of anxiety and apprehension to the urgent signals of fear. Fear mounts and panic occurs when a woman in labor is isolated or abandoned. Glib reassurance, however, is perceived by a woman in labor as indifference or profound ignorance of the alerting purpose of pain signals.

The response to pain signals for a woman in labor is affected by fatigue, isolation, or abandonment and disorientation in time and space. Cognitive controls are stressed under these circumstances to the point where pain can be boundless and self-controls are lost.

Fatigue impairs cognitive functions. Prolonged fatigue is in itself painful. It is in the nature of labor in childbirth that the maximum effort demand is at the end of hours of controlled mental effort. Without minimizing the pressure-pain of childbirth, the fatigue is as hard to cope with as the pressure, or even harder. The fatigue is not just sleep hunger or sleep deprivation, although these do disadvantage a woman in labor. The fatigue is a product of muscular exertion, like that of a marathon runner in an important race, with an increase in lactic acid and a decrease in available tissue oxygen to produce severe, sustained pain.

Fatigue is reduced when a woman can let go, not to relax, but to cognitively allow the baby to descend and to be born. This requires a faith, trust, or hope that body boundaries and intactness are not destroyed despite the signals to the contrary. Fatigue is reduced when a woman can delegate cognitive control and vigilance to at least one but preferably more persons who know her as a person, her changing situation in labor, her current and imminent condition, and who do not leave her. Attending persons who leave periodically or intermittently, no matter how available on call, increase the woman's tension vigilance to the pain signals. An unknowledgeable attendant also increases the woman's vigilance. Fatigue and vigilance are incompatible: control is lost and the pain of spiraling physical and emotional pressure signals becomes overwhelming.

Because pain is many faceted in labor and not simply lineal cause-effect, relief of pain must be programmatically broad to reduce or eliminate the excessive overlayments of pain signals and to promote the effectiveness of a woman's capacity for control. Medications are a good adjunct for a team of attending physicians, nurse, and husband or other family member. But medications are cortical depressants and should be used judiciously at the beginning of the second and/or third phase of labor depending on the woman's capacities for coping with the accelerated pressures of the next phase. Medication is not a substitute for care. Overmedication, often well-intended, is not only hazardous to the infant but deprives the woman in labor of cognitive controls over the spread-effect of pain. The depression of cortical controls often frees forebrain rage (Magoun, 1958) that nullifies all other relief measures. Without any medication, however, rage can also develop when controls and relief are inadequate.

Preparation-for-childbirth classes are useful adjuncts in reducing pain by enriching the cognitive control side of the equation, providing there is a team of the attending physician, nurse, and husband, each with their own complementary contribution for pain reduction and control supplementation. Classes, however, are not substitutes for professional help because as labor progresses awareness of anything other than the internal signals is obliterated and knowing what to do is not coordinated for appropriateness of time and situation. The hazards of hyperventilation are comparable to overmedication. Bad timing of intra-abdominal pressure causes more cervical lacerations and exhaustion than would occur with a passively spontaneous delivery.

It is nursing care that prevents too early dissipation of body boundaries. The responsive awareness of the condition of the woman and the progress of the labor is communicated by eye-to-eye contact, verbal confirmation, touch or counterpressure, and cooling or restful massage. It is nursing care that helps a woman's coping capacities in defining the source, beginning, and ending of pressure pain, in conserving energy for the long process and between contractions, in conserving controls in orientation in time, rate of progress, and distance traveled to the goal of delivery. It is nursing care that assumes vigilance for safe passage. Continuous nursing attendance, especially after four centimeters of dilatation, reduces a woman's anxiety and prevents the build-up of fear. Medication will serve the same purpose, but there is a heavy cost in side effects for any medication sufficient to substitute for nursing. In a long labor, nurses have to be relieved or alternated: judgment is impaired by fatigue. An independent evaluation of the progress of labor by the doctor, whose focus and expertise lie in delivery rather than in labor, ensures reliability in judgment and vigilance. In the doctor's symbolic representation of delivery, his or her appearance raises a woman's hopes and reduces the intensity of pain. Hope raised too often and fruitlessly, however, converts into despair.

Labor rooms tend to be isolation rooms. The presence of a family member is helpfully supportive but not sufficient when the volume of pain signals increase. The helplessness can be reinforced in the absence of the knowledgeable and effective controls of a skilled professional. The entrapment of both husband and wife produce fear and anger, more painful overlayment. If husband and wife are completely isolated from help, outside a hospital, there would be fear but also a recruitment of their own inner resources in some responsive action and no anger. In a hospital, with help all around but not present, isolation becomes abandonment in need, and anger is aroused at the injustice. The anger is addressed to the partner or to the baby.

7

Time and Space
in Childbearing

The subjective experience of time and space, physical and social space, changes as extensively and accommodatively as the body of the childbearing woman. The altered experience of time and space is a product of the formation of a maternal identity and the pursuit of the maternal tasks. The change is promoted by the rising levels of hormones, estrogens and progesterone, and the growth of the child in utero. The end result of these changes in personal time and personal space is a relatively greater tolerance and sympathy of the biological mother than that of any other adult for the infant and child who lives in a world of forever-time and miniscule space.

Pregnancy, labor, and the postpartum period, each phase of childbearing is too long, endless in time in the subjective experience. As long as nothing seems to happen in pregnancy and in labor, time is empty and endless. Retrospectively, however, at the end of pregnancy and after delivery, in the awareness of how much happened, the "time went so quickly."

Time and Space in the First Trimester

The psychosocial pregnancy really lasts only eight months from the onset of awareness that there might be a pregnancy. For some women awareness is even later, and time for maternal identity formation and maternal tasks is shortened. Too little time for pregnancy, for labor, or for postpartum recovery raises the anxiety level to fear, and in labor, with the added anxiety about body intactness produced by pain, to terror. Urgent crowding of activities into a foreshortened space of time makes for high energy demand, and sometimes there is not enough energy. Sometimes the activities cannot be executed at all within the abridged time.

Time is a measure and frame for ordering behavior and activity. From the time a woman knows that she is pregnant all plans, commitments, and engagements are regulated in reference to the expected date of confinement. Continued participation in employment, school, or clubs is decided in terms of the expected date of confinement. Invitations are accepted or rejected depending on the timing of the social function in relation to the time of delivery. The life space and activities are organized around the preemptive expected date of delivery. Planned events for the family are moved ahead in time if they fall near the important date. Anniversaries of birthdays and deaths that occur in the month of the expected date of childbirth are seen as omens, and there is a recalculation of the expected date to move it closer to the anniversary day of a happy event or farther away from the anniversary day of a death.

In the first trimester of pregnancy the expected date of confinement is light years away. A woman has no subjective experience in the present of being pregnant or awareness of a child in the first trimester. All a woman has to orient herself to is the absence of a feminine function, amenorrhea, and a magical estimate of a delivery date. Worse than finding oneself between a rock and a hard place is to find oneself between nothing and a mirage. Present time in the first trimester of pregnancy is empty time with nothing happening, boundless emptiness, a void, and a burden. In self-defense, a woman continues her ongoing activities and commitments, grateful for the social demands and commitments. She spends much of the time of the first trimester sleeping.

Time is life-time. The emptiness of early pregnancy life contrasts sharply with the fullness of adult life so that there may be resistance to changeover, to giving up, or to taking "time out" of life to have a baby. For some women, life's activities are not all that meaningful, productive, or useful so that changeover in experience and in having a child at this time is rewarding. But empty time is burdensome in pregnancy.

Time and Space in the Second Trimester

Experientially, the second trimester of pregnancy begins with quickening, the feeling of life within. The novelty, change, and companionship of the growing fetus replaces the void of earlier pregnancy. Time is bounded and contained from the discernible present to an end point months away in the future. Time is no burden. The second trimester is the best time of the pregnancy. The hormonal assist ensures tranquility and energy to enhance life qualitatively. The slight prominence of her pregnancy is noted socially, and there is social respect for what the woman is doing and making.

The turning inward to the contents of her pregnancy is accompanied by a withdrawal of time, interest, and association from social spheres outside the immediate family. There is a reduction in the extent of time and space, social and geographic, that she occupied before. There is the formation of a new social space of transitory relationships with women in her immediate neighborhood who have children and who are or have been pregnant. More time is spent in the immediate presence of her mother and sisters. Women who do not have their mothers or sisters accessible spend more time in clinic waiting rooms as long as there are peers present and accessible, or in mothers' classes, for peer interests.

The second trimester focuses on the child. Inner space replaces the outer radius of world space. It is a time for leisurely walks alone or with her husband, for window shopping in the evenings when there are fewer hurrying adults. The crowded time-space of the adult world is not for the woman becoming a mother. Her pace of walking and moving is leisurely and serene; she is not going somewhere or getting something. She is receptive, responsive, and totally lacking in aggression. If she is employed, her employer wishes she would snap to and get with the job at hand, but she continues doing her own work, which no one else can do for her, in a serenity and composure that everyone finds charming and unassailable.

The second trimester of pregnancy ends, in the subjective experience, with the woman's awareness of her vulnerability, at about the last half of the seventh month. The growing fetus is no longer contained comfortably within her own body, but projects into space. The weight of the mass is high and forward, disturbing the gravitational pull and postural model. It takes physical effort to get out of bed, out of a deep chair, upstairs, or onto a bus. Her movements in physical space are curtailed and physical space is constricted to the home and the immediate vicinity. If she has to travel, she avoids going alone, not only because of her vulnerability, but also for the orientation provided by another's postural model. The adult male's vigorous and aggressive movements and postural model, however, are not consonant with the woman's efforts countering the gravitational pull and her uncertainty about her changing body boundaries. Each trip outside the home becomes more exhausting.

Home is a haven. Home is also a confinement. There is a wish, often a wish put into action in the third trimester of pregnancy, to make a sentimental journey and to link in again with the outer world she belonged to earlier. The sentimental journey is to her mother's house if that is far away, or to take a trip with her husband somewhere again, or to go swimming or camping again, or to meet with the girls at work for lunch again. The yearning for that larger affiliative world space is denied if it is perceived to be detrimental to the maternal task of seeking safe passage for her child and herself. The wish remains through labor as a promise to be realized when this child is old enough.

Time and Space in the Third Trimester

Time-space in the third trimester is filled with trivia. It takes so long to move, to dress. A woman becomes irritable and sometimes hostile, but amazingly not angry or rejecting, about this slow rate for just system maintenance. The slow pace and inefficient movements of the newborn and toddler in eating, in dressing, in standing and walking, and in communication are later accepted by the same woman with an impressive tolerance and understanding of his condition. "He can't help it." The subjective experience of the woman in slow-motion is of relatively short duration and yet is deep enough a learning for empathy and compassion of considerable duration in the extension of this learning and "knowing" to the condition of the child.

There is, however, another sense of time in the last trimester of pregnancy, and that is of time running out. As the day of delivery approaches, pregnancy time terminates. There is an urgency to get ready, ready for delivery and ready for this child in the setting of the home and family.

The sense of time running out combined with the feeling of physical vulnerability produces the growing awareness of the woman's own mortality. The ominous feeling is greater in the multipara than in the woman entering her first experience of childbirth, because she knows intimately the pain and trauma and has a more extensive collection of data on the hazards possible. Both the primigravidous and multigravidous women try to get their minds off the subject of death by staying busy. The activity preoccupies thoughts and fills time so that it is not so oppressively heavy.

The activity is directed toward providing for the woman's intimate family while she is gone and in case she does not return. The curtains are taken down and laundered; loads of personal laundry are washed, ironed, mended, sorted, and put away; floors are scrubbed;

closets and cupboards are scrubbed; bills are paid, the last will and testament is formulated; arrangements are made for the care of the children. Almost all of the activity is done silently: the persons closest to her become anxious and uncomfortable if she speaks of her possible death or the provisions that should be made for such an eventuality.

Sleep is disrupted by the dream images of delivery or of the child she delivers. She prefers to stay awake, to do something to get her mind occupied. The chosen activities do not require concentration or movements that are rapid or strong. The repetitiousness of the movements, as in ironing or scrubbing, are rhythmical and comforting, like a lullaby or a rocking chair. Through her own experience, a woman learns what is comforting or consoling when there are no answers, no solutions, and no escape. She will use these learnings to comfort and to console her child through his difficult situations.

The awareness of time running out, perhaps of life-time running out, is a singularly lonely experience. There is a dread of dying, but not of this loneliness. There is an estrangement, an isolation from others, but this is not experienced as oppression or desertion. This aloneness is acceptable and comfortable. It is in sharp contrast to the aloneness of physical vulnerability where another is sought for and held onto so desperately. There is a quality of peace in being alone, in doing what one has to do, and in surviving quite well what has to be endured alone through inner resources of faith and pragmatism. Without physical pain or dismemberment, the prospect of death is not all that dreadful.

It is not so much the constriction in time and space of the third trimester that is burdensome but the pregnancy itself. Time and space comprise the framework of a living world. During pregnancy a woman occupies two worlds in time and space, an inner world and an external "real" world. The two worlds are disparate but mediated through the mind and body of the pregnant woman. Synchronization between the two worlds is possible until the eighth to ninth month. Then the child becomes much larger, occupies more space, and is much more active while the woman's activities are reduced in rate and scope and effectiveness.

The cumulative mass of the pregnancy, once nurtured with pleasure for every pound of gain, now weighing anywhere from fifteen to fifty pounds and of a size almost equal in length to her own torso, is now seen in terms of delivery. In the imagery of fantasy, the prospect of delivery vaginally becomes awesome. The vulnerability to external injuries and intrusions upon the body and its boundaries is augmented by the fantasies of the child coming out forcefully, rending the woman's body, and hurtling to the floor. The dangers in delivery make it imperative that she be close to the hospital. Closeness is measured both in time and in space. The fantasy of delivery as explosive or splitting is manifest in her dreams of the earth splitting, or coming upon chasms, or walking down staircases that disappear. A woman is not alone in these fantasies of childbearing. A husband, neighbors, police, firemen, and almost everyone else fantasize a destructive explosion in childbirth, and rush to get a laboring woman close, in time and space, to where control over delivery can be exercised knowledgeably.

Time and Space in Labor and Delivery

The coordination and synchronization of action in time and space holds a very high value (Rubin, 1968b). Knowing what to say or what to do when the time for saying or doing is past, and the situation itself has past, is useless for action. Human culture values the exquisite coordination of action in time and space of the musician, dancer, sportsman, trapeze artist, and juggler. High levels of achievement in coordination of action and space attract large admiring audiences. What is entertained is the aspiration to achieve effective control of self in exquisite coordination and synchronization with time and space. Success is the summary term for the successive practice and preparatory inputs for action, mental or physical, to effect control of self in pinpoint time and particular space. Control is of self, not of time or space. Luck, good or bad, has to do with the conjunction of time and space, space as events, situations, or place, in which self is active and in control of self.

It is the self-control in relation to time and space that is of paramount importance to the woman in labor and delivery performance. The woman who has a "false" call or "false" labor may be in the right place at the wrong time in relation to her own performance or activity. It is like the runner who starts the race before the race is started, or like the person who responds to an invitation and arrives at the right place a week before the party is scheduled to begin. The humiliation is high, the self-concept is low. The falseness is not applicable to the labor but to the person in action and in knowledge. The audience reflecting the self in action is a public one in the hospital, a resonating one on return to the home and neighborhood. The pain of this humiliation is so great that a woman who has had one false labor will delay calling for help or returning to the hospital when labor resumes until it is almost too late. She can endure the pain of contractions better than the humiliation repeated. It is the concern for safe passage, her own intactness, and the survival of the baby that override the danger of repeat humiliation.

Actually, there seems to be no such thing as false labor. A woman starts in labor with uterine contractions many times in the last three or four weeks of pregnancy. Contractions stop and labor does not progress when a woman fears the baby is premature or immature, when the prospect of her possible mutilation is too great, when she has cause to feel that she and her child are rejected, or when she is exhausted from sleep deprivation and emotional tension. The uterine muscle contractility is not under voluntary controls, but it is responsive to the involuntary inputs of the reticular system and limbic or survival system of the brain. Labor can stop progressing anywhere up to four centimeters of dilatation, the point where increased and usually irreversible momentum is established. There are confirmed reports, however, of women with uterine dilatation of six centimeters walking around, conducting their lives for about two weeks before resuming and completing labor. The uterus is not an isolated organ; it is a system as open to the mental apparatus as it is to the circulatory and hormonal systems.

Uterine contractions are spaced in time. There is a rhythmicity and predictability in the contractions that are in themselves not unpleasant. It is the force of the descending fetus against the woman's bony frame that can be quite painful. An observer can palpate the pressure on the thoracic cage in midlabor by full-sized twins or the protrusion of the movable coccyx just before the end of labor in a typical labor. Women with a tight pelvic inlet for the baby feel the pressure in the hips and radiating down one leg, or at the symphysis, the cross-bones of the pelvis, depending on where the prominence of the baby's head is positioned on entry into the maternal pelvis. A baby uses its head quite effectively to leave the uterus and enter the outside world. There is a directional assist to the baby's head in the shape of the mother's pelvis, but this results in a lot of pressure on the mother's lower back in the last half of labor. A uterus in very good tone and effective for rapid labor puts more force against the mother's back. A child lying back-to-back with his mother is in a position where the uterine contractions are less effective, so labor is longer, and the riding of the prominence of the baby's head against the mother's sacrum is harder and longer than that of a baby facing a woman's back.

Relief from pressure-pain, once the baby has entered the inlet of the pelvis, is effected by reducing the weight and pressure on the woman's back: turning the body onto the side, rhythmical arching or rocking of the pelvis as done with dysmenorrhea, or counterpressure on the sacral pressure point, as done with any counterpressure to pain, such as toothache or headache. Women in labor provide this relief for themselves spontaneously as long as they are not too exhausted to move. The ischemia of the uterus at the height of the contraction adds pain to pressure-pain, and women spontaneously hold still during the sharp acme of a contraction.

Increased peripheral vascularity adds discomfort to pressure-pain. There is headache and the face, neck, and palms are covered with perspiration. The covers are thrown off the torso and feet to cool a body that has become unbearably hot. The increased body heat produces a dry mouth and throat. Fear adds to the dryness of the mouth and throat to produce a white gluelike plaque of mucus on the teeth and inner lips. Cooling washes, cooling compresses to the eyes, an ice bag to the head, cooling sips of water or ice cubes are received as gifts of relief. Rhythmical massages of the back relieve tension, provided there is no added friction, pressure, or generation of heat. Each of these relief measures received by a woman in labor is given by her to her child after delivery when the child needs relief or comfort.

But it is time superimposed on layers of tension, discomfort, and pain that makes labor burdensomely painful. There is a progressive withdrawal from outer space and a turning toward inner space as labor progresses. Awareness is withdrawn in concentric circles of space: from outside the room to only what is in the room, from what is in the room to what is in or on the bed, from what is in or on the bed to what is going on inside her body. There is a progressive attentiveness to the contraction, as though listening for the coming and going of the contraction. Life space is filled with the contractions, their coming and her preparation for them, their sway and her coping with their impact on her, and their going and her being able to let her guardedness down.

In this confined space of being, time is marked by the frequency, duration, and intensity of contractions. The woman uses the formula of Rate × Time = Distance. Distance is full dilatation, ten centimeters, the end of labor. Rate is determined subjectively by the force of the most recent contractions and her capacity to sustain and endure the force. Time is the time-space between now and the end. In the last phase of labor, seven to ten centimeters, a woman with moderate sedation will sleep so deeply between contractions that she is unaware of the intervals between contractions. Although the intervals at this phase are in a time ratio of four-to-one to the contractions, in the subjective experience there are no let-ups, no spaces between contractions, only a steady, incessant state. The after-effects of soreness from the pressure of each contraction is remarkably unnoticed during labor. But the fatigue of cumulative tension and self-control, combined with the cumulative lactic acid produced by uterine muscle exertions, is very much noted. It is the fatigue as much as the pain of labor that makes time such a necessary measure of the self and of the situation in labor: "How much longer?" "What time is it now?" "I can't go on any longer."

Time also serves to orient a woman in labor, to anchor her in the larger world. In early labor she uses the clock to note the onset of labor, to verify that contractions are occurring, to establish a point when she calls others, to determine how fast she needs to move, and, if there is doubt about true labor, how long the contraction lasts. A long slow labor disorients her in time: by time of day, morning or evening, or day of the week. Disorientation in time, such as occurs at the end of labor when ten minutes feels like an hour in subjective time, causes diffusion in self-orientation. A woman searches for a clock to mark the time delivery starts and ends. Years later she can still recall what time labor started and what time labor ended in delivery of this child.

Time defines a beginning and an end to an event, situation, or condition. In the flow of events, situations, and conditions, time in hour, day, or date circumscribes or puts a boundary around a particularly significant event for cognitive control and separation out from what is true and present and what is true and past. Women overdosed with cognitive depressants to minimize the awareness of pain have difficulty ascertaining a beginning or ending of pain. They also have an increased, pervasive sense of anxiety because they have less control of themselves in time-space. The woman who has had scopolamine in labor or a general anesthetic for delivery has difficulty realizing that she has delivered, that she is no longer in labor, no longer in pain. It can take quite a while before this woman marshals sufficient evidence to backfill for the end of labor and delivery events and the beginning of the neomaternal and neonatal events.

Cognitive awareness marshals the inner controls to coordinate self, event-time, and situational-space. Pain that is unrelieved and persistent, however, floods (Schilder, 1970) the body and mental apparatus with noxious sensations. Body boundaries become diffuse and the ability to delineate what is self and what is environment is reduced. Loud noises in the environment are sensed as added pressure in a pain-filled body. Nevertheless, a woman dreads loss of control in pain and works hard not to cry, scream, or soil the linen with blood, urine, or feces. If there is a loss of control, she is an object of shame in her own self-esteem, and, she assumes, in the estimation of others. The loss of control of the contents of the uterus, liquid, blood, or the fetus descending with rapid momentum arouses fear or panic, not shame.

When the fatigue of labor reduces her energy and effectiveness in coordinated control of her actions in event-time and situational-space, a woman welcomes surrendering control to another. Even the guided synchronization of respirations with contractions is submitted to responsively and in gratitude. A cue for when to sleep, when to let go or when to ready, and when to take deep breaths reduces the level of anxiety to a remarkable degree and with it the layering of pain.

Time and Space in the Puerperium

The subjective experience of time and space in the postpartum phase of childbearing is anchored in the delivery event. Like a magnet in a field, delivery serves as a point of orientation for both the pregnancy and postpartum phases of childbearing.

With childbirth there is a deliverance from intense physical and mental pain and from the imminent threat of dismemberment or death. The relief is profound, hoped for but never really expected, as though born again to live, and valuing the privilege of life as never before. In this context, the child is a gift twice given of life itself. The miracle of life, its wonder and beauties, are attributes of this child, no matter how homely he may appear. This experience in death, to the point of tasting it, and life given again twice over forms a matrix of bonding unique to the biological mother. There is a spiritual, religious, and philosophical experience. The ethos and meaning of life is enriched. The gift of a child takes on the dimension of an entrustment and responsibility for a life. The concept of her own life-time becomes less finite and less subject to the personal caprice of freedom to do with her own life as she pleases, not in deprivation but in privilege.

There are surprisingly few instances of women who, given a live and complete child, do not experience the poignant relief of deliverance and accentuated love of life. These few instances occur in situations in which social acceptance is severely withheld or in which pain has gone unrelieved. Unrelieved pain is subjectively experienced as social rejection of the self. Being rejected as a person tends to produce rejection, an antipathy toward life, the child, and the self.

The surge in elation and well-being in being alive, safe, and having been given a child is followed by a sustained taking-in of life. The life space is circumscribed in the simple, life-sustaining functions (Rubin, 1961a). There is a real appetite and pleasure for sleep and food. The social acceptance and tributes of others are compatible with the woman's joy in a new life. The responsive behaviors of others give resonance to the good feelings and significance of life. A woman takes these tributes in with the same pleasure as food and sleep.

The physical care and ministrations to her body in relief of the residual aches and deprivations of labor, in the healing of open wounds, and in the promotion of restoration in body functions is taken in, in restoration of the self-concept and self-esteem. Events, situations, and conditions in labor and in pregnancy are reviewed. Missing elements are backfilled for wholeness and then summed up for perspective: it was worth it; it was a good or a terrible pregnancy. The review and summary provide a debriefing for an intense experience. The ministrations provide a decompression for the intense physical traumatization. Together they serve to complete the intense mental and physical experience of childbearing and childbirth, to finish them so that they become past experiences, put away in memory to free both mind and body for future experiences in a new life.

The taking-in phase of the postpartum period involves a centration in space equivalent to that of early labor and late pregnancy. In duration time, the centered taking-in phase postpartally is equivalent—three weeks—to the preparatory labor phase at the end of pregnancy. In the last three weeks of pregnancy, subjective space progressively decreases to the delivery point. In the first three weeks postpartally, subjective space progressively expands from the delivery point.

The subjective experience of time during the first three weeks after delivery is related to her own activity. Since motor activity is reduced by residual fatigue, a lowered and impoverished circulating blood volume, and residual aches from skeletal and tissue pressures, movements are slow and labored. She depends on the activities of others for orientation in time and for her own behavior: time for meals, time for the baby, time for visitors. If there is pain, and there usually is from swelling at the sutures, from hemorrhoids or abdominal distension, uterine contractions, headaches, or breast engorgement, time is endless and burdensome. Sleep deprivation and sleep disruption added to sleep hunger lead to disorientation in real time.

It is in this behavioral mode of receptivity, of taking-in, in the constricted action-space and time, that neomaternal behaviors are begun. There is a taking-in, cognitively, of the child. The whole child, the macroscopic appearance, characteristics, and behaviors, and the rules of conduct in the mother–child subsystem are absorbed through all sensory modalities. There is a cognitive imprinting, the formation of a cognitive map to know everything about this child. There is an eager, appetitive quality to this taking-in behavior.

There is also an appetitive receptivity to her husband as lover and to her other children. The primipara cannot wait to return to her husband. The multipara has more to do in planning and reorganizing the family constellation, forming a cognitive map of relationships and interactions within the altered family structure: how she will introduce the new child to her children, how she will get her older child up and off to school before she bathes her new child, how she will have so much help. These plans tend to remain at the fantasy level, but there is an ideal, a goal to move toward. There is very little initiated or sustained activity in the three-week receptive, taking-in phase. The mind is eager for a full life, but the body is still healing in intactness of structure and function, and energy levels are depleted by the fatigue of labor and delivery. The gap between the ideal image and the self-image enlarges in the home setting.

The fatigue in the postpartum period is superordinate. Just as vulnerability dominates the end of pregnancy, fatigue dominates the three or more weeks following delivery. The upright position is hard to maintain. There is not enough energy for activities to be executed satisfactorily in the upright position. She sits whenever possible, yearns to lie down, to let go, but the ideal image, her "should" system, pushes her on.

Sleep disruption superimposed on profound fatigue creates a sense of victimization. Babies who cannot differentiate night and day and who get hungry as though hunger is a disaster every three or four hours are incompatible with a nuclear family in an abbreviated lying-in period. The sense of victimization is symmetrically experienced by the husband—"What about the father?"—who is also tired and sleep deprived. Ideas of infanticide, matricide, and patricide are not rarities.

Confined personal space and amorphous time is not within the husband's experience and this provides him a broader, more realistic perspective for husbanding. The social isolation that occurs with the centration in time and space for the postpartum woman in a nuclear household reduces contact with the real world. The contact socially helps to maintain self-boundaries and to maintain an openness of the self-system and the maternal–child system to a larger system. Without the social contact as interface between systems there is entropy: disorientation, depression, despair.

The disorientation, depression, and despair are more pronounced in the primipara than in the multipara. Most multiparas learn from their experience as primiparas to ensure sleep and physical recovery before returning to the isolation of the nuclear household. The multipara dreads the postpartum isolated space-time, her powerlessness, the literally out-of-contact depression, and the paranoid feelings that could lead to infanticide or homicide. If there are older children, contact and orientation in real time is helped, but the fatigue can be oppressive.

The orderly comings and goings of people in the household, time for meals, adult-level stimulation, ordering of simple tasks for beginning and ending times, and a change in routines help counter the depression and disorientation. But in the first postpartal month, in contrast to the excitement surrounding delivery, in the lack of body intactness and energy for body support or movement, and in the centricity of conceptual space, a woman is powerless to initiate and effect controls.

The end of the lying-in postpartum period coincides with the essentially completed bodily involution and recovery. Body intactness is restored; organs are restored in size and place. There is a body boundary and a postural model. There is energy for the erect position and motion. And the baby sleeps through one feeding so that there is a blessed six to eight hours of uninterrupted sleep. In real time this occurs three weeks after the delivery day for most women, longer for women who had a caesarean section or other physical complications at delivery, such as hemorrhage.

There is symmetry of the subjective experience in the three weeks before delivery and the three weeks after delivery in time and space, the postural model, and the rate of motor activity. Before delivery there is an overhanging threat of loss of intactness, wholeness, or life and an increased alertness for danger. After delivery, there is a relief and joy in life, then a dulled level of awareness characteristic of fatigue and sleep hunger, and an actual loss in body intactness and function. The subjective experience in the last three or four weeks of pregnancy has a definitive end point in time-space and event-action, in delivery. The subjective experience in the first three or four weeks after delivery has no ending, no definitive time or action-event to demarcate the end of a stage-situation of the self.

In the seemingly endless flow of actions and experiences, a time-space marking the beginning and ending of a situation or state is essential for self-orientation. Schooling, for example, goes on and on from the age of three to eighteen or more, but it is demarcated into units that have a beginning and an ending and are progressive. There are rites of passage in promotion and in graduation that give awareness and orientation to the end of one stage, the beginning of another. Birthdays, marriage, delivery, christening, confirmation, and retirement are rites or social celebrations of the completed passage of an experiential state, converting a situation into an event, an entity, complete and finished. This identification and separating out of what is passed and what is present releases energies bound in attitudes and behaviors of the past for the present or the future.

There is currently no endpoint to the lying-in or neomaternal stage in American and some Western societies other than the child's baptism. Discharge from the hospital to the home is seen, quite correctly, as a rite of passage, as the end of one experiential event and the beginning of another. But it is also seen as signifying the end of the larger childbearing experience, which it is not. There is, therefore, an added overlayment of disorientation in attitudes and expectations by the woman and her family that adds unfortunate stress on the nuclear family and the woman's feelings of sanity.

Women spontaneously effect an end point in time and space to the lying-in stage of childbearing when they have physically recovered. Independently and without awareness of the general practice, they energetically burst out into sociable space and sociable time (Rubin, 1961b, 1977). Most typically they leave the baby at home. There is a similarity and symmetry in time and function of this bursting out of the home into the sociable world with the sentimental journey of late pregnancy. Postpartally it is a sentimental reaffirmation of attachment bonds, but it is also a drive and a readiness to reenter the adult world in time and space.

8

The Fourth Trimester

Delivery of the child is the climax but not the end of the childbearing experience. There is still the physical involution from the expansive growth of pregnancy and the recovery from the labor and delivery experience. There is still the identification of this child and the development of maternal behavior in the interaction system of mother and child. There is still the adjustment and accommodation of the constellation of relationships in the family and household to include the new member.

Following delivery the physical structures and functions of the body that served the woman so well as nourishing host and protector to her unborn child recede and are restructured for simple functional objectives. The changeover is not without functional disequilibrium. In addition there is the recovery process from the efforts of labor and the loss of intactness from the traumata of the expulsive forces in delivery.

With the birth of the child there is a massive shift in orientation to the child and to herself as mother of this child. There is transition in location of the child from the innermost body space to the external, environmental space, from the child in fantasy to the known real child, from the futuristic "someday, a child" to the immediate present "now, this child of mine." And there is a transition in the identification of self as mother from the predominantly receptive mode of taking-in to taking-on and actively doing and being mother of this child. The greatest part of the relocation and reorientation is achieved in the first month postpartally, but the binding-in process is not stabilized until the second or third month.

Under conditions of acceptance, each member of the family is quite willing to welcome and accommodate the new family member. The newborn, however, does not join a family but stays in his own world within his own orbit of eating and sleeping patterns, acutely vulnerable to his own limitations and needs, unable to communicate or to respond. The newborn's contributions to the family are more symbolic than real, and his initiatives tend to be intrusive, demanding, and disruptive. The malodors of the regurgitations, urine, and feces and the scatter of his possessions and equipment are irritating. The newborn is asocial.

The burden of socialization, through mediation, interpretation, protection, and reading of the newborn's expressivity, falls to the woman as mother. In the specialized functions of the maternal–child subsystem (Parsons & Bales, 1955) the microscopic developmental transitions of the newborn from the uterine to the external world can be fostered, protected, and supplemented by the mothering activities of the woman on the baby's behalf to make him socially acceptable. The major breakthroughs from the mother–child subsystem into the family system occur when the baby develops to the point where he sleeps through the night, when he can see and recognize another and the recognition elicits a smile, when he can stand and walk about in this world, when he tries to communicate in speech, and finally, when he can dispose of his own urine and feces without inflicting the odor and sight on anyone else. With these cumulative achievements the child moves out of the specialized mother–child subsystem into the family system.

The specialized mother–baby system within a family is often perceived as a wedge, intrusively disrupting the integrity of the family by its exclusivity and its usurpation of time for established lines and styles of relationships. The resentment of the displacement is experienced by every member of the family, including the woman as wife and mother of other children. It is often hard to see the trade-off benefits of change that involves loss.

The exclusivity and intimacy of the mother–child subsystem is a territorial problem for the husband becoming a family man and finding the husband–wife relationship relegated to a special subsystem within the family. It is also a territorial problem for the child who was previously the baby and is now moved deeper into the complex family system. A woman who has a baby, however, does not deny the legitimacy of her newborn child or the special relationship because of the intensive and extensive experience of binding-in to the child during pregnancy. It is the woman's own personal loss in the special relationship with her husband and with the child who was her baby that makes her aware, in regret not just in sympathy, and energizes her to "make it up" in a wellspring of affection and consideration after delivery.

The reconstruction of the self-system, the mother–child system, and the family as system is begun immediately after delivery in eager anticipation, a product of the binding-in process, and in faith and confidence, a result of the favored outcome of the delivery experience. The puerperium is the end goal of the long preparatory and readying process of pregnancy and the travails of labor. There is a release of energies pent up in the waiting out of the pregnancy course, a realization of actualization, and a yearning for reunification and wholeness in her family.

After the seemingly endless waiting out of pregnancy, waiting for labor to begin and waiting for labor to end, the theme of the postpartal period is "can't wait." The primipara can't wait to go home to be reunited with her husband; the multipara can't wait to see, hear, and touch her children who are at home. A woman can't wait to see and hold her newborn. She can't wait until she regains her figure. The woman's time frame has changed from "someday" to "now."

This new time frame is particularly useful in its synchrony with that of the newborn, whose time frame is "right now." The differential between maternal and infant time frames, of the "now" and the "right now," is a compatible one in the first two or three weeks of the puerperium. Since this is a period of acute vulnerability for the newborn, when his cries express acute distress, the compatibility is fortunate. Beyond this period a mother becomes impatient with the differential in time frames and wishes he would wait a minute. By the end of the fourth trimester when the baby can see and has built up a repertoire of experiences to form a narrow range of predictive expectancy, his time frame for "now" is less pinpointed and can span a give or take of ten to twenty minutes. This achievement is a great relief and a gift of time to the mother. By then, however, the mother's time frame has enlarged and commerce with the baby in "now" includes "soon" and "later."

The limited time frame of the child's conceptual capacity and action can be stifling and exhausting. For the adult, "now" is an extrapolation between yesterday and tomorrow, between experience and objectives. A mother has "more patience" with the limited time frame of childhood but not so much patience that she can accept all of the child's needs for immediate gratification, all the "dawdling" and "taking forever," or his endangerment by the lack of foresight in the "now" framework of childhood.

The woman's capacity to participate in the "now" time frame of the child and to gradually push for the enlargement in his conceptual time-space provides the context for the endearing companionship and directional guidance in the child's long and lonely course of growing up. Occupation of now-time is not without its stresses to a mother, however. Sustained now-time is empty in sameness and is endless because there is so little change in action or in focus. A mother caring for an infant in acute now-time finds each hour and each day infinite, prolonged, and exhausting with nothing to show for it, no end point. Now-time without relief is confining, exhausting, and disorienting to a healthy adult. The disorientation of empty time-space is a threatening experience. It is a common experience of the puerperium, starting in the second week and becoming progressively cumulative in the isolation and entrapment without relief from the endlessness and pointlessness of now-time. Shame and depression follow from and add to the disorientation. The worst case is that of a woman with two children, an infant and one less than a year of age, in the isolation of a nuclear household. The least severe is the case of the woman who has other adults in the household during the day as well as during the nights. But then she must suffer the adult conceptual time-frame that admonishes against "spoiling" the infant—because he will never succeed in making the team or succeed in business if he cries all the time.

In the exhaustion from unending now-time or from its effect in the fear of losing her mind, a healthy woman protests and seeks relief. The relief takes many forms, and each woman may try several forms to effect an equilibrium and her own balanced mix of now-time with her child and of the conceptual time-frame of adult life. At no time during the first years of childbearing, however, is there a sufficient proportion of adult-type time for self-actualization. But when the growing child is bored or depressed in the loneliness and endlessness of now-time, a mother knows from experiential insight that relief lies in companionship and in activity that is novel.

The major thrust of the newly delivered woman in reconstruction of the self system, the mother–child subsystem, and the family as system is focused on the mother–child system, on her own effectiveness as mother of this child, and on his survival and well-being. A woman is aware of the interface and interdependence of the systems and that the mother–child system is the fulcrum, not a wedge, for the successful reconstruction and well-being of the family and of the self. In the normative course of childbearing, the first half of the fourth trimester is indeed the puerperium, the period of this child.

Maternal–Child Subsystem

There are two members, partners of equal significance, in the maternal–child subsystem. Maternal identity, maternal behavior, and the quality of life, maternal and familial, is anchored in the developmental age-stage, sex, physical condition, and behavior of this child.

The initial arrival and presentment of this child is crucial. During pregnancy a woman seriously considers the highly variant possible conditions of the child and its attendant situational consequences for her and for her family. The dread and fear of the various possibilities is a factor in labor, in holding back on the progression of labor, and in dreading to see the baby. "Is it all right?" is the prevalent question during pregnancy, at delivery, and during the puerperium.

The mother of a stillborn child feels denied, rejected, and deprived of wholeness and intactness in the self and in the family. Restitution, not reconstruction, is slow and incomplete. There is always a void in the self system and in the family.

The mother of a premature has a very incomplete delivery with an incomplete infant. There is no end of one phase of childbearing and the beginning of another. There is identity diffusion and a continuance of the pregnancy as if still awaiting delivery. There is constricted energy and space for action and the images of the child are of nightmarish quality. The mother of a child with a congenital defect feels denied and rejected in her wishes and expectations and confronted with her own defectiveness in making a child. There is a deactivating shock and a profound bereavement (Lindemann, 1944) for a remarkably short period of time. The bereavement seems to stop at the protest stage, in vehement denial that a defect should be met with rejection. The resultant energy and activity of a mother in securing remediation or compensatory adaptive modalities for her child and the close, firm durable bond with this child of hers is awesome testimony to the capacity for courage and altruism of the human spirit. The protest phase of bereavement (Lindemann, 1944) also produces the "why me?" aspect in the intimidation of the overwhelming burden of caring for this child. The painful uniqueness is relieved in experience with other mothers whose situations are as bad as or worse than her own and in finding people of goodwill whose consideration and help reduce her burden. Pity, however, recycles the protest in all its aspects. A mother of a child with a defect avoids the public and its condescending pity.

"It does not matter what the sex of the baby is, as long as it's healthy." This is a pregnancy statement; the prayer is for a living, whole, and well baby. Given such a child, the gender does matter. A man wants a son and a woman wants a daughter. Someone is going to be disappointed and there will have to be another pregnancy to give her husband the son he wants or to get the daughter she desires. The last thing a woman wants to even think about postpartally is another pregnancy. But if the second or the third child is of the same gender as the first child, a woman feels despair, not just disappointment. A series of same-sex children leaves the parent of opposite gender rejected and unfulfilled. A woman is more comfortable, can empathize with and understand a little girl at all ages. During the neonatal period sex differences are not prominent. But a boy does have penile erections in voiding, in bathing, and when he is held after a feeding. This is charming but dissonant in the relationship and causes some distancing. Whether it is maternal distancing or the little boy's angularity, a boy baby tends to be less cuddly after the neonatal period.

The condition of the normal, healthy neonate is in itself an enigma. The newly delivered woman is eager to have, to nourish, to care for, and to protect her baby. But a neonate is much harder to care for than a baby. There is no experience of the neonate to provide even a familiarity with his appearance, size, functional behavior, and personality at birth. There are so many changes during the first week in the appearance and tonus of the newborn that it is difficult to establish what is a temporary and transient feature and what is a true, permanent feature. The newborn manifests the duration and dehydration of the labor experience, the pressure of resisting pelvic structures in descent and birth, and extensive coloration changes with oxygenation on exiting the uterus, on crying, and at rest. There is edema of the presenting part in labor, there is edema of the eyelids from the prophylaxis, and occasionally there are extensive bruises from forceps. There is often a dry scaly skin abdominally and usually long fingernails. In the search to identify this child, impressions oscillate between beautiful and ugly, attractive and repulsive, alert and responsive or limp like a rag doll.

There is no consistency in the amount and style of eating by the infant during the first week of life, so there is no predictability of his performance or his needs. Measures taken and plans made to ensure a more satisfactory feeding often become unnecessary or irrelevant. The apparent randomness and inconsistency of his behavior make identification and orientation thin and insecure. There is dependence on nursing expertise for definition, insight, and understanding of the infant's behavior for stability, security, and self-confidence. Dependency is undesirable in its infantilizing properties, and asking for help is self-demeaning unless the dependency is legitimized. But without help or with too little help in interpretation and understanding, the irrationality of the neonate's behaviors can be overwhelming, producing rigid and inflexible maternal behaviors, or producing premature and antipathetic polarization between mother and infant.

The neonate is in a stage of transition from a uterine world to a world as we know it. His behaviors are an admixture of adaptiveness to the experiential situations and conditions of both worlds with a greater proportion of behaviors appropriate for a uterine world.

The neonate looks but does not see. As sole occupant of the eventless uterine world, there is nothing to see and sight is useless. Daylight is a new experience. Strong light is painful, but the neonate enjoys having vision and gazes avidly when his energies permit. The gazing increases in frequency and in duration and is most prominent during a meal. The gazing is nonperceptive—perception requires a framework of experience and cognition—but provides contented pleasure. An infant is extremely near sighted and has no peripheral vision, but within the limits of his spatial access he patently enjoys vision in the progression from active gazing, to seeing and holding, and to recognition and searching.

With limited vision, the infant uses the tactile mode predominantly. Sounds, pleasant and unpleasant, are received in the tactile mode as a stroking or pounding of the aural fluid and cilia. Babies like to be talked to and enjoy hearing rhythmical, caressing sounds. They also respond to stroking of the head and back. Taste is more in the tactile texture and viscosity than in flavor. The dominance of the tactile mode in infancy and early childhood further demonstrates the spatial awareness of the child's self in a world where nothing exists that does not come into direct propinquity with the body. It is through the tactile mode of passive and active experience that a child learns about himself and the world around him and establishes a body boundary of secure containment between self and the world.

In utero there is no change in climatic temperature, no discontinuity in the source and supply of food and oxygen, no transactions internally with digestion, elimination, or respiration, and no transactions externally with events or people. Without change, discontinuity, or action, time is infinite, unsegmented, and without experiential meaning for past or future location and allocation. Any change, discontinuity, or transaction in utero would be fatal. After birth the pain of a climatic temperature drop of 20° to 30°, the pain of hunger, or the pain of pressure of the first formed stool marshal the infant's awareness and energies to imminent danger. Air is forced out of the lungs in a strong cry, all four limbs flail, and the circulation is increased, reddening the face and torso. The energy is mobilized but the infant is helpless for accommodative action. Fortunately, the urgency and desperation of the infant's cry mobilizes the empathetic anxiety of the hearer, adult or child, to intervene on behalf of the baby.

The neonate's capacities to marshal and to sustain effort are particularly remarkable when compared with the effortlessness of uterine life. After birth an infant works at pumping air into and out of his chest, rests awhile, and then resumes breathing. As the intercostal muscles develop, breathing requires less effort. The nasopharynx is short, coordination of the musculature to permit swallowing and breathing is not too effective, so the infant stops in feeding to take deep breaths, then resumes sucking and swallowing. Food and wet burps can flow through the nostrils if a baby sucks more than he can swallow or if his position while swallowing or burping is a recumbent one. Until the circular muscles of the mouth, the buccinator muscles of the cheeks, and the drawing muscles of the tongue are developed by usage, feeding takes effort and time. An adult can be dismayed at the length of time it takes an infant to consume a half ounce, an ounce, or three to four ounces of simple food. But an infant never protests the effort, the time, or the fatigue of working with as yet undeveloped muscular equipment. On the contrary, the infant seems to get gratification in attaining comfort and satisfaction through his own efforts. The fatigue and deep sleep following work is accepted and the next feeding is welcomed with enthusiasm and eagerness. A healthy child enjoys using his resources of energy in an effort to produce a satisfying experience and is miserable when he does not have the energies or capacities to overcome a situation through his own or assiste efforts.

Both active and passive movements are possible and present in a uterine world, where the surfaces are smooth and well lubricated, where there is no resistance, and where weightlessness obtains as a relative absence of gravitational pull. The mother's walk provides a rhythmical, gentle, rocking motion. When his mother stops walking to sit or lie down, the infant as fetus in utero can cross his legs, turn around or do a somersault; motor activity is pleasurable. After birth the passive movement of being carried is like being home again. Being carried or rocked in rhythmical motion is an instant relief from the pain signals of hunger or of being put into a cold, clammy bed. When vision is better developed, being carried is the secure and comforting way of enlarging the spatial world. What is not available after birth is the muscular energy and body framework to overcome the resistance of surfaces and the pull of gravity. An infant can raise his head for an instant but he cannot change his position and he cannot pull out a limb that is pinned down under the weight of his own body. The sheer joy in motor activity, active or passive, is manifest in the pleasurable games of babyhood and is a major characteristic of well-being in childhood.

The uterine world is an environment of supportive containment and finite in its boundaries. In any direction that the infant as fetus moves in the uterus there is contact and feedback. After birth the loss in support, containment, or contact with finite borders produces a startle, a generalized grasping movement, and then profound fear or panic. The response will be the same whether the infant is dropped in space, placed on his back or side without support so that he rolls, or put into a position where on extension of his limbs there is no contact, only infinity. This terror of boundless space, of movement in space uncontained, unsupported, and without contact, is not unique to the newborn but endures in the nightmares and fears of childhood and adulthood. When bundled, swaddled, or supported in bed in the prone position so that with any movement of the arms, legs, or torso there is bounded space for contact, the infant is content and secure.

The reciprocal of the infant's need for contact is the maternal need to hold her infant. Maternal "holding" is an enfolding of the infant within the largest and most sensitive surface of her arms and bringing the infant onto the surface of her chest, particularly her breasts, for a complete encirclement and containment of the infant in maximal body surface contact. The infant responds to maternal holding by curling his trunk, head, arms and legs onto the maternal body surface for maximal contact. The cuddling is experienced by the mother as a gratifying responsiveness to her. The complementarity and full trust in contact is a shared experience of security and pleasurable contentment. The act of giving birth is not completed for a woman until she can hold her baby. The child remains a phantom, unreal, until he is experienced again and again in the mutually responsive and rewarding holding/cuddling embrace. For the infant in full contact in the mother's embrace, there is no danger from cold or hunger, and the passive movements provided in the act of being held, by her singsong speech, or by her bodily movements help make this new world very compatible with his feelings of security, trust, and faith (Erikson, 1956). A woman denies herself this affirmative bond with her newborn child only under conditions of severe stress or pain in herself or in her baby.

The comforting peace and tranquility that heals many hurts, and the full, nonverbal communion in the warm contact with her infant is one of the most gratifying experiences in having a baby. Equally gratifying is the state of serene contentment manifested in her baby as a result of her ministrations. The serenity, induced and shared in the reciprocal relationship between mother and infant, is the substantive bond, the gift given and received each to the other, and the goal to be attained again and again in the maternal identity.

There is pleasure in discovery of the newborn child, his attributes, characteristics, and behavioral capacities. The neomaternal woman requires a reorientation and relocation point of identification of her infant. The location of the child outside her own body is an adaptive process requiring confirmation as long as the enteroceptive stimuli and the body image of pregnancy persist. The child's functional properties outside the uterus come as dysjunctive surprises. The neomaternal woman has to ask if the cry or the burp emanates from her child, and she is arrested in motion by the sneeze, hiccups, voiding, and defecations produced by her child. Although she is quite prepared and eager to feed her baby, the child's capacities to suck, swallow, and burp come as surprises that are pleasurable, inducing respect and pride in his unexpected abilities.

Unattended and unsupported, the neomaternal woman's identification of her newborn baby's features and characteristics in appearance and function are remarkably thin and cursory. The causal interpretations of his behaviors are predominantly negative in quality.

Back to back with the experience of vulnerability in pregnancy and of the dangers in labor and delivery, the woman is less than sanguine about the uncoordinated movements and the strange or dysfunctional behaviors in her infant. Aspirations, choking, bleeding, eruptions, rashes or distress signals evoke anxiety. Which manifestations are "normal" and which are not, and what does one do to make a differential distinction, or to take effective safeguarding measures? The tension and anxiety serve the woman as mother well because the infant is highly vulnerable and there are few degrees of freedom in time and action when an infant is endangered. There is little humor or playfulness in the insecure, unstable, uncertain neonatal/neomaternal period. The characteristic vigilance of the maternal identity develops early. The vigilance intensifies with experiences of actual or threatened loss of wholeness in the infant. Given the vulnerability and the low predictability of the neonate at a period of low levels of physical tonus and energy, the responsibility as protector can be overwhelming.

Self System

It takes nine months from childbirth for a woman to feel like herself again: whole, intact, functional, and in goodness of fit of self in the world. Traditionally, when women nursed their babies at breast, this duration of nine months for recovery and reconstitution was accepted and expected. Without a concrete and visible symbol of the childbearing experience, each woman now believes that she alone requires so much time to heal and to reconstruct and that, therefore, she is less of a woman. The model of womanhood, somehow, is the primitive woman who gives birth in the field and then resumes working the field immediately. The rest of this anthropological tidbit, that the motivation is the spectre of starvation, that this woman of the fields ages prematurely and dies before the age of 30, does not enter the mythology of the ideal childbearer.

It is the disparity between the expected and the real, between the ideal image of self as woman, wife, and mother and the experience of self in body postpartally, that produces the self-disparagement. The self-depreciation results in depression and in hostility. The depression is a sense of hopelessness or despair that occurs in roller coaster fashion on the third, fifth, and seventh days postpartum. The depression becomes characteristic of the second and third weeks of confinement within her own lowered energy levels and continues in inverse relation to the feedback of competence and rising self-esteem. The hostility is a self-depreciation without despair or hopelessness, has a higher energy level than depression, and is directed primarily at self, and, by extension, to those belonging to her, such as her husband or child. Whereas depression is privately personal and apathetic, hostility disparages loved ones in a spread-effect. The spread of hostility is incompatible with self-control and self-esteem and therefore generates further self-depreciation.

The feelings of depression and hostility are unexpected, unwanted, and resonantly dissonant (Festinger, 1957) with the expected feelings of the momentous achievement of childbirth. When elation gives way to depression, when love is replaced by hostility, and the surge of generous giving is replaced by apathy or disparagement, there is a recycling of the lowered self-esteem, a disorientation, and a vivid fear that she is losing her mind. The situation is exacerbated in societies that disallow a lying-in period for physical recovery and demand fully developed maternal behavior during the neomaternal stage.

The pain of the negative feelings, the mismatch of self in a world, and the perversion of what should be a magnificently beautiful entry into the state of parenthood make the fourth trimester of childbearing most difficult. The primipara is stunned and ashamed, dreads the postpartum period as much as or more than labor in a subsequent pregnancy, and takes elaborate precautions to ensure help. The help, however, rarely materializes: the neomaternal woman rarely requests help and is so involved experientially that she cannot objectively define her needs.

Recovery from the traumata of labor and delivery and reconstruction of the anatomical and physiological structures for the nonpregnant state are necessary before a woman feels like herself again, actively and constructively participating in the current life space. But

in the puerperium, the early stage of the child, postpartum requirements are often subordinated or neglected.

In labor, the coccyx is usually displaced posteriorly by one to two
centimeters just before full dilatation. Earlier, the sacrum bulges as
much as one centimeter as the baby starts descent through the pelvis.
The low sacral pressure is particularly severe and prolonged when
the baby presents posteriorly, the back of the baby's head riding on
the maternal sacrum. With a large baby or twins, the maternal thoracic cage projects two to three centimeters with early contractions.
The rigid bony structures of thorax, sacrum, and coccyx are bent to a
point just short of fracture and are just as painful. The position for
delivery in current obstetrical practice and the pressures of the baby's
continued descent on the woman's back are also painful. Postpartally,
there is backache and the attendant guardedness and restriction in
movement. But women rarely complain. On the contrary, a backrub
promoting circulation and healing is perceived as an unexpected gift
of relief.

There are pressures on the soft tissues above and within the
pelvis during labor and particularly during descent of the baby. No
two labors are the same. Some descents pinch the kidneys or bladder,
the sciatic nerve, or the rectum. Lacerations of the cervix, the vagina,
and the urinary meatus are common. Protrusion of the rectum, hemorrhoids, is not uncommon. The soreness of the soft tissues of the
pelvic vault is generalized. A woman sufficiently rested and returning home to her husband in a very receptive mood is dismayed to find
intercourse aversively painful. The vaginal vault tends to remain
weakened so that cystoceles and rectoceles can occur with heavy lifting within the first two months postpartally. The low back pain and
vaginal fullness are coped with by reduced mobility.

As the local anesthesia wears off and healing starts, the perineal
episiotomy becomes hot and edematous with increased circulation.
With either hemorrhoids or the engorgement of the perineum there is
pain which increases on standing, walking, or sitting. There is a
sense of fullness or pressure as though everything inside is falling
down. There is a lassitude as with a low-grade fever and there are
headaches. Sometimes there are bruises on the tuberosities, the obstetrician's thumb pressures, to add to the discomfort. It takes about
two or three weeks for complete healing: two weeks with warm sitz
baths or compresses to the perineum and cool compresses to the hemorrhoids, three weeks without any relieving treatments. Women complain very little about the pain but the loss of intactness and support
cause anxiety, an overlayment of pain, and there is careful guardedness in movement.

The woman who has had a delivery by caesarean section also has edema at the suture line, lassitude, headaches, and the anxiety about loss of intactness. Like the women with hemorrhoids or perineal sutures, acts of laughing, sneezing, or coughing increase pressures on the sutures and increase the sense of vulnerability of the body boundaries. Women after a caesarean section avoid turning from side to side, reaching, and sitting up in bed. They also avoid abdominal pressure contact with their newborns and are therefore deprived of much of the holding and cuddling contact with their infants. Infants delivered by caesarean section need supplementary holding and contact sessions to reduce hyperactivity.

In a woman delivered vaginally the third day postpartum is the day of major physical stress. Anesthesia has worn off, peristalsis returns, hormonal levels of estrogen and progesterone are at their lowest, lactation starts with engorged vascularization of the breasts, and the infant is listless with physiological jaundice. Whether breast or bottle fed, the baby is apathetic about food, and feeding sessions, so very important to the mother as a test of her capacity to nurture and to give, result in failure. In the now-time, "tomorrow" or "next time" is irrelevant and not reassuring to a new mother. If the breasts are engorged, there is malaise, low-grade fever, throbbing headaches, and a desperate need for the baby to nurse and relieve the breasts. Aspirins, compresses, and uplift support to the breasts can also supply relief at this time.

The return of peristalsis to the gastrointestinal tract produces a barrage of uncomfortable sensations which cause a centration of attention on the inner activities of the body. Added to the edema of the soft tissues in the pelvis, the flatus pressures are urgent and frequent, disrupting all other normal activities such as socializing, meals, and feeding or holding the baby. Hemorrhoids and perineal sutures interfere with evacuation and partial evacuation brings no relief. Some six to eight hours can be consumed in this struggle of evacuation of the bowels. Women become depressed and feel "like a baby" who cannot even perform such a simple function, and despair that they can ever be mothers. The woman who has had a caesarean section has acute abdominal gas pain. Relief is immediate with the insertion of a rectal tube. A woman resists an enema as long as possible, preferring a fully controlled evacuation by herself. There is a silent determination to avoid the pain and humiliation of inadequate bowel function by abstaining from milk and other gaseous foods, by avoiding large meals during the sedentary living, and by taking prune juice or laxatives.

There are uncomfortable discharges and odors postpartally that a woman copes with silently and immediately. There is an increased amount of perspiration, the diaphoretic discharge of the hydremia, sufficient to soak the night gown and bedding. The vaginal discharge of lochia is twice as long as the menses in duration and increases in flow with any upright position or activity. The woman who has had a caesarean section has, in addition, the mucoid plaques in the mouth, similar to that of women having fear in labor. But the postoperative woman cannot cope alone with the discharges, accretions, perspiration, or tangled hair unaided. The more immobilized a woman is postpartally, the less she can effectively provide for herself the grooming that relieves the encrustations and malodors emanating from the increased metabolic changes of the puerperium.

It is the immobility, the confinement within a body, that is the central characteristic and problem of the puerperium. Mobility in space is restricted by anemia, the gravitational pull on sutures, the unsupported internal organs, and the uncontrollable rush of lochial flow. It is the immobilization, the body drag and counterweight, that frustrates the neomaternal woman in her zest for living, activity, and creativity. There is nothing comparable to the entrapment within the limits and boundaries of one's own body to produce depression, hostility, and disorientation.

The intimate knowledge of this experience serves a woman as mother in infant care and childbearing. In essence the central problem of infancy and childhood is the entrapment of the infant or child, in illness or wellness, within the severe limits of functional mobility. The child's response to confinement or immobility is depression, hostility, and disorientation.

The single largest factor producing the postpartal immobility is profound fatigue. The original source of fatigue is the labor process itself. The depletion of oxygen supplies to the muscle fibers is manifest in the effort required, and the short sustainability of this effort, of the woman just delivered to raise her head, hold her baby, or hold a glass of water. Turning her body or maintaining an upright sitting position is more than she can do unaided and more than she can endure for more than a few minutes during the first two days.

The exhaustive fatigue of labor is followed by the more pervasive fatigue of anemia. The physiological hydremia of pregnancy, a hydrated red blood cell circulation that has its counterpart in the fetal circulation, provides the adaptive vehicle for oxygenation and nourishment of the pregnancy. The hydremia contributes to the woman's decreased activity, promoting the duration of the pregnancy. In labor the hydremia exacerbated by a superimposed dehydration promotes the profound fatigue experienced with contractions and expulsion.

Postpartally, the hydremic character of the circulating blood is replaced gradually over a period of weeks by the more typical iron-rich circulatory system. Before the more typical circulatory system is established, however, the anemia of pregnancy is compounded by the blood loss of delivery and by ten days of heavy lochial flow.

The tingling sensations in the soles of the feet when a woman stands up after no more than eight hours in bed, the sensation of faintness or dizziness on walking that causes women to hold on to something firm, the propensity for fainting in an airless bathroom, and the massive fatigue women experience after twenty minutes in maintaining upright positions of sitting, standing, or walking are caused by the oxygen depreciation in anemia. The decreased appetite and the energy expenditure for securing good but not necessarily convenient food when the woman is home alone and unattended further exacerbates the lowered supply of nutriments to the body tissues.

The massive and perseverant fatigue is accompanied by the apathy and decreased perceptual acuity always present with anemia. The household is a "mess," body grooming and dress are neglected. The dysjunction between the self-image as competent, resourceful, and well-organized and the self experienced in this situation of the puerperium is confusing and threatening to her stability. Except for the part-time help from a hungry and tired husband, there is no help and no relief for the woman isolated in the nuclear family household. There is a dogged, determined holding on to sanity, to life, and to the neonate in the treadmill series of obligations and responsibilities (Rubin, 1967d). As in labor, the woman does not see this costly perseverance as courageous, which it is, but as a matter of integrity.

The fatigue of the puerperium is overlayed by sleep hunger, sleep deprivation, and sleep disruption. Sleep deprivation and sleep disruption begin in the last month of pregnancy and increase exponentially in labor so that by delivery there is acute sleep hunger. With careful nursing management, the postpartal woman averages seven and a half hours of night sleep, always disrupted by her own needs as well as those of the hospital environment. This amount of sleep plus an hour nap is a maintenance level to handle the day's needs, but does not compensate for the cumulative sleep hunger unless it is continued for six or seven days (Kleitman, 1963). At home, with a baby to feed and care for, the sleep disruptions are of longer duration, every three or four hours, not enough for a complete sleep-dream cycle. Sleep deprivation and sleep hunger are severe in the first month of the puerperium and continue through the fourth trimester for as long as the infant requires three, two, or one feeding during the night, or has indispositions such as colic or illness.

Sleep deprivation is a recognized hazard to morale, to the ability to problem solve, and to the self-control necessary to prevent homicide (Kleitman, 1963; Dement, 1972). The sleep-deprived neomaternal woman has problems in morale; she can get irritable or depressed. Sometimes problems do not get solved and sometimes there is an impulse to infanticide or homicide. Her husband and other family members also experience sleep deprivation with a baby that has not learned that daytime and nighttime activity patterns should be different. But sleep deprivation under postpartal or postoperative conditions, when sleep should be increased for rest and recovery, is an extreme deprivation prolonging the fatigue and reducing the effectiveness of tissue healing and reconstruction of the self and relationships within the family.

9
Body Image and the Image of the Child in the Puerperium

Lying in the recumbent position after delivery, the woman's discovery of the flattened abdomen is a source of real pleasure, an orderly and rational consequence, a testimony that childbirth has been accomplished. There is a feeling of miraculous wholeness, and, if the baby is intact and whole in all its parts, a sense of marvelous completeness. The sense of completeness, a rare and very special feeling, makes the demands and sacrifices of the pregnancy, labor, and delivery "worth every minute of it." The physical and emotional painfulness of labor and delivery as an experience in cognitive awareness is suppressed in the completeness and fulfillment. The woman's sense of completeness is renewed and reaffirmed with the fullness of contact in holding the infant's body to her own body. It is also renewed in the circular and symmetrical feedback of eye contact, the baby's smile, and in the baby's contentment and pleasures.

The sense of fulfilled completeness, transitory and renewable in its nature, provides the motivation and the capacity to cope with new tasks and new problems and the strength in courage and endurance to persevere where others would resign in despair.

The woman whose infant is not whole and intact or who is deprived for some reason of holding, of eye contact, of the smile, contentment, or pleasure of her child feels very incomplete, a sense of hollow emptiness. Such deprivations do occur frequently in small unit doses in the typically normal experience. But in the postpartal now-time, the deprivation and sense of incompleteness seems extensive and motivates the woman to recruit her energies and resources to restore the symmetry and wholeness. When the deprivations persevere and are intractable, a woman continues to feel incomplete, less of a woman, with something seriously missing in herself as a person and something missing in this relationship with this child.

Sleep Patterns

Dream images during the first week of the puerperium unravel the confusion and disorder (Kleitman, 1963) of the feelings and emotions experienced in labor and delivery. Dream content postpartally tends to be of massive struggles against overwhelming obstacles. When dream content is peopled with others, the persons are those of significance at a former period of her life, whose indifferent or negative attitudes toward her are or should be now altered. Spontaneous dream disruptions are rare despite the frequent nightmarish proportions of the struggle content. When spontaneous dream disruption does occur, the woman leaves her bed to go to see her baby, or to visit in a lighted area with someone in a neutrally social conversation. Despite sleep hunger, women delay going to sleep, waiting up for the ten o'clock feeding, and then visiting, changing clothes, bathing, or setting hair before retiring.

Sleep during the first postpartal week is deep, with a very short first or induction phase and a long dream phase. It is not easy to rouse a woman in postpartal sleep. When a woman is roused, she is startled and disoriented in the desynchrony between the involvement in dream content and the mundanely affectless situation on arousal.

Postpartal sleep is very much like sleep during labor. In labor there is an elision of other sleep phases and a prolongation of the dream phase of sleep. In labor a woman falls into deep sleep in the five-minute interval between contractions so rapidly that there is no time to reposition her body in a supportable position. The woman in labor needs little encouragement to fall asleep again in the next interval between contractions. On being aroused by the next contraction, a woman is startled and disoriented, requiring reorientation to where she is and what is transpiring. Rapid eye movements are not characteristic in labor or in the puerperium, suggesting that dream content is less scenic and more concentrated on inner experiences.

In the last month of pregnancy, sleep is so much more in the classical phase pattern (Kleitman, 1963) that the arousal hour when the woman could not return to sleep can be assumed to be a dream disruption. Dreams of the last month of pregnancy are anticipatory, dealing with the wishes and fears of labor. Dreams are different for each woman but the themes are similar. A representative dream in anticipation of labor is: she is in bed in her room and there are a couple of men, thieves or rapists, at the front door and battering the door down. In the next scene she is frantically tying the strips of bed sheet into a rope and then sliding down the rope from the window to the ground. The last scene is of herself serenely walking away into the sunshine with the baby in her arms. A frequent dream about labor is being chained to a bed and then being split apart. Splitting apart and hurtling down a divide or precipice are recurrent anticipatory dreams of labor. A very typical wish dream is that she goes into labor and in the next scene she is wheeling the baby in front of her as she strolls in the sunshine; she has skipped labor and delivery altogether. In the few dreams of the baby at this period, other then being lowered or carried, the baby appears as a full-faced apparition, a dark and hairy-faced animal, often a cat. There is a deliberate avoidance of going to bed early in this last month of pregnancy in the hope that she becomes so tired that when she does fall asleep the fearsome anticipatory dream images will not occur.

Dream images during labor summarize the immediately present experience. Most dreams during labor are not recalled. Under scopalomine, the woman who is almost fully dilated struggles with getting something like the refrigerator door open, a door that is stuck and will not open; or struggles with putting something like a pie down carefully so it will not drop or break; or struggles with a three-legged stool that cannot stand up without the fourth leg.

The image evoked in the descent of the infant through the vaginal vault is that of a "trailer-truck barreling through." The very rapid delivery is "like driving a car without brakes." After a local anesthetic is administerd in preparation for a vaginal or caesarean delivery, and the surrounding confusion and inner turbulence are abated, there is a not uncommon image: the self separates out from the body and weightlessly floats above, where she can dispassionately view her own body on the delivery table and what is transpiring around her. This is felt to be a phenomenal experience, not an image, characterized by peace and tranquility.

Postpartal dream images are retrospective, a reworking and reexperiencing of labor and delivery until there is a condensation of the multiple, seriated feelings of struggle and fear. The child does not appear as a separate and independent entity in the content of these dreams.

The Developing Image of the Child

The memory of the images of the child in fantasy and in dreams during pregnancy provides the anticipatory set, the only experiential basis for "knowing" what to expect in the appearance and behavior of the newborn child. The images in this memory bank are vivid, fragmentary, recurrent, and inconsistent in their oscillation between the idealized and wished-for child and the dreaded "monster," "pig," or "hairy animal." It is this pooled anticipatory set that makes a woman both eager and apprehensive at each introductory encounter with the appearance, intactness, and behavior of her newborn. The apprehension and hesitance in approach continue until the collection of anticipatory images is replaced by concretely identifiable characteristics that are consistent and stable enough for recognition and a real "knowing."

The most persistent image of the child during pregnancy, logically enough, is that of an internal organ: bloody, without shape or skin. Medical films and illustrations of the fetus reinforce the image. Watching the delivery as an action event is quite separate from seeing the baby. The incompletely oxygenated blue coloration, the smeared blood, and the vivid redness of the child in crying are more apparent and more disturbing to the mother than to anyone else. The hair, fingers, and toes, even to fingernails and toenails, of the newborn are more exciting and more gratifying to the mother than to anyone else.

The anticipatory set of dreaded images of the child has a preparatory function in providing some degree of protective insulation against extreme shock (Deutsch, 1944). In instances of congenital malformation, incompleteness, or anomalous structure, the fears are confirmed. There is a stunned numbness and a heavy sense of having wishes rejected. The preparatory function of the fantasies and dream images serves to protect the woman with a stillborn child as well. But if the mother of a stillborn child is denied the opportunity to see or to learn of her child, including hair color and quantity and sex, the fantasies of the dreaded images and the sense of rejection are elaborated.

The woman's active searching and discovery of the child's parts and their detailed constituents, including folds, dimples, and textures, reconstructs the image of the appearance of the child in very concrete and substantive terms. The work of image reconstruction occurs in cyclical waves. First there is a verification of the stability of the already discerned features and properties of the child. If there is stability, then the identification of the child progresses to further searching and discovery. In both verification and further searching, discovery of a discontinuity in the baby's skin surface arrests the process of identification. The central focus becomes the discontinuity itself: the abrasion, dry and scaly skin, the bleeding from the cord or the circumcision, the cleft lip or the pilonidal cyst. In the next encounter, verification starts with the discontinuity.

During pregnancy, the fantasies of the child begin with the image of an adolescent or teenager, move to school-age child, to preschool child, to a toddler, and finally to a baby. The image of the age-stage of the child gets progressively smaller as the pregnancy advances. A woman "gives" her unborn child the treat foods age-specific to her image of the child. There is a parallel interest in clothing for the age-stage fantasies of the child: from evening gowns and prom wear, to cute frilly dresses or jacketed suits, to the adorable outfits for toddlers' dress or play, to the serious business of no-gender baby clothes that are "so small."

By the end of pregnancy, the image of the child in appearance and behavior is that of a baby six months of age and weighing about fifteen pounds, the ideal baby. This image of the baby evokes some overwhelming body images when contemplating labor and delivery. The hostility and fear a woman has about the size of the baby in the eighth and ninth months of pregnancy promotes the separating-out from the pregnancy. But the size of the baby is a threat only as it impinges on the body-self image. During most of pregnancy and after delivery, a woman desires her ideal baby, a big baby. The question on delivery, "How much does he weigh?", is filled with hope. Six pounds or less is disappointing and even demeaning: such a long gestation for so little.

A woman is unprepared in fantasy and in imagery for a baby "so small." The parameters of the baby are hard to determine when he is wrapped in a blanket, so there are several misses in the execution of the intention to reposition the baby. Picking up, putting down, and turning the baby require attentive concentration and deliberate movements. There is anxiety about moving the baby in space. Some of the anxiety is because of the woman's reduced available energies, but most of the insecurity is because the object parameters, the body boundaries of the infant, are yet to be defined. A woman will position herself to receive her baby and hold him and herself in the same position until the nurse removes the baby and then she can move again, reposition herself.

That "anything so little could be so perfect" in form and function, an esthetically pleasurable miniaturization, is miraculous. All the more reason to be careful, so a woman lets, encourages, or requests others to hold or move the baby. She observes closely how the baby is held and moved and delights in the recognition of her husband's awkwardness and discomfort in holding something "so little." Repeated experiences in contact with the infant help establish the baby's boundaries. But lifting the baby into a basin of water and holding the wet, soapy baby in a bath reactivates the fear of falling, breaking, or splitting and renews the awareness that there is no firm hold, conceptually or operationally, on the mass of the baby's size.

In the dreams and fantasies of the child during pregnancy, the images of the baby are fleeting and transitory, appearing from and disappearing into nowhere. The experience with fetal movements has the same transitory quality. The fleeting, transitory images are tantalizing, stimulative to the curiosity and search for concrete and stable images. During pregnancy the searching heightens perceptual acuity for signs, symptoms, and omens (Rubin, 1970). After delivery there is an intense desire to see, to touch, and to examine the baby (Rubin, 1961a). There is a hunger to hold and to hold onto the baby, to feel the substantive weight and mass of the baby as a reality instead of a fleeting mirage (Rubin, 1972).

The woman who plans to place her child in adoption may prefer not to see or to hold her newborn so that the image of the child is maintained at the level of a dream or fantasy. The woman who has a child with congenital defects hopes it is only another dream image, transitory and impermanent, and avoids holding the baby. The woman who has a stillborn baby is ambivalent about holding her baby, knowing she cannot really hold onto or have the baby, and yet needing to know that she has had a baby.

If a woman cannot hold her newborn, she does not feel that she has a baby. The events and experiences of labor and delivery in relation to the child become as another dream, another fantasy, vivid in memory. But holding is in itself transitory, episodic, and discontinuous. The concept of constancy is acquired in actions and interactions that are essentially consistent, continuous, and predictable. In the meanwhile, in the uncertainty and instability of the image of the child, the woman's anticipatory set is for loss of the child or his wholeness in structure and in function. The variety of prenatal images of the child provide the attitudes of seriousness and apprehension as well as those of joy and gratitude that coexist during the puerperium.

The carryover and continuity of prenatal imagery and expectations serve to insulate the newborn with a protective shield of maternal alertness. In ensuring safe passage for her child antepartally, a woman addresses the environmental risks to the baby. As a product of the multiplicity of the images of the baby postpartally, a woman focuses in on the baby itself. The centration of attention on the child and the alertness to hazards in the environment combine to form the particular protectiveness of the maternal woman.

The Mother's Body Image Postpartally

There are no fantasies or dreams in pregnancy elaborating the image of the body-self as convalescent postpartally. There is little or no anticipatory apprehension or protective vigilance in respect to her own body after a safe and successful delivery. There is instead an anticipatory set for wellness and resumption in continuity of the body-self before the interlude of pregnancy. Postpartally, pain is met as an intrusion or a setback more often than as an ominous warning or threat.

The dreams a woman has that she will walk in the sunshine with her baby in her arms are realized by most women in the institutionalized routines and customs that form for her rites of passage: being wheeled out of the delivery room with the baby in her arms, having her baby's name announced and then having the baby presented to her, the formal procedures of discharge from the hospital with the baby in her arms, the visitors from far and near to see her and her baby in the hospital and at home. The social climate of attentiveness and pleasure is like sunshine. Institutional routines and social customs, in behalf of the woman and her child, especially when performed with a touch of elegance, are perceived as confirmatory evidence of passage to a new day, a new life.

The expectation that the woman's body weight, mass, and girth gained during pregnancy would disappear with birth of the baby is not met. On taking the upright position after delivery, the discovery of the abdominal size and mass, like a six-month pregnancy, is an appalling and dysjunctive anachronism. Disparaging terms like useless, fat, or blubber are used to describe the abdomen and the figure. The scales are approached with an admixture of hope and dread and are read with disbelief and dismay. The slow, belabored gait and the wide stance to support the pelvic mass are more typical of the last trimester of pregnancy than the expected freedom of movement following childbirth. Dream content, body feedback in action, and the continuous after-image or phantom sensations of the weight and movement of the baby in utero combine to produce a loading for the experience of being still pregnant rather than being freed of the burden of carrying the pregnancy, of having been delivered.

There is, in addition, a nostalgia for the intimate and pleasant experiences with the child in utero. There is a sense of emptiness, of the body and of the self. The emptiness is relieved in the contact with and responsiveness from the infant. However, the transitory and un-stabilized image of the newborn contributes to the body-self image as being still pregnant. The body-image and situation of pregnancy are in themselves not unpleasant, but relative to reality and the expecta-tions of self now that delivery is accomplished, this is an anachro-nism, a seductive regression in experiential time and interpersonal space.

There is a determined and aggressive turn away from the seduc-tion of the body-self image of being pregnant toward the ideal and real self. As early as the fourth day postpartum a woman begins to aggressively take on the organizing, planning, and execution of the care of the baby beyond simple feeding. By the fifth day there is a determined denial of the pregnant body-self image. If this is the day she is to return home from the hospital, it is particularly important to her that her dress and shoes are sexy, attractive, and nonpregnant. The woman who returns home without her baby, because it was still-born, premature, or hospitalized for treatment, may wear maternity clothes, holding on to pregnancy. But the woman who returns home with her baby disdains maternity clothes for her body-self image and is quite willing to give the maternity clothes away, get rid of them, anything but use them to outline the archaic body boundaries of pregnancy.

The aggressive turn toward the renewed self is limited, anchored in the archaic but real body. Body boundaries, body mass, and body tonus do define the self in action. The aggressive bursts in taking actions compatible with her self-concept increase narcissistic sup-plies. Even though all roles are performed, however, the quality and involvement in performance is felt to be of a low, perfunctory, and unsatisfactory level. There is hostility toward the body-self image, an apathy and neglect in the nourishment and care of the archaic body image.

In the isolation of the nuclear household, the diffusion in body-self boundaries increases. Social contact and social interaction help define the parameters of the self. The interface in social contact pro-vides a sense of controlled containment of the self, a good feeling. Without events or action, time and space are undefined and additive to the diffusion. The woman's own resourcefulness and energies for activity are depleted by fatigue, sleep deprivation, and apathy.

The sense of unrelatedness, interpersonally and in time and space, can become acute. The fear of losing her mind arouses anxiety and mobilizes an aggressive holding on to self, to sanity. Without consolidated body and ego boundaries, the hostility and aggressivity include a husband as alter and baby as an extension of self. The threat or actual loss of self-control provides circular feedback to reinforce the unloved and unlovable body-self image. In the depletion of narcissistic supplies there is no pleasure in self, in baby, in husband, or in the situation of the confinement.

The body image and subjective experiences postpartally are symmetrically similar to the body image and experience antepartally. There is progression antepartally and retrogression postpartally, so that the first month postpartally and the ninth month of pregnancy are highly similar, the second month postpartally and the eighth month antepartally are similar. Both the third and fourth trimesters follow an experience of heightened narcissistic gratification in making and having a baby. Both trimesters contain the experience of body-boundary diffusion, restrictions in time and space orientation, diminished mobility, hostility toward self and the baby, and the feeling of entrapment in an unlovable and poorly functioning body.

The estrangement and isolation from relatedness in the first month postpartally is analogous to that of the experience at the end of pregnancy. The vulnerability toward physical dangers of the eighth and ninth months is transferred and located in the child. The disorientation and fear that one is losing one's mind postpartally is not all that different from the behavior at the end of pregnancy when extra locks were put on the doors and when every strange sound or strange person elicited apprehension. What is different, however, is that the hostility toward the child, the anger at the situation of being pregnant, and the wish to separate out resulted in labor and delivery. Postpartally the hostility, anger, and the wish to separate out leads to impulses of infanticide, and this is indeed frightening. The fear of loss of self-control which existed in anticipation of and during labor is even more overwhelming, an insanity, postpartally.

Separation of Self from Baby

Relief from the oppressiveness of the puerperal situation is provided by the woman herself. As soon as body intactness is restored, a matter of three or four weeks for most women, the woman removes herself spatially from the child and from the confinement of the home and sets aside time in which to find and to be herself, the self in good continuance with her pre-pregnant, recognizable, and predictable self.

There are no models and no support in custom or practice for this ending of confinement in modern Western societies, so each woman uses her own initiative and her own style of resources to break away for time-space in which to locate herself. Multiparous women accept invitations during pregnancy to banquets, weddings, or parties that fall on a date close to the end of the first postpartal month. The invitational date then becomes a goal, an end point, and a boundary to the endlessness in time and space, the hiatus in a postpartal identity.

There is precedent for this healthy breakaway for narcissistic supplies of self-worth in the eighth month of pregnancy. This is a time when a sentimental journey to the woman's mother or a luncheon date with her colleagues at work or the baby shower with friends is necessary to reaffirm the continuity and relatedness of the self. The trips, such as accompanying a husband on a business trip, during the ninth month of pregnancy are rare and are more out of fear of being left alone for labor. There is a similar dread of being left alone in the third and fourth weeks postpartum, a more diffuse kind of fear of loss of self-control. It may be the diffuse fear that gives the reentry into the outer world postpartally its characteristic qualities of determination and urgency.

An evening on the town with her husband is the desired release from the confinement and void of the puerperium. If the ideal cannot be met, then a visit to the beauty parlor, the bar, a shopping area, even unescorted, is necessary. The common features of these self-renewal essays are that the baby is left at home; that it is a dress-up occasion for a reconstruction of the body image; that there is passive participation in a pleasurable social environment that contrasts with the solitude and isolation of childbearing; and that there is the being served specially prepared foods which help reconstruct self-esteem and provide a symbolic communion with adult society in its pleasurable aspects.

The precondition for this essay at the end of the first month is that the arrangements be made for a surrogate to watch and care for the baby. A surrogate is not a baby-sitter but someone who values the baby, who knows this baby, and can watch with eyes and ears for what does not occur, such as cessation of breathing, as well as what does occur, such as a fire. It is only with these safeguards that a woman can leave the baby at home to keep an appointment with her self in the world. Even so, after a couple of hours away from the baby, the images of what might be happening to her child and the distance in polarization and separation from the child become burdensome and reunion becomes imperative.

There is guilt on return to the baby. The guilt is derived from the "selfishness," the narcissistic gratification that for the first time has excluded the baby. The more successful the breakaway has been, the greater the guilt. Out of guilt, there is a surge of love and care for the baby to "make up," not just to continue as before. With her own replenished supplies in gratifications and pleasures, a woman's giving of herself is more spontaneous and more generous.

The capacity for guilt is a component of the maternal identity. Maternal guilt is not a simple replication of social values and standards. It originates in the intimately personal experience of having been delivered, of having been given life and a life. Gratitude and the sense of being entrusted operate to set a high standard of ethics and morality in the maternal woman's personal behavior. The positive and pleasurable experiences of the growing child renew and reinforce her gratitude, her appreciation, and her entrustment for the gift of life. Acts of commission contrary to this sense of personal entrustment produce guilt and the consequent corrective behaviors. It is the experiential knowledge and appreciation of life as a gift that becomes the guiding principle in attitudes and behaviors for herself and for raising a child in deportmental and interpersonal values.

Maternal guilt does not usually occur before the end of the first month postpartum. Forgetting that the baby exists in external space, the inability to come up with the right magical solution to the baby's needs every time, the inability to find the baby an object of great charm and value all the time, and the ungenerous withholding or hostility result in shame, lowered self-esteem, or in anxiety about her rationality, but not in guilt. Moreover, there is little conceptual separation of self and baby: the baby is an extension, a part of self.

With the restoration of her own body intactness and the deliberate separation in time and space from her baby to relocate herself in the context of her larger world, there is a change in perspective. The distancing from the child in time, space, and objectives is a polarization (Deutsch, 1944) to form two differentiated individuals. On returning, a mother perceives her child more clearly and more wholly from a refreshed and larger perspective. Moreover, there is a constancy in the child in objective reality: it is the woman who goes away and returns, appears and disappears, not the child. The relief in finding the child still there where she left him and still the same is one of security in constancy. There is a self and there is a child. There is polarization and a special relationship of two individuals based on, but different from, the unity of mother–child as one. The neomaternal stage is completed with polarization. Third-person intermediation in the mother–child relationship is no longer necessary: there is a knowing of the baby with a reliability and predictability; there is a confidence in self as mother generated by recovery and mastery of function.

The relationship between two individuals, mother and child, benefits from the completed identification of the constituent "I," "you," and "we." The binding-in process of pregnancy and the polarization following the neonatal–neomaternal phase of the relationship goes into a holding pattern during the second and third months postpartum. As the baby develops in vigor and functional capacities, his reciprocity in the relationship enhances the value of the "you," the "I," and the experience of "we." By the third month postpartally the baby's smile in recognition and in anticipation and his actively contented behaviors fulfill the ideal image of the baby of the woman's dreams and fantasies during pregnancy.

The maternal identity is achieved and stabilized in some magnificent programmatic ordering even before self as a person and a woman, her own full identity of self in the world, is achieved. That sense of identity, when she feels like herself again, is achieved when her body image in action in the world is contiguous and consistent with her self-concept, about eight or nine months after childbirth. The woman who again becomes pregnant before the eighth or ninth month postpartum does not feel "caught up," "herself" again.

10
Identification of the Child

There is an intimate relatedness with an unknown and unknowable child during childbearing. For the greatest part of a chronological year, there are major accommodative changes in a woman's life style, in her life space, and in the possession and control of her own body in behalf of and in response to an unidentifiable child. The neutered "it" or "the baby" represents an idea, a generalized abstraction of principle, transcending the "reality" of the embryo and the fetus on the one hand and yet, on the other hand, unanchored in the objective referents of personhood: sex, size and shape, condition, appearance, and behavior.

The maternal tasks volitionally undertaken in behalf of the unborn child are not conditional on the actual characteristics and behaviors of the child. A maternal identity is developed in a sustained act of faith independent of the specific characteristics of this child. The unconditional love of a mother for her child originates in the binding-in process of pregnancy.

There is a pursuit of the ideal, a conscious drive for perfectability in making a child and in becoming a mother. In a progressive realization of the gift of life, there is a centration on the ethical and proper actions and interactions of human behavior. The idealism, the pursuit of perfection, and the critical evaluation of the interactive effects of behavior become the moral imperative, the maternal "should" system, guiding the woman's own behavior and that of her childrearing later.

Prenatal Identification

The child conceived and borne in love is anticipated as a gift that enhances the receiver. The favorable anticipation of the child by husband, parents and children, relatives and friends amplifies and sustains the purposefulness of a woman's pregnancy and childbirth.

There is, however, remarkably little narcissism in the achievements of becoming pregnant and in completing a successful pregnancy. There is instead a profound humility accompanied by uncertainty and insecurity throughout childbearing. In the first trimester there is the uncertainty about the pregnancy itself and a sense of vulnerability to loss by mishap, miscarriage, or "bad luck." The uncertainty and insecurity are abated in the second trimester in the enteroceptive communication and feedback from the child within. But the sense of vulnerability remains and increases markedly in the third trimester with the extension and thinning of body boundaries and with the labored mobility.

There is a drive to reduce uncertainty by acquiring information, insights, and confirmed probabilities (Rubin, 1970). The felt presence of the child within accentuates the drive to reduce uncertainty and to increase security. The discordance between the subjective but real experience of the child and the objective denial by others of such a presence until birth has an isolating effect. There is a resultant reality testing that is not limited to the external "real" world. Signs, omens, dreams, and anecdotal case histories bridge the credibility gap between subjective experience and objective remoteness. In the maternal character, it is not instinct but a perceptive awareness that the concrete and objective "reality" does not necessarily encompass all truth or validity. In the turn to idealism and perfection, in the creativity of making and becoming, in the extraordinary nature of the gift to be given or denied, and in the ongoing uncertainty and insecurity, there is an inceased orienting toward and conviction in the omniscience and control of a Creator. Signs, omens, dream images, and the experience of others are not ignored. Wishes are replaced with prayers.

As a woman approaches the end of pregnancy, the importance of the baby's gender is relegated to a position secondary to the primary concern of the condition of the child at birth. She "doesn't care" whether it's a boy or a girl, "as long as it is healthy and normal." The search for models of what the child could be like has resulted in a large and varied population of possibilities. Possibilities for replication include congenital and genetic conditions of occult internal deficiencies and of manifest structural anomalies. Despite the low statistical incidence of cerebral palsy, mongolism, or cardiac anomalies, a woman ready to deliver feels that she is the statistical "one," one in ten thousand or tens of thousands. The multigravidous woman has acquired a larger and more extensive sample population of what could go wrong. The nurse becoming a mother has a skewed sample population of possibilities: spina bifida, hydrocephalus, dwarfism. The dread of the outcome of delivery is as great or greater than that of coping with pain and the fear of dismemberment or death in labor. The multigravida and the nurse enter labor with more dread and are more guarded in looking at the newborn immediately after delivery.

In anticipation of the wished-for child and in the spent patience with the physical and social limitations of pregnancy, a woman cannot wait for delivery. In the dread of an imperfect or incomplete child, a woman is in no hurry to confront delivery. A woman who has reason to expect an imperfect or incomplete child, such as a premature, will hold back and have a prolonged labor in an otherwise unobstructed labor.

Despite the compounded fears, women go on into labor and do deliver. Women deny that this involves courage, claiming only a many-faceted fear. There is strength in the number of models who have successfully coped with labor and delivery. The multigravida has her own experience as model, a model that is not always reassuring. Nevertheless, the multigravida is more pragmatic, perhaps fatalistic because there is no turning back, and goes on in faith, trust, and hope. Despite the dry mucoid plaques in the mouth and the cold clammy feet typical of fear, the multigravida has a shorter and more effective labor. The explanation that the relatively rapid labor of the multigravida is attributable to the physical powers, passageway, or passenger is not supported in evidence. There is more change in personality growth than in physical structure with repeated maternal experiences. In the primigravida there is growth and transformation from narcissism to moral masochism; In the multigravida the capacity for moral masochism grows and is transformed to a capacity for grace.

Some women want to be "knocked out" for delivery not only to avoid sensate feelings but to avoid thought as well. But most women in labor cope with the thoughts and fearful images in the same way that they did on their own initiative in the third trimester of pregnancy: with increased physical activity, with focusing and occupying their minds with something, anything and with avoiding isolation and abandonment. As long as the woman is not alone, there is magnificent control and direction of activities in getting to the hospital. In the first phase of labor the physical activity is discharged in walking and talking. The walking can be in the room or in the hallway. The place is less important than the movement. Talking can be conversational, a monologue or just listening to others, but the objective is to occupy and to hold the mind on something other than what is to come. The walking and talking activities require a partner in whom the woman has confidence. There is a holding on to the partner in walking about, in the content and style of conversation or speech, and in eye contact.

The advent of the second phase of labor, four centimeters of dilatation, is heralded by a decrease in expendable energy. The woman can no longer support her body in the upright position and cannot support speech in more than short, necessary sentences. The cervical opening decreases the feeling of intactness. Some women try to continue talking between or during a contraction just to maintain contact and divert their thoughts, but they soon fall into a fatigued or medicated sleep between contractions. With the onset of another contraction, however, the woman seeks eye contact, hand contact, or speech contact and actively moves her legs and arms. The body torso is too heavy and too hot to move freely.

The nature of the compounded fears changes. Considerations of the child recede as pain increases. There is apprehension with the beginning of each contraction. There is an attentive "listening" with the onset of a contraction, an identification of the contraction and a preparation for holding on for the onslaught. Eye, hand, and speech contact become less casual, more desperate, as the cervix opens wider and the pelvic bones distend further with each contraction. The fatigue of readying for the repeated contractions under conditions of drowsiness and the deliberate progressiveness of pain-pressure makes time itself, as a measure of the number and volume of contractions yet to be coped with, a feared enemy. Anger and hostility toward self and others in the situation often replace fear. As a sudden change in behavior, anger and hostility usually signal entry into the third, hardest and shortest phase of labor. The anger is short-lived with an effectively caring response. There is relief from entrapment in the marshaling of all available energy to push the baby along for delivery. Clock time becomes a symbol of the ending and the beginning; the emotions and sensations fade in memory but the clock time of deliverance and birth is not forgotten.

Once delivery occurs, whatever the outcome, fear disappears. Fear has the protective function of recruiting resources for impending situations of danger. The emotion is an assessment of the self in coping with or controlling the magnitude of the situation to come. There is a gradient in feelings and emotion dependent on the degree of noxiousness, threat, or destructive elements of the situation and on the length of the interval in time and space before the situation occurs. Feelings of uncertainty, anxiety, and apprehension are at the lower and midlevels, and emotions of fear and panic are at the higher levels of intensity of response (Arieti, 1960) to the estimate of self in an indeterminate and threatening situation. Attention is focused on self in the situation. Pulse and respirations accelerate in preparation for the action of planning and instigating measures to reduce the noxiousness of the coming situation or to fortify the self in coping with an unavoidable or unalterable situation. At all gradient levels, help outside the self is sought. Reduction in the pain signals of these feelings and emotions is achieved when outside help is effective in fortifying the self in coping capacity, the situation is obviated, or the situation is delimited and broken down into unit dosages compatible with coping capacities.

In the uncertainties and apprehensions of pregnancy, a woman seeks outside the self for enrichment of her coping capacities and takes preventive measures to obviate disastrous or noxious situations. She recruits the help of persons whose knowledge and skill can effectively control the crisis situation of childbirth. It is important that obstetrical competence be combined with a knowing of her personally, particularly her coping capacities and limitations. The woman attending a clinic, where obstetrical practices are usually excellent, has apprehensive overlayment because no one knows her. The excellence of the practice of obstetrics is irrelevant, even threatening, in the crisis of self in a situation of multiple dangers. Women prefer a private obstetrician, a personal doctor "who knows her." There is added stress when her own doctor is away on vacation or on another case. A close member of her family, her own nurse, and a skilled obstetrician collectively provide a sense of control in the situation: someone who knows and cares about her, someone to help her cope with the situations, and someone who can mediate or control the situations of childbirth.

In childbearing, the maternal woman's skill in helping her child in addressing situations of uncertainty, anxiety, apprehension, fear, or terror is impressive. In the limited capacities of the growing and developing child there are numerous and frequent situations evocative of degrees of fear. The inability to cope with a strange or forbidding place, person, action, or experience is a characteristic and prevalent experience of childhood. Maternal awareness and response is immediate and takes the form of lending ego to the child. There is a repertoire of helpful measures in supplementing the child's capacities to cope that range from proximal contact, going or staying with him, delimiting the situation in terms he can understand, and offering feasible coping approaches. There is an obviation of situations of threat or danger that the child could not possibly cope with. There is a dividing up into stages of the unavoidable situations or experiences so that many or all of the unit steps are within the child's capacity to cope, alone or with help. These skills in helping another are learned in direct experience, particularly in stress situations such as labor, by receiving skillful help.

Identification at Birth

Deliverance from pain, from fear, and from the restrictions of the pregnant state is a profound relief raised to sheer joyousness in the birth of the child. The joy in receiving a child at birth is a factor of the condition and gender of the newborn. The perfect child exceeds expectations: the imperfect child is not wholly unexpected. Yet there is a numbing sadness when the newborn is not whole and healthy.

The gender of the child is of paramount importance to a woman and to her family. During pregnancy most of the signs, symptoms, omens, and social games relate to the sex of the anticipated child (Rubin, 1970). The primigravida tends to desire a son to give to her husband. By the third trimester of pregnancy, however, the binding-in fantasy of how it will be when she has a child is richer with a girl-child than with a boy-child. Whatever the social or cultural pressures, the prospect of life with boyhood and manhood lies outside a woman's experience and presents a remote, stereotyped, and just plain dull promise. It is not the child but the self who is rejected when the child is born of the wrong gender. A woman's disappointment lies not in the child but in having to go through another pregnancy and another labor in the foreverness of childbearing to give her husband a son or to receive a daughter, an outcome of no certainty. For either the woman or her husband, the absence of a child of the same gender is more than a disappointment; it is a lifelong deprivation.

Despite the depletion in energy and the fatigue of labor, the need for determination of the newborn's condition, sex, and size preempt the hunger for sleep and for food. These determinations provide the answers withheld during the pregnancy and serve as orientation foci for a new relatedness. The initial determination of the child's condition, however, is an acceptable best estimate, gratifying but without certainty or finality. Confirmation of the baby's good condition by others affords welcome objectivity and reality testing, but there continues to be an ongoing independent verification of the baby's condition by the mother herself.

The situation of the biological mother in identifying her newborn child is complicated by the historical experience of pregnancy. Locating the child outside the body-self is not achieved by the delivery experience alone. There is a psychological counterpart to the physical process of separating out from the incorporated unity of pregnancy. There is a sorting-out and disengagement from the no longer relevant and operational contexts of the hypothetical identifications and preliminary relationships of pregnancy. There is the construction of a stable and constant image of the child as object in external space. And there is an extension, transformation, and elaboration of the maternal bonds and the maternal identity in the present relationship.

There is an eagerness to replace the indirect and inferential sources of information about the child, the various and transitory models and images of pregnancy, with direct observation. There is a visual and tactile hunger for primary observations (Rubin, 1961b). The enteroceptive stimuli of pregnancy and their resultant imagery fostered incorporation and binding-in; the visual and tactile drives following delivery initiate the externalization and objectification of the neonate. Visual contact has primacy in the identification and location of the child and for self-orientation in relation to the child.

The anticipatory set of the imagery generated in fantasy can temporarily obstruct the urge for direct visual contact with the newborn. This is manifest when a woman asks if the baby is all right at birth before she dares to look at it. It is also manifest in the decelerating approach of the woman rushing to see her baby who is hospitalized for prematurity or surgery. The woman traumatized by delivery, however, as with a caesarean section, a general anesthetic, or exhaustion from labor has little unbound energy for either fantasy imagery or direct visualization of the child.

The initial view of the child is molar so that color or generalized activity, such as that of crying, is more apparent than the features. In the configurational gestalt, the background delineates the unfamiliar object in the foreground and the child itself is not seen in the isolette, under the treatment lamp, or in the midst of intravenous tubing on initial viewing. The background paraphernalia has to be dealt with and separated out from the image of the child before the child can be seen, identified, or recognized.

There is remarkably little pleasurable smiling in the woman observing her newborn child. The smile is a product of recognition and there is little that is recognizable in the neonate to the neomaternal woman. The work of identification precedes recognition. For the neomaternal woman, identification of her newborn is a process of discovery, not a single act. Although each encounter with the baby provides additional identifying information, most of the observational findings are made after a feeding, when her work of feeding is done and the baby is quiet.

The work of identification starts peripherally and progresses toward the central torso of the child (Rubin, 1963). Face and hair, hands and feet are visualized and inspected for wholeness and intactness. If there is wholeness and intactness, there is tactile approach, instrumentally to improve visualization and then to elicit more information on texture, contour, temperature, and moisture content of the baby's face, hands, feet, and hair. The process is recycled at each encounter during the first week until discoveries are confirmed and stabilized for recognition and predictability.

The actions and functions of the newborn's facial structures are particularly rich and varied in discovery content: the facial grimaces in sleep or in burping, the eyes opening, the sneezing, gagging, sucking, crying, yawning, and the production of tears. The behavior and facial expressions of the neonate have no precedent in the fantasy imagery of pregnancy, so these discoveries have an element of surprise, usually pleasurable surprise. The delightful surprises of the child's behavior and expressions contribute exponentially to the maternal bonds of affection.

Each element of appearance and behavior identified in the child is linked and bonded into the self and family systems at the time of discovery in a process of claiming. The eyelids, eyelashes, or eyebrows, the shape of the nose or nostrils, the size and configuration of the ears, the amount, color, and texture of the hair, the contour of the hands and feet and of the fingernails and toenails—each element of each feature is "like" her own, or her husband's, or their other children's. The loud or whispered burp, the working up of a storm when hungry, and the falling asleep when fed are "like" her husband's, her own, or their other children's behaviors. The linking by association of each of the child's features or behaviors to persons the woman cares about, who belong to her, and to whom she in turn belongs and by whom she is cared for, is a claiming of the child as belonging in the composite and intimately significant sphere of the family.

Claiming is self-initiated, an active pursuit of high significance to the neomaternal woman. The prenatal social game of guessing the child's sex is replaced by social corroborations and discoveries that the baby's mouth is shaped "like hers," that he has his father's dimples, that the hairline or whatever is identifiably "like hers" or someone dear to her. It is most gratifying when her own family members identify, associate, and claim features or behaviors of the newborn as being "like mine." The randomness in replication of features and characteristics of family members makes discovery particularly interesting, honors a wide number of family members, and enhances the attractiveness of the newborn in its union of diverse personal attributes.

Claiming moves the identification process beyond a simple inventory of parts and beyond simple judgments of attractiveness to awareness of the composite of attributes of those persons the woman loves. Each feature is the child's, but also another's. There is a surge of desire to nourish and cherish this child in its collective representation. The novel and creative mix of replicated attributes of loved ones and of self produces an awed wonderment about the promise and potentials of this child.

Claiming is a problem in situations of indeterminate paternity, rape, or incest. There is difficulty in conceptually locating the child. Identification of this child is limited, cursory, or aversive. Maternal bonds with the child are not amplified or reinforced.

Naming the child is another form of claiming, an affirmation of the child's existence and belongingness. Naming is an important process of deliberation, negotiation, and compromise in giving and honoring husband, maternal and paternal parents, self or other relatives. The name of the designee, the name stem with an adjustment for gender, or the first letter are replicated in the first or middle names of the neonate. Whether the name honors a family member or represents a remote hero or heroine, there is a test for alliterative consonance of the child's name with the family name.

Identification and Action–Interaction

The identification process also includes the nature of the relationship, the goodness-of-fit of self and child in situations of action and interaction. Each early encounter is an inquiry into the nature of the relationship. In the asymmetry of the power relationship, her own capacities and competence in giving at each episode of action-interaction is critical, and the response of the newborn serves as the basis of self-evaluation.

The giving and receiving of food is the primary vehicle of direct action-interaction. Feeding becomes the criterion of self-esteem as mother of this child and of the goodness of fit in this relationship. The significance of providing and giving food is a continuation of the sporadic and generous essays in feeding the unborn child during pregnancy. But there is an immediate necessity for feeding the newborn and an immediately observable response of the newborn that did not exist prenatally which add pressure to the neomaternal performance. When the hunger stress of the child is assuaged and contentment replaces distress as a result of her successful actions in feeding, there is a satisfying sense of the goodness of fit in the relationship.

The pressure on performance in the feeding of a baby in panic with hunger stress is intense and disadvantaging. To the neonate hunger is a novel experience, a threat to survival. An older baby is more sanguine about hunger contractions. But it is the neonate that the neomaternal woman encounters. A frenzied, exhausted, or weak neonate has difficulty grasping the nipple. Frenzy and exhaustion can be prevented and the weak grasp and suck of the less vigorous newborn can be compensated for with a softer nipple. But such alternatives of action are possible only after being able to distinguish the situation of the child from the nature and kind of child itself, an advanced stage of knowing and understanding based on prior identification of the child and his behaviors.

The neomaternal woman works intensely to achieve goodness of fit in the feeding interaction. There is preparatory readying to ensure optimal conditions for the feeding by positioning to receive the baby, by ensuring no interruptions from phone calls or for bathroom needs, and by reviewing any problems that arose in the previous feeding interaction. Replication in mimicry or role play of the best or most successful modeled or advised feeding is worked at and brought to bear on this feeding. The concentrated effort in achieving goodness of fit in the feeding/eating situation is manifest in the perspiration that appears on the woman's upper lip and in her palms and by the aching stiffness of her body from the absolutely still position she maintains while the baby eats.

The earnestness with which a woman approaches and works at achieving a goodness of fit feeding interaction makes her particularly sensitive to failure and rejection. The infant's refusal of the nipple, to take food, or to burp is perceived with dismay. If the infant eats well for another but does not eat well for her, this is perceived as personal rejection. A wet burp, gagging, or vomiting arouses apprehension about the child's condition and, if his condition is satisfactory, is perceived as rejection of her care. In early feedings the infant can gag on mucus, grimace with a food of new consistency, and take a little more food when he really needs to burp, so that when he does expel the swallowed air the overlayer of food is expelled, too.

Overeagerness to feed the baby often precludes the infant's capacity to participate in the interaction. Forced entry into the mouth, jiggling of the nipple, breast, or bottle, and stimulation of the cheek or other parts of the baby's body send unintended and disruptive tactile communications to the infant. A healthy newborn enjoys eating when he is ready for food. The overdetermined position of the breast or bottle above the baby's mouth does not allow for the short nasopharyngeal structure of the newborn so that swallowed milk often is expelled through the nostrils. A baby cannot eat well lying flat on his back. The impatience of an active woman collides with the small baby's need to develop lip, buccinator, and tongue muscles and with the fact that eating is muscular work for the neonate, requiring rest breaks and a chance to replenish oxygen supplies. The rhythm of a rocking chair and a quiet, nondiverting conversation help discharge an overabundance of intentional energies of the mother and help set the more leisurely and permissive pace of action-interaction for mother and child. A pillow under the woman's supporting arm provides the desirable position for the baby's eating and reduces maternal fatigue: the baby's head becomes heavier and hotter as his eating progresses.

The third neonatal and postpartal day is not conducive to the goodness of fit in the feeding relationship. Either or both the woman and child have major physiological changes that preempt attention and militate against successful action-interaction. The breast-fed neonate has a normal weight loss before milk supplies arrive on the third day and tends to be either more passive or more aggressive at breast. The breasts engorge on the third day, are hot, heavy, and painful, and the woman needs the passive baby to be more effective in drawing off the milk and the more aggressive baby to be gentler. Most neonates have lassitude, irritability, or a slightly elevated temperature, even without patent jaundice, on the third day. The novel sensation for the infant of a formed stool in the lower intestine and in evacuation causes the same distress crying as in hunger, but this is not relieved by feeding and continues without relief until final evacuation of the stool. The postpartal woman has an equally trying day of preemptive physiological demands. There is a return of bowel function but no healed and intact musculature to facilitate elimination. Hemorrhoids are engorged or the repaired perineum is edematous and pulling against the sutures. In addition to the central focus of pain or discomfort—breasts, bowels, rectum, or perineum—the postpartal woman has headache, difficulty with the upright positions of sitting or standing, and is irritable.

And depressed. After a long day of frustration, discomfort, and inadequate functioning physically and in relation to the newborn, there is cumulative disappointment and fatigue. Husbands often take the night off to tend to other matters on the third postpartal evening, but even if a husband does visit that evening, the woman is too irritable and tired to have a satisfying visit. The self-assessment is of being "like a helpless baby," struggling for an evacuation, to sit, stand, or move about, and of being "neither mother nor wife." The depression contrasts sharply with the earlier elation in delivery of a healthy child and in the pleasure of having a child. The incongruity between her apathy and depression and what she realistically "should" feel adds to the general feeling of loss and unrelatedness.

The determination to achieve goodness of fit in the maternal–child relationship is not diminished by the setbacks of the third

neonatal-postpartal day. On the contrary, the determination to succeed is accelerated with relief from pain, improved mobility, and a
good night's sleep.

It is in maternal touching that inquiry into the nature of the
relationship, the qualitative identification of the "you" and the qualitative response of the "I" in relation to the "you," is elaborated (Rubin, 1963). Neomaternal touch is hesitant, uncertain, tenuous, and
lacks the secure possessiveness of later maternal touch. Neomaternal
touch, mostly fingertip touch, is receptive, enquiring, a learning
about self and about the other in progressive claiming and binding in
to a "we-ness."

Visualization precedes touching. Touch is inhibited if the neonate
is wet with amniotic fluid, blood, spilled or expelled food, tears, urine,
or feces. Later, a woman uses an intermediary object to dry the child,
but in early neomaternal stages, a woman is immobilized and ap-
palled by the wetness. The body boundaries of the child are not yet
identified and established. It is through repeated sessions of touching
that the image of the child's body boundaries is established. It is also
through repeated maternal contact and touch that the young child
develops his image of his own body boundaries, delineating what is
contained within his body-self and what is external, outside his body-
self.

Fingertip touch exposes the smallest maternal surface for body
contact. But the fingertip is richly endowed for taking in sensory
information, and at fingertip distance visualization is improved. Delineation of the features of the child is promoted by fingertip exploration. There is a light touch that "reads" contours, shapes, size, textures—"smooth," "soft," "silky."

The light fingertip touch evokes the newborn's response of tropism, turning toward the stimulus and contracting the muscle tissues
around the point of contact. When the response is read as a frown or
grimace, the woman infers displeasure, stops, apologizes to the infant,
then resumes explorations at another part.

Outlining the baby's lips can produce a "grimace," a "smile," or a
"kiss." All responses of the child are communications, a very welcome
and even delightful nonverbal dialogue. But the smile, the kiss, and
the little hand that envelopes the exploratory finger are in a very
special class of communication: a mutual claiming, each of the other,
another shared bond in experience together.

Fingertip contact is limiting in effectiveness for instrumental and
manipulative acts such as holding the offered breast or bottle, and in
turning, dressing, or bathing the baby. But it is optimally suited for
qualitative discoveries about the child, about the self, and about the

media of communication. The apprenticeship in reading microscopic behavioral responses of the infant, no more than communication cues, develops into the maternal skills in reading the nonverbal behaviors and responses of the child as expressive communication. The developed capacity to read nonverbal behavior as a message cue of the child's inner status in situational experience leads to a knowing of the child in an uncommon but highly characteristic maternal intelligence. Since all cues are direct, personal messages in communication of inarticulate feelings, there is sensitivity and responsiveness, one to the other. The maternal woman responds in ego strength with lifesaving or life-enriching actions. The child in turn responds to the maternal cues of pleasure-displeasure, approval-disapproval, within the limits of his capacities for action.

The newborn changes daily in appearance and in behavior. The edema of the eyes, of the presenting part in delivery, and of the face and body in general is reduced within the first three days. Muscle tonus that is quite flaccid at birth improves rapidly during the first week so that the infant can hold his eyes open, head up, purse his lips to hold the nipple, and sustain the work of eating for a longer span of time with better coordination in swallowing and breathing. Within the first two weeks, the expressive cry changes in timbre and intensity with the enlarging repertoire of experience from the predominantly panicky to include protests and commentaries. New functional capacities are phased in: crying and sucking at birth, urinating shortly afterward, defecating a solid stool three days later, tears and perspiration by the end of the week, the recognition smile two months later. The capacity for food goes from less than half an ounce at a feeding the first day to two to four ounces by the end of the first week, to six or eight ounces by the end of the second week, and to an addition of a teaspoon of cereal at nighttime by the end of the third week. As the capacity for food intake increases, the frequency of feedings decreases.

Missed observations of change in the neonate, especially changes in weight, appetite, capacity for food, and responses to temperature change, are typical of the neomaternal period. The fluidity of change and growth in the neonate runs counter to the woman's need to identify and to stabilize the image of her newborn. Without a stable baseline of identification, change is not discernible.

In the first three days postpartally, feeding-identification sessions with the newborn are of very short duration, a factor of the intense recruitment of energy from depleted stores of energy for these desired tasks. Despite the excitement of a safe delivery and of having a perfect child, the woman's energy is bound into the process of recovery from pain, discomfort, fatigue, and dysfunction. Since each identification session starts from the point of previous discovery in a confirmation of the finding and its stability and then progresses to a larger radius of exploration, identification in a period of short duration is incomplete. Repeated sessions make for progressive, cumulative, and thorough identification. If there is a problem in the baby's intactness, in wholeness or in function, however, there is centration on the problem and a limited extension of the radius of identification. The centration continues as long as the problem remains. If the problem is transient or remedial, such as poor sucking, scratches, dried and cracked skin, caput, or forcep marks, the centration is of relatively short duration. If the problem is less transient, such as cleft lip, prematurity, birthmarks, or imperforate anus, the centration remains the focus of identification of the child and her maternal identification in relation to the child.

Identification and the Changing Infant

The increments in the behavioral repertoire of the infant are a surprise to a woman seeking identification and a stable image, a "knowing" of the newborn. Many increments in the behavioral repertoire of the infant are apt to be missed or misread by the postpartum woman. Many of the problems in locating and identifying the neonate's behavior occur at nighttime or during the night when the woman at home is tired and depleted in her stores of energy. The last feedings of the day or those during the night are impatient, the bottle is not warmed enough, and the baby is not satisfied, is distended abdominally with gas pains, or is returned to a bed that is cold at nighttime temperatures and clammy even if the sheets are not wet. The response of a healthy baby is a cry of protest. The response of a healthy adult, whether an exhausted woman or a tired spouse, to the deprivation of rest or sleep and the continuation of demands for another's relief, is hostility, reluctance, and anger. Any person free of pain, exhaustion, and sleep deprivation can magically solve these problems: a larger, unhurried meal at night; warm fluid, whether spiked with spirits of peppermint or not, for colic; a crib kept warm while it is empty, or maintaining the same warm body contact of mother and child in bed. Real problems in the baby's condition are not manifest only in the small hours of the night.

There are fewer missed or misread cues of the baby's behavior by the end of the neomaternal period. Identification is replaced by knowing. Discovery and surprise are replaced by comfortable predictability. In establishing the identity of the child, the maternal identity in relation to this child is established. In knowing the child there is a knowing of self in relation to the child and a more active, more securely certain behavior with or in behalf of the child.

In the polarization through identification and knowing of the child as a separate being, elements of the relationship experienced in the unity of pregnancy persevere and endure. The unity in space and interaction time of pregnancy is retained to form one of the qualitative attributes of maternal behavior and character and, also, one of the harder problems a woman as mother has to cope with in a lifetime. Spatial proximity is a phenomenological necessity for the welfare of the child and the comfort of the woman's maternal identity.

In the early neomaternal period, if a woman cannot see or hold her newborn child, there is a feeling that she has no child, that it does not exist. There is no attendant feeling of anxiety at first, just a sense of emptiness, a personal void. The quiet child in another room is forgotten. The still-pregnant body image and the psychic energies consumed in recovery and in an active household are contributing factors, but essentially the baby, unseen and unheard, is not integrated in the neomaternal woman's schema of external space. The baby's cry from distant space elicits a startle of reorientation, recognition, and, if the interval has been of several hours, a guilt-like anxiety. The multipara, particularly, tends to keep the baby nearby, in the same room, where she can "see and hear" him. There is no sanguine sense of object constancy during the neomaternal period. A woman has to "go see" or "see if the baby is all right" if she awakens during the night or the baby is separated from her for hospitalization. At the third or fourth week postpartum, when the woman's body boundaries are restored to intactness and there is a bursting out from the confinement of the puerperium for adult social interaction, the existence of the baby in distant space and without directly immediate stimuli is first manifest. There is real discomfort in the spatial separation, however, and mounting anxiety until reunion is achieved and the child's existence and condition are ascertained.

There are times when the presence of the child is too constant, but as soon as the baby or toddler is "too quiet" in another room, or is not visible or audible outdoors, the maternal woman "has to see" what is happening. Each increment in spatial distancing between a woman and her child evokes resistance, anxiety, and self-discipline in accommodation to the maturing child's enlarging sphere of physical space. Whether the spatial distancing is for starting school, going to camp, evenings or overnights with friends, or for leaving home for college, work, or marriage, there is maternal pain and anxiety. The maternal woman waits for her child to return from school, waits up until her child returns from an evening date, visits her child away at camp or college, and urges the child to write or phone, to bridge the spatial distance, to maintain contact, to ascertain that he is "all right."

There is a reciprocal mirror-image but more acute necessity for the child to be in proximal space with the mother. In the adaptive transition from the finite uterine world to the external world of infinite space, the child needs proximal, body-surface help. The maternal enfoldment of the infant in her arms, in a blanket or in the bed, replicates the uterine situation of contact, postural support, temperature regulation, and motion. The consistency and continuity with previous spatial experience promotes the transition to the external world by providing a haven of security until the child develops sufficiently to cope with friction and gravity.

A baby "borrows" the mother's bodily vigor for positional change, postural maintenance, and movement through space. The mother is an extension of the child's self, making for a wholeness in action and in the discovery of pleasure in the world around them. Even the temporary absence of the mother in proximal space leaves the baby, toddler, or preschool child unwhole, reduced in capacities and resources, depressed or vulnerable in the confinement of the limitations of his own body (Spitz, 1945). The growing child's explorations and novel experiences by himself are adventures in living, providing there is tactile, visual, or verbal contact with the mother at the end of each such experience. No matter how trivial or banal the child's experiences or how inarticulate the child's show-and-tell, the maternal woman enjoys the contact session, prolongs the contact by questions and appreciative elaboration. This is not an insignificant nurturance of the child's ego strength, the strength that makes it possible for the maturing child to increase the spatial distance from his mother and family. When there is deprivation of the mother in proximal or accessible space, the child is apathetic or resistive to novel living experience and has low-self confidence and low self-esteem (Freud & Burlingame, 1942).

The biological mother experiences the child not only as an individual but as an extension of herself. In action and particularly in feelings there is a highly permeable border between the actions and feelings of the child and the self. Not only does a woman open her own mouth when she offers the nipple or spoon to her baby, but she feels shame and rapidly makes amends when her baby soils on another, as though she herself had committed the act. Emotions and feelings have a spread-effect and are readily communicable even without causative stimuli to another, but to the biological mother the child's experiences in situation and in feeling are experienced as her own. The hypodermic needle penetrating the child's skin, the bleeding cord, the bruises and scrapes in the child's experience are felt experiences of the mother. When the child is anxious, fearful, happy, or content, she becomes anxious, fearful, happy, or content. The feelings and emotions of the mother are, in turn, experienced by the child as his own (Erikson, 1963). The child does not have the maternal cognitive capacity to determine causal determinants of feelings and emotions. In infancy all feelings originate in self or in mother as an extension of self. The maternal cognitive capacity to discern situational orgins of feelings and emotions and her ability to experience the child's emotional signals as her own, without the intermediation and dependency on language, enables the woman as mother to avoid or minimize noxious situational stimuli and to maximize, repeat, or elaborate situations productive of the more pleasurable feelings and emotions of her child and herself.

Appendixes

Appendix A
Methodology

In these appendixes the method of study and two case protocols are presented. These are original recordings, the editing limited primarily to punctuation, and represent short-term or cross-sectional studies. The marginal identification of behavior and the discussions are written by the author.

The clinical field is a rich resource for a variety of investigative methodologies in the understanding and care of patients. We have used hospital records for demographic material, surveys, structured and open-ended interviews, and the experimental method with test variables. But the most productive method is one most akin to that of the naturalist in the field. This method is hypothesis-free and therefore a means of discovery rather than being only confirmatory.

The naturalistic method of study focuses on a Subject in action, involved in a situation and in a setting that is a natural and accepted part of the Subject's situation. The nurse-observer is an identifiable and functional part of the setting and a helpful adjunct in the situation. As observer, the graduate nurse has the advantage of being able to relegate medical, nursing, and hospital procedures into contextual background, as an independent variable or given, against which the Subject's behavior and responses can be foreground, the dependent variable.

An observation session was not considered complete until it was recorded. In training and practice, nurses are skilled observers and recorders. These skills are developed by faculty as independent observers, in clinical and postclinical conferences and in written feedback and discussion following the reading of the recording. A recording session including behavioral identification and discussion takes about as long as the observation session itself. The reliability of recall is improved by recording before another observation session is made with the same or another patient.

The recorded observation becomes the data base, the protocol. It becomes a learning tool, an evaluative instrument for quality and adequacy of services, a basis for designing an observational schedule for nonverbal behavioral studies (see Dunbar, 1977, and Richardson, 1979), and for further research. The protocols can be entered and reentered with each new research question or hypothesis.

Depending on the research question, a unit of behavior is established for analysis of the data. A typical unit includes one action (attitude or response) of the Subject and one object or referent (implicit or explicit) of the action. The protocols of some twenty to thirty Subjects are then examined, and the unit of behavior is determined and coded (no more complicated than the first letter of the action, a slash, and the first letter of the object or referent). Using the same unit and the same behavioral definitions and determined objects of behavior, the unitizing and coding are done again by an independent coder. If the definitions are complete, the percent agreement between the investigator and independent coder of the same protocols tends to be high, 80 to 95 percent.

The coded units are distributed on a large worksheet with actions across (dependent variable) and object or referent down (independent variable). Subsets of dependent and independent classes of variables may be used if the data support subsets, that is, Body: appearance, completeness or intactness. The unit would then be coded for subsets, too. The classes in independent and dependent variables are derived inductively from the data. The independent classes of variables are relatively simple: the patient says the object is a particular treatment, part of her body, her baby, the doctor, or her husband. The dependent variables require more defining of the categories and their boundaries. Emotions are generally too soft ("nervous," "scared," "fear," "dread") within and between patients for classification purposes. Classifications on the variable are worked at until they are definitive, exhaustive of the data, and on an equal plane of abstraction for all classes. Once this is done, the coding is possible and simple. A study is as good as its classification systems.

Each worksheet is identified by the patient's initials, parity, and social data. If the study covers days, weeks or months, there is a separate worksheet for each time period for each patient. After distribution of the units, the columns and rows are totaled (subtotals for subsets) for each worksheet for each patient and for each time period. Patterns and trends begin to emerge that could not be visualized from raw data. Computer-processed data do not show these patterns emerging. All totals, down and across, including all subsets, from all patients are then totaled by time and by parity. In the average study, each protocol generates 200 to 300 units and in the grand total of all subjects the $N = 3,000$ to $5,000$. Low-density behaviors and objects become meaningless as either idiosyncratic or nonproductive in this study using these categories. It is with these final worksheets that hypotheses and questions of comparison between groups and over time can be tested statistically. Tables and graphs promote visualization. One is now ready to report findings in responsible and measured statements.

Appendix **B**
A Case of Cognitive Dissonance

Patient: Dorothy M.
Age 22, Black, Married
5th month, 2nd trimester
Gravida V, Para IV

L.M.P. August, E.D.C. ?
Nurse: Ruth Hrizo

Except for maternity dress, body (? self) image is one to be neglected

I couldn't decide if Mrs. M. was wearing an uncombed wig or if her hair had been straightened and needed combing, badly. She wore an old camel colored coat—one bad tear near the pocket, cuffs frayed, buttons missing. She also wore loafers with gray wool socks, but they were in much better condition. I can't remember her dress except that it was a maternity dress. She wore no rings.

Mrs. M. and another patient were sitting together in the waiting room. Mrs. M. looked very familiar, so I approached her. I soon found out that she had been here in the clinic earlier this week—reason for being familiar.

I was surprised at how easily she talked. She got right to the core of problems. (A crisis situation.) She had come to Planned Parenthood recently. She had been examined and told she was pregnant and given an appoint-

Surprise

ment. "Oh, no, was my first reaction. It took me about a month—no, I mean a week to get used to the idea." "How will I manage?" seemed to be the major concern.

She talked quickly with little concern about my comments. She needed a listener. Her husband had left her two months ago after seven years. "He got tired of babies, I guess."

During the course of her conversation, I learned about Terry, a boy, aged 4, and Randy, a girl aged 2, and another boy, Tyrone, who died at the age of 2. I couldn't place Tyrone because she would refer to him and then quickly drop the subject to go on. She had "given all my baby clothes away, except a bunting of Randy's and a snow-suit of Terry's which were never used." Diapers had been torn up. "All except two which I used for dust rags. I was so glad to get rid of them. I had a ceremony."

Finished

The crib had been sold to a sister-in-law a couple of months ago. "I guess I will have to buy it back." Her mother was "on welfare like me, so you know she can't help me. My father is dead." I suggested that perhaps she would receive gifts that would help. She said that her brother James said that he would pay for it, if it was a boy and was named James for him. "But I don't trust him, he don't buy anything for his own kid. He has a baby named for him already." Another brother would pay for a girl if it was named Raymie Lynn for him. "I like boys' names for girls."

*Conditional acceptance
Note change in time
frame from past self to
future self*

She said she dressed her little girl in slacks. "She can wear dresses when she goes to school." She talked proudly about her children then. She told about them trying to make her breakfast and breaking a whole dozen of eggs to get them into the skillet. "When I came downstairs, there was egg everywhere. Boy, did I whip! They cried and said that they 'were only trying to make you breakfast, Mommie,' but I sent them upstairs."

She then told me the problem that she was having with Terry refusing to let his sister Randy use his little potty. She then went on to tell me that Terry wants anything but another baby. "He said he wants a horse or a kitty or a puppy, 'Bring home a puppy, Mommy.' "

For some reason, Mrs. M. then told me about one of the nurses that she "hated." She identified her as the tall nurse who usually worked in Dental Clinic. She was in the Emergency Room when Mrs. M. came in by Police Ambulance with her mother during her first pregnancy. "I told her that it was coming and she said that she was a nurse and it wasn't coming. I had one bad pain and it was born. She said that she was real sorry afterwards but that didn't help. My mother doesn't get mad but she was swearing at her." This story was repeated with the added information that she was fifteen at the time and that this was about a five month gestation that died at the time.

"Like"/model, self

Mrs. M. told me that all her babies had been born on the seventh of March. I think she was telling me that this baby would be born then also. One baby weighed 4 pounds, one baby weighed 3 pounds, and one baby weighed 2 pounds.

The depletion syndrome in a multip with premies. —And "like"/model, her children

The last baby, Randy, stayed in the hospital four months. "It didn't seem like I had a baby. I never saw them until the day I went home and then I didn't see them again until I came to get them. I called everyday, but it seemed like I was calling about a girl friend's baby. When Randy came home, I heard her crying and I thought, I wish that baby's mother would get that baby and change it's diaper and give it a bottle. Then I thought, That's mine!"

When she was in on Monday, she had been examined by a medical student and "a man in a suit." She said that her sister-in-law ("well, I call her my sister-in-law, she goes with my brother") worked at the clinic. She had been in the room with her on Monday and they had "laughed and carried on so that she said that we were going to get her fired."

She was called into the office at this time. After I weighed her and found that she had gained two pounds since Monday, the conversation quickly moved to food. She laughingly told me that she loved chocolate sundaes and bacon rinds. She said that she and a girl friend had stayed up until midnight the night before and had played with one of the kid's games, Uncle Wiggley, and they had eaten peanut butter crackers and Pepsi. At this time I moved her into the examining room.

A kid's food and a mother's food

She continued to talk about food. She said that she loved pork, but it was hard to imagine such good meat coming from those beasts that ate garbage. Seeing I wasn't shocked, she continued. She told about wringing the neck of a chicken when she was five. She got to the part where she should have given a hard snap but got sick, dropped the chicken and ran into the woods. Her mother was mad at her but "I was only five, imagine?" I asked if she had been living on a farm then. She said that she had been living on a farm in Alabama. She and her family had come north when she was seven. Besides wringing the necks of chickens and saving the dishwater and garbage for the hogs, she remembers "there was nothing to do." They never celebrated Halloween and for Christmas, they received fruit and nuts. "We never got toys. Our first Christmas up here, my brother got a bike and I got a doll. We were wondering about all those fruit and nuts when we were little. Old Santa got mixed up."

I said she liked it better up here, then. She certainly did. "Down there you lay in bed and looked up at the stars. The chickens ran under the house. There were snakes everywhere. I wouldn't go to the bathroom at night; I had my little pottie right under my bed. There were cotton snakes in the cotton fields. There was a big snake that lived in a tree beside the house. We used to feed him. Our mother yelled at us, but there was nothing to do. You fed snakes."

Her mother wants her to return (to Alabama).
They had been back once for a visit. She told
about telling her cousins about the Christ-
mases up here, about wringing chicken's necks
and about nothing to do. She said that if her
mother wanted to go back, she could but she
wasn't going.

Dr. Dym came into the room at this time. I
was startled by the change in her. She was extremely quiet. He looked at the chart. As I
helped her onto the bed and was getting the
sheet fixed, she told me that one doctor had told
her that she wasn't pregnant. Before I could
find out more, Dr. Dym started the routines.
He felt for the height of the fundus, measured,
listened for fetal heart sounds. He had a per-
plexed look. He questioned her. Yes, the dates
were right—she had the last normal period in
August but had been spotting monthly. That's
why she had thought she wasn't pregnant and
had gone to Planned Parenthood. The doctor
there had told her she was pregnant and had
told her to come to regular clinic. She had felt
life, she thought, about Christmas but she had
thought at the time that it was her nerves. She
got sick just the night before—like morning
sickness.

"Like"/model, general
other

Dr. Dym did a pelvic exam and said something to me about a long cervix and then to
both of us, "Just what I thought. Have her get a
pregnancy test. I don't think she's pregnant."

Her expression was one of total bewilder-
ment. I told her to dress and then wait for me.
When I came back with the instructions for a
pregnancy test, she was sitting on the chair in

Dissonance

the office saying, "I don't understand, I just
don't understand." I explained slowly what she
was to do for the pregnancy test. She looked up
and said, "What? Another one?" At that I asked
her to come out to the front desk and wait for
me. We called to the lab and got back a report
of a pregnancy test that had been run on the
9th of January. It was negative.

After some difficulty, I got Dr. Dym's attention and told him about the negative test. His answer was to tell her to come to a Gyn Clinic. (He was very involved with another situation at the time.) I hesitated then I decided that it wasn't helping anything by letting her sit. I told her that the test had been found and that it was negative. I told her the doctor would check her on Monday. She shook her head and said, "I don't understand. I don't know what to do."

I decided that maybe she needed to hear it from the doctor. I asked Dr. Dym to tell her what had been found and what he wanted her to do. Although obviously busy, he came out and told her, "Well, Dorothy, seems you had a test and it was negative. We'll want you to come back to the Gynie Clinic and we'll see if we can get your periods regulated for you." Then he was gone.

Her first question was what was Gynie Clinic? I told her it was the Monday afternoon clinic for nonpregnant patients. She asked for *Dissonance* her appointment book. I looked for it. It had been thrown out. I couldn't even find it in the waste basket. I had to return to her without it.

I told her how hard it must be to think pregnant and then to think not-pregnant. It must be hard shifting so fast and often, that I felt confused, myself. She asked me what to do. *Dissonance* Whatever I said, I don't think she heard me. She had just remembered that she had even *Dissonance* had a note written by the Monday's doctors to tell her Welfare Worker that she was pregnant.

That reminded her that she would not receive her check until the following Friday and that she could not come into the clinic until after it came. She started over to the desk to make an appointment when her "sister-in-law" came up. Mrs. M. told her that the doctor had said that she wasn't pregnant. "That's good!" she said. Mrs. M. repeated "That's good?" I was startled at the glibness of the *Dissonance* statement myself. Mrs. M. wavered between me and her sister-in-law. "What should I do?"

Before I could answer, the sister-in-law started to talk to her and to walk away with all indications for Mrs. M. to follow. They left together.

Discussion

This unusual case highlights the distress of cognitive dissonance (Festinger, 1957). The surprise diagnosis of pregnancy some two or three months ago is still the presenting crisis situation today. Nevertheless, she has done and is doing a lot of work in preparation for becoming a mother and having another child. She puts away the concept of her being finished with babies and begins to face anew how it will be, that she will need the crib again. She has sought acceptance for her becoming a mother again, received outright rejection from her husband and a permissive acceptance from her family of origin. This young woman is poor financially but rich in familial attachments. She has pinpointed the financial problem and has already taken the initiative of getting a note from her doctor to her welfare worker that will increase her income to accommodate a baby. She has backfilled in memory to find her last normal menstrual period ignoring, as one does in cognitive dissonance resolution (Festinger, 1957), the intervening and atypical menses since then. This makes her five months pregnant and from her own experience of premature labors, she has little time left. This may be why she is pressured in having her four-year-old son learn to share and why his preference for a pet to a baby is a bit less amusing. This may also be why she rejects the idea of moving back to Alabama at this time.

Note that there is no experience of a child within. She may have felt fetal movement at Christmas, but none since. She may have had morning sickness the night before last. She is fishing for signs, as one does in the first trimester. Despite her expectations of a premature, she is loading in food treats such as chocolate sundaes, peanut butter crackers, and Pepsi as for a school child, not a premie. There is an idea of a baby, but no experience of a baby. There is a wish, preferably a girl, and a psychosocial binding-in at the level of a two to three month pregnancy.

The diagnosis of not-pregnant is a shock in expectations and orientation of self in a world. "What should I do?" In some ways her experience is like those women who have a spontaneous abortion in the first trimester. But she lacks the experience of body image involvement and the anticipatory feelings of anxiety and fear. She is less prepared, more destabilized. She has not accepted the not-pregnant idea or self-image. How could she? Each doctor has a different story and one doctor gave her an official note saying she was pregnant. Anger at the doctors who gave her such a costly run around would be a normal summary of the feeling. But she is not summarizing an incomplete experience. She is making another appointment. She needs more information to support, refute, or substitute in a cognitive mapping and an orientation of self in a world to know what she "should do."

Appendix C
The Early Puerperium: A Case

Patient: Joanne H.   Nurse: Barbara Moulton
Age 24, White, Married
Gravida III, Para III

Unprepared?   *Delivered July 11 at 3:37* A.M.   *(E.D.C. Sept. 8)*
Low forceps, midline episiotomy
Male infant, 4 lbs. 12 oz., condition good

Tuesday, July 11th

Mrs. H. was coming out of the bathroom when I arrived at her room. A practical nurse was standing by the bed and assisted Mrs. H. back into the bed. Mrs. H. was dressed in a hospital gown, which she was holding together at the back, and hospital slides that she was having trouble keeping on her feet. Her hair, dark and short, was disarranged and she did not have any makeup on. Mrs. H. is about five feet, five inches tall and of medium build. As she got back to bed she rolled over on her side, facing the door. I was standing inside the door; the other patient in the room was feeding her infant.

Body image, at this time and in this situation, low

Pt.: Ohh.

N.: Hard work, getting up and down the first time?

158

Pt.: Uh huh. But it felt good to get up.

N.: Mrs. H., I'm Miss Moulton, a graduate student in Nursing, and I am interested in mothers who have had premature infants and from all the records you had one this morning, right?

Pt.: Yes. Have you seen him? Is he all right?

N.: Yes and he seems to be fine, kicking his legs and moving his arms about.

Pt.: Does he still have that forceps mark on his face?

N.: Yes.

Pt.: How long will it take before it goes away?

N.: Several days anyway.

Pt.: Does he have all his fingers and toes?

N.: Yes, I counted them all for myself and they are all there. Did you see him in the delivery room?

Pt.: Yes. When they put him on my stomach for just a few minutes. All I saw was the forceps marks and he had a cut on his head. It was bleeding.

N.: Sure it was a cut?

Pt.: Had blood all over his head, looked like it.

N.: I didn't see anything when I looked him over and I didn't see any note of it on the physical exam sheet. May have been blood from you.

Pt.: He had to cut me. Does he have any hair?

N.: Yes, some real black hair.

Pt.: Is he all right? Has Dr. S. seen him?

N.: He's fine and the resident physician in the premature nursery has checked him. I didn't see any note on the chart about Dr. S. being in yet, but I can check next time I go to the nursery.

Pt.: Wouldn't he come to see me after he looked at the baby?

N.: Yes, I would think so. He probably hasn't had time to come over yet and the baby is in good condition.

Pt.: He takes care of my other children. Had to take my little girl to him the other day. She had swollen glands and a sore place in her mouth I was worried about. Is the baby really all right?

N.: Yes, he is and if you want you can go see him anytime today.

Pt.: Have to wait for my robe and slippers.

N.: No, you don't; we can find a gown and slippers if you want to go before they come.

Rejects image of body/self in hospital gown and slippers

Pt.: No, I'll wait for my own. My husband will bring them after lunch. Did my doctor say I could go?

N.: He has an order on your chart for you to be "up as desired after six hours" and the nurse at the desk says that means you can go. We'll just have to use a wheelchair since the nursery is on the floor below and you might get weak standing and walking that far.

Too distant?

Pt.: Why wasn't I put on the same floor with the nursery?

N.: I don't believe there are too many beds for obstetrical patients on that floor.

Pt.: Oh. . . . When will they start feeding him?

N.: Probably after 24 hours; each doctor has his own routine.

Pt.: What will they give him, Enfamil?

N.: Not at first. They try glucose—sugar water—first and then formula. They are using Enfamil in the nursery for most of the babies so maybe he'll be on it when you take him home. Did you use it before?

Pt.: Yes, with my last baby.

N.: How many children do you have?

Pt.: Two, a boy, five, and a girl, four. With my boy, I used dextri-maltose and it was too sweet or something; he kept spitting. But with my girl, she was on Enfamil. I like it. It's so easy to fix: just unscrew the top and screw on a nipple, that's it.

Models and expectations, "like"

N.: Were you surprised to have this baby early?

Pt.: Yes and scared, too.

N.: Why were you scared?

Pt.: With my other two, I delivered about 30 minutes after I started in labor. My husband wasn't home and I knew I was early, almost eight weeks. You know, I was in the doctor's office at 3:00 o'clock on Monday and he said the baby was real low and for me to go home and go to bed, lie down.

"Like"/model, self

N.: Were the other babies on time?

Pt.: They both were a little early, not like this, just a week or two.

Expectations "like"/model, self

N.: How much did the other two weigh?

Pt.: My boy was six pounds and my little girl was five pounds and eight ounces when I took her home.

N.: Did you have to leave her and come back for her?

Pt.: No, she went home the same time I did.

N.: This one weighs four pounds and twelve ounces. Seems like your babies are coming smaller each time.

Fantasy here?　　**Pt.:** Umm . . . Don't want any more (said loudly, emphatically).

Roommate: This is my last. I'm getting too old.

Pt.: This is all I want. My first was six pounds and my little girl was five-eight when I took her home and this one is four pounds twelve ounces. Don't want no more.

Roommate: It's a lot easier to say not going to have anymore, so I'm going to do something so I won't.

Pt.: I'll just watch myself a little closer because I sure don't want anymore and three is what I've dreamed of having. It makes a nice size family and that's all we can afford now.

She rolled over onto her back and looked toward the other patient and her infant.

"Like"/model, baby　　**Pt.:** Her baby is so cute but it looks small. Guess mine will look even smaller.

N.: Probably so, but he's all right and he'll be eating before long and gain weight real fast once he starts eating.

"Like"/model, baby　　**Pt.:** My others ate real good and gained real fast. Hope he does. Ummm . . . I'm so tired. Haven't had much sleep since I had the baby.

N.: What time did you come in?

Pt.: My water broke about 9:00 and I was in here by 9:30. I was sitting on the couch and
"Un-like"/model, self　　it really soaked the couch, and I had pains with this one. I didn't have no pains with my others.

My last one came 24 minutes after I got in here and I just live about five minutes away.

N.: You mean your water broke and you came right in and delivered?

Pt.: With both of them that was the way it was, no pains at all. With this one, I came over here and didn't have it for hours and the pains kept coming and the doctor said I wasn't dilating. They wouldn't give me nothing for the pain, either. But it wasn't bad.

"Unlike"/model, self, so disorienting, confusing, "scary"

N.: I noticed they gave you a saddle block for delivery.

Pt.: Uh huh. First time I had that; with the others I didn't have nothing. They didn't want to give me anything last night; 'fraid it would hurt the baby. But he had to use forceps and cut me, so he gave me the saddle block. It wasn't bad. My legs felt funny when they started waking up.

"Un-like"/model, self

N.: Yes, it does feel funny when the feeling starts to come back. You seem so tired. Why don't I go now and come back later to talk with you and take you to the nursery, if you haven't gone by then? Okay?

Pt.: Uh huh. I am tired and would like to take a nap. When will you be back?

N.: I have class from 1:00 to 3:00, so right after that I'll come back. See you then.

Pt.: Bye. Do you know who can visit the baby?

N.: Parents and grandparents, but I don't think there would be any questions unless there seemed to be a crowd. Why?

Pt.: John's mother will be coming, I know, this afternoon. And what times can we go?

N.: Today you can go anytime but the regular visiting hours are 11 to 11:30, 4 to

4:30, and 7:30 to 8. Anything I can do before I go?

Pt.: No, except will you hand me that piece of paper with his footprints on it? I don't want to lose it.

As I handed the sheet to her she looked at the prints then at the information—weight, length—and said them aloud.

Pt.: Umm . . . They said in the delivery room he wasn't quite 18 inches long and on here it says 18.

N.: So close, maybe that's why they put 18.

Pt.: 3:37 was the time he was born. Thought it was later.

N.: That's standard time, so our time it would be 4:37.

Pt.: Oh. (Sighed) So tired.

N.: Why not try to catch a nap. I'll be back later. Bye.

Pt.: Bye.

As I arrived back to her room later she was sitting up in the bed, dressed in a pale pink cotton gown with bra, underpants, and sanitary belt on. Her hair was up in rollers and she had lipstick and glasses on. Her husband and mother-in-law were standing by the bed.

Pt.: Here's the nurse I was telling you about. Thought you'd forgotten.

N.: No, just had class and it ran over a little. Waiting to go downstairs? This must be husband and grandmother.

Pt.: (Nodded) We went when my husband came but want to go back at 4:00, if you can get me a wheelchair.

Husband: When I first came I asked if we could go to the nursery and the nurse at the desk took us down.

N.: Nice; I'm glad you didn't wait for me. What do you think about that new boy of yours?

Pt.: He doesn't look so small.

Husband: Sure was moving a lot.

N.: Yes. He was moving about a good bit this morning when I was down.

Pt.: He has all his fingers and toes, I counted them, and even has fingernails. Think he has more hair than the others had, but he doesn't have any eyebrows.

Complete.
"Like"/her children
"un-like"/her children

N.: He has some but from where you were standing you probably couldn't see them.

Husband: That place on his head looks better. It was like a cut this morning, but it just looks bruised.

M.-I.-L.: From what?

Pt.: You know, the forceps: they had to take him.

Husband: The doctor said it was better to take him than to let her push him out, hurt him less. They just cut her a little bit.

M.-I.-L.: Had all my babies at home, didn't have any of that. Who does he look like?

Ready to claim

Pt. I don't know; he has Janis's nose. You'll see him.

N.: Ready to go now? I don't believe they'll mind you coming early since it's your first day. I'll go get a wheelchair and be right back.

When I returned with the wheelchair, I helped her into robe (yellow) and slippers, then into the chair. Husband pushed chair. As we went down the corridor:

Pt.: Want to remember to watch my robe if I get up out of the chair and then sit back down. I got a spot on it before. Seems like I have more bleeding after I lie or sit and then get up.

N.: The blood collects in your vagina as you're sitting or lying down and with movement you will tend to notice more flow.

Pt.: This is the second gown I've had on since he brought them. Don't want to mess it up, too.

As we arrived at the nursery:

N.: Want to stand up?

Pt.: No, think I'll sit. I can see him all right if they do like they did earlier. Will they move his bed out so we can see him?

N.: Yes, She'll come in a minute. Looks like she's busy right now.

Claiming and identifying. **Pt.:** He looks just like my little girl. He
"Like"/her little girl looks bigger than she did yet he weighs less. She was only 17 inches long, too. He's 18.

N.: She must have been a dainty little girl, with small bone structure. How much did you say she weighed at birth?

Pt.: When she was born, she weighed five pounds, ten ounces. She lost some and when I took her home she weighed five pounds, eight ounces.

N.: How many days were you in the hospital that time?

Pt.: Four days.

Husband: You're staying till Sunday this time, so you can get five days' rest. She can't let anyone wait on her or take care of things. She has to do it, just like now. He told her all along to take it easy and to rest each day.

Pt.: I rested when I got tired. Can't be down all the time, have to keep house and look after the other two.

M.-I.-L.: She had someone to help with the kids but she just wouldn't take it easy.

N.: It's a little hard to give up doing everything when you really don't feel bad.

M.-I.-L.: Just like yesterday. He told her to take it easy and lie down. When she called me she said she was going to get up this morning and take it slow doing her wash, that she had to get it done. That's how come I was over there when her water broke: her sister and I went over to do the wash so she wouldn't have to do it.

Pt.: I just don't like for anyone to have to do my work. I felt all right.

Self-concept

Husband: Look, he's moving all about and making faces.

Pt.: He was awake when we were down before. What's that big thing on his cord?

N.: That's what they use for clamping the cord. They take them off after 24 to 36 hours; then the cord dries and comes off.

Pt.: With my little girl, they had a thin plastic thing on it, not as big as that.

N.: This is just made by another company, probably, but it's the same type thing. . . . How old did you say your other two were?

Pt.: The boy is five and Janis, my girl, is four.

Husband: That boy is something. Momma, you know when I was with him downstairs while you and Dad were visiting Joanne, someone went out with a new baby and he came to tell me the baby was so tiny and measured with his hands, like this (showed with his hands:

about six inches). Then, you know, the other day he was talking about seeing some frogs and showed me how big and he had them about this size (measured about 36 inches).

M.-I.-L.: He got scared last night when Joanne started to cry and everyone was rushing around.

Pt.: That was because everything was happening so fast and he saw me crying and he didn't know what was going on. Did he cry long?

M.-I.-L.: No, he soon quieted down, after we got him to the house.

(He really won the race)

Husband: We were here in about 15 or 20 minutes after her water broke. They had to call me, I wasn't too far away and we only live about five minutes away. They called the doctor by the time I got home and we just came on over. I went through a red light coming and I looked in my mirror and there was a cop. He followed me to the emergency entrance then drove on by.

Pt.: I told him to slow down, that I wasn't going to have it right then.

Husband: Didn't want my car messed up and I wouldn't have known what to do if you'd had it. The others came so fast, I wasn't taking any chances. Lucky Mama was with you. What would you have done if you'd been by yourself?

She shrugged her shoulders and looked up at him then turned back to watch through the window as she had been throughout the conversation above. Husband then questioned how long infant would have to stay in incubator and in hospital.

Pt.: They said I could hold him before I go home. He's so small, just like a doll.

There was conversation as to whom he looked like and of how the other two children had looked when born and how they had acted. All three participated but mostly mother-in-law and husband with Joanne correcting or adding to once in a while. Her eyes and attention seemed to be riveted on her baby as though taking inventory of everything she could see.

Claiming, "like"

Taking-in

We were down there about 15 minutes when she sighed, as though tired.

N.: Ready to go back to bed?

Husband: Yeah, better get you back; this is the second time since lunch you've been down here.

With that he started to push the wheelchair toward the door.

Pt.: Are you sure Dr. S. will come in?

N.: I'm quite sure he has been notified but will check before I leave this afternoon.

Husband: He's probably so busy he hasn't had time. The baby is all right. That doctor last night that checked him came and told me he was fine.

Pt.: Yeah, but . . .

Dr. S. knows her and her children, she knows him

Husband: I have to take Janis tomorrow to see him so I'll remind him if he hasn't been in.

N.: He'll probably come in after office hours now since it's so late now.

Pt.: He was really busy the other day.

Back to the room. Assisted her into bed. Husband and mother-in-law talked about home arrangements and neighbors who had asked about her and whom he had called or not called. I excused myself and returned when I saw them leaving.

N.: Now how about me washing your face and hands and back and giving you a backrub to help you relax before suppertime?

Pt.: I'm so tired, a backrub sounds good. When I was in here before there were some students learning to give backrubs and I really got a lot of them.

Taking-in

As I returned with supplies, she and the other patient were talking. She was noting that she had been up since 6:00 A.M. the day before. That she had gotten up, cleaned house, and gotten some things ready for the baby— clothes, bassinet—and her gowns, sanitary belt and panties for the hospital and then she went to the doctor's office. As I was preparing the water, I heard her say:

Pt.: He told me to lie down, but, you know, it hurt to lie down: the pressure of the baby or something bothered me. When my mother-in-law and my sister were doing my wash, I got up and went to the basement and just sat on a hard chair: I was so uncomfortable.

As I bathed her, she was quite passive. As I started to clean her perineum, she tensed slightly but then relaxed. During this time, she asked me why I was "interested in mothers who have had premature infants"? I told her I had worked a great deal with premature infants but not too much with the mothers, so I decided to find out how the mother feels and what a nurse can do to help her.

Pt.: You're already a nurse, though?

N.: Oh yes. For a long time. This is specialized work on a Master's level, specialized study in maternity nursing.

As I came to the perineum—

Pt.: I tried to clean myself, but it's hard to reach back there.

N.: It sure is. Have you been using the wash cloths and soap and water?

Pt.: Trying to. We're supposed to put the cloths in that mesh bag?

N.: Yes and use a fresh one each time.

Pt.: Thought I'd put these pants on. It makes me feel better: it holds the pad in place. (She also had on a sanitary belt.)

N.: Have your stitches bothered you?

Pt.: No, except when I was sitting up so long this afternoon. He said something like he was going to sew me up differently or something.

N.: It's a short episiotomy and looks real neat.

Pt.: Last time I tore but he didn't sew me. It left a tag hanging and it gets in my way. Did he fix it this time?

N.: Let me look closer. You mean up here (Touching near anterior labia)?

Pt.: Yes.

N.: No, it's still here. You probably would be sore if he had repaired it. Does it really get in your way a lot?

Pt.: Well, sometimes. But guess I'm getting used to it, had it this long, now.

N.: Are you urinating all right?

Pt.: Yes. Didn't have any trouble. It don't burn like it did with the last one.   *"Like"/model, self*

N.: Good.

Pt.: Why did they catheterize me twice after I had the baby?

N.: Twice?

Pt.: Once in the delivery room after he sewed me and then that student that was with

Intrusive

me did it again before they brought me up here. I told her I could go and she said, no, he had ordered it. I don't like to be catheterized: it doesn't feel good.

N.: No, it's not a pleasant procedure to have done to you, but some doctors like to be sure your bladder is empty before you are transferred up here.

As I cleaned up the bedside table, etc., and got her fresh water, she seemed to doze a little. Then supper trays came.

N.: Well, no rest for you now. How about some food then maybe you can catch a nap before visiting hours tonight.

Taking-in

Fixed her supper and then excused myself and went to eat. When I returned, she was lying back in bed with overbed table pushed to foot of bed. Supper tray was empty of food.

N.: Looks like you were hungry.

(Hadn't seen baby.)
Taking-in

Pt.: Uh huh. Didn't eat much for breakfast or lunch. This tasted good. Is there a place visitors can go eat here?

N.: Only the coffee shop. The cafeteria is for employees only.

Pt.: Oh. At Allegheny General the visitors can eat and anybody can eat in theirs. It's real nice and the food is good. My father was there for several weeks and we ate in the cafeteria almost every day.

Note

That's another reason I couldn't take it easy: I had to go over there to see him every day. He died three months ago. You think that had anything to do with my going early—all that confusion and being upset about him?

N.: I would think if it had had anything to do with you and the pregnancy, it would have happened earlier. Can't really tell, though.

She raised herself to the side of the bed.

N.: Going somewhere?

Pt.: To see my friend in there. (Nodded toward the bathroom)

N.: Need some help?

Pt.: No, I think I can do it by myself.

She came out of the bathroom and went to the closet.

N.: Can I help you?

Pt.: Just need another pair of pants. These have some blood on them.

N.: Leave them there and I'll rinse them out for you.

She came out shortly with pants in hand, rinsed out, and looking for a coat hanger. Went to closet before I could, helped herself and fixed them just so on the hanger.

N.: You are independent, aren't you?

Pt.: I feel all right and the sooner I can rinse them, the easier it is to get out.

N.: That's true. Ready to get back in bed now?

Pt.: Uh huh. (Climbed back into bed.) Do you work two shifts? You've been here all day.

N.: No, I don't have any special hours, just when I think I need to be here or when the patient needs me is the way we work. Of course today I had that class and then when I left you this morning, I went and read awhile. I wasn't working all day, just part.

Infant brought out to the other patient. Joanne watched while the nursery nurse helped the other patient then she turned away, toward the door. The staff nurse came in and questioned both patients about their need for sleeping pills at bedtime.

Pt.: No, not tonight, so sleepy can go to
sleep without, but the night before I go home,
I want one.

Staff nurse then questioned about the
need for a laxative. Negative reply from both
patients.

Pt.: What kind of laxative is it that's
white and brown, liquid? It really works. They
gave it to me last time I was in here.

N.: Milk of magnesia and cascara?

Pt.: Yes, it was strong but it worked.
What do they give now?

Other patient noted what she had been
given the night before.

Pt.: Guess I better take something tomorrow night.

N.: You look sleepy, so I'll go. You'll have
time to catch a short nap before time for visitors. Want anything before I leave? Comfortable?

Pt.: I'm fine.

N.: I'll see you in the morning about 9:30
or 10:00 and take you to see your son. Bye.
Have a good night.

Pt. I will. Bye. (As I got outside the door,
I could hear her say "thank you.")

Wednesday, July 12th / Postpartum Day 2

Joanne was in bed, head of bed raised. She
had on a pink gown, hair in rollers, lipstick
and glasses on, smoking a cigarette. She was
watching the other patient feeding her infant.

N.: Hi, how are you today?

Pt. Better: slept last night. (To roommate): What time was it when I went to sleep?

Roommate: About 10:00. She was sound asleep and I went across the hall to talk. It was so hot, I couldn't sleep.

Pt.: If I hadn't been so tired, guess I wouldn't have. Woke up about 4:00 and asked for a pain pill.

Both patients laughed.

Roommate: Do you know the night nurse?

N.: No, why?

Roommate: Well, she has cotton white hair and she must be in her seventies. I couldn't sleep, so I turned my light on to ask for another sleeping pill. And she came down here to find out what I wanted. And when I told her she told me if I'd stop reading—I was just reading to see if I would, could drop off—and turn the light out and close my eyes, I could go to sleep. (They both laughed at this point.) She gave me another pill and turned the light out and as she was going out the door said, "Close your eyes now and go to sleep."

Hostility at being dependent and then infantilized

Pt.: When I wanted that pain pill—cause my stitches were bothering me, you know: drawing—this morning about 4:00, she came down here with her flashlight. And I had this light on. She told me to turn the light off, I didn't need it on. When she got me a pill and then I didn't have any water and she had to go all the way back down the hall for it. (They both laughed.) She looked so funny with her little flashlight on, walking in here. She's too old to be working.

Hostility: dependence and then infantilization

Laughter a good resolution

Roommate: I like the older nurses, not that old, but older nurses take care of you better than those young ones. That one that came in yesterday to take care of her . . .

Pt.: Yeah. She came in here right after I got here and all I asked was could I have a cigarette before she gave me my bath. And she

Need to take-in: cigarette, care

said, "Go ahead, here's your water for your bath when you're ready to take it" and turned around and walked out. All I wanted was to smoke one cigarette.

Roommate: I was telling her that when I came on this floor, an older nurse came in and bathed me all over. I didn't have to do a thing.

Pt.: I sure didn't feel like washing myself, but I did down to here (both hands placed on lower abdomen and pubic area), and that was all.

Touching + caring about need to take-in = Nursing. Early linen change = housekeeper?

That nurse came back in here after awhile and changed my bed, but she didn't touch me. I did it all. Don't they teach these young ones how to nurse anymore, you know, take care of people like they used to?

N.: Yes, some are taught to care for people and do it while others are taught and don't do it, and I guess some aren't taught to care for patients. I should have known to ask you how much care you had received rather than at the desk. She told me you had had your bath and been taken to the bathroom. I could have given you a bath rather than just that piece of one in the afternoon.

Pt.: Oh, but that felt so good yesterday afternoon. I got up and took a shower this morning.

N.: Already?

Sleep disruption?

Pt.: Yeah, about 7:00 they came and stuck a thermometer in my mouth and after that I got up, was so hot and sweaty.

N.: Sounds like the two of you had an interesting evening and night last night. Did you go to the nursery last night, too?

Pt.: My husband and I went down and they were feeding him and Dr. S. came as we were leaving. Oh, I want to get hold of him, but he's so small.

Dr. S. came up here after he checked him, said he was all right and maybe I could take him home when he weighs 5-2 or 5-4, if he's doing all right. Did you see him this morning? (I nodded) What was he doing?

N.: Sleeping, on his tummy with his bottom up in the air.

Pt.: (Laughed). Wonder how long he'll have to stay.

N.: I would guess about 1½ to 2 weeks if he eats okay and starts to gain soon.

Pt.: He had, what do you call it, phlegm?

N.: Mucus?

Pt.: Yes. Last night he was spitting some up. But Dr. S. said that was all right.

Dr. B., her obstetrician, came in, checked her breasts and fundus, questioned her about her stitches. They exchanged comments about the size of the infant. He said he would wait to circumcise the baby until he got bigger but before he went home from the hospital.

Pt.: You do that, and not Dr. S.?

Dr.: Yes.

Pt.: How will you know? Will they call you?

Dr.: Yes. They'll call me several days before he is to go home.

When Dr. B. left, I asked if he did general practice or just ob.

Pt.: He does general practice now. Used to do just maternity but the pills made his practice drop. I like him: he's delivered all my babies and I just have confidence in him, I guess.

He knows her, she knows him

N.: Does he have an office close to here?

Pt.: No, we have to go way over to _____ Rd. Do you know where that is? (I didn't.) Well, it's about 25 or 30 minutes' ride from here. We used to live in that section of town before we moved over here after my little girl was born.

Joanne looked toward the other patient, who was burping and talking to her infant.

A void   **Pt.:** I can't keep my eyes off the baby. She's so cute. I wish I could just touch mine. It doesn't seem like I've had a baby.

N.: Need to hold him to know it?

Pt.: Uh huh. This is like being on a vacation, no baby or children around.

Phone rang. Apparently her mother.

Finished with being pregnant?   **Pt.:** Couldn't help it, Mom. I just had it early. . . . Don't be upset, you couldn't help it cause you weren't here. How could you tell I would have it now instead of August? . . . Everything is all right. . . . You know, Mom, I got up Monday morning and cleaned house and all, then decided to get the bassinet down and the crib sheets and things and got my gowns and things for the hospital out, even bought a sanitary belt when I went to the store. . . . You know, I always come a little early, but this was seven weeks early. . . . I just thought I'd get things ready. No, I was feeling all right in the morning. . . . Mommy don't let Grannie upset you: you couldn't help it if you weren't here.

She was recounting some of her labor and delivery experiences as I went for the wheelchair. As I returned:

Claiming, "like"   **Pt.:** Mom, I have to go now: it's time to go
Unlike: small   see the baby. You coming this afternoon? . . . Yes, you can see him. . . . Oh, looks like John. He's so small, though, Mom. See you this afternoon, Mom. Bye.

Pt.: Can we go now?

N.: Yes. All ready?

Pt.: I need to go to the bathroom before I go.

When she came out of the bathroom, I helped her with her robe.

Pt.: Do I need to comb my hair before I go down there?

N.: You can, if you want to, but it's not necessary. Do you want to?

Pt.: Umm, no, let's go. (She got into wheelchair and we moved off.)

Pt.: Last night I was counting his fingers and toes again. My husband said I shouldn't, that they were there, why keep counting?

Recycling the identification for wholeness

N.: Why not?

Pt.: He said it wasn't right. But I just have to know everything is there: he's so small.

(H. is superstitious)
Again: wholeness

N.: Have to make sure, huh?

Pt.: Uh huh. You know that piece of paper they give you with the footprints on it? Well, I keep looking at it and keep counting his toes.

Wholeness

N.: All there?

Pt.: Yes. (Smiled as she said this.)

As we entered the nursery viewing area, the incubator was moved over to the window. The infant was on his tummy with head to side and had spit a small (minute) amount of formula and mucus. Nurse turned him on his side.

Pt.: Oh, why is he spitting up?

N.: Probably had a little too much or some mucus needed to come up. He's sleeping through it all.

Pt.: Maybe they ought to turn him back on his tummy.

N.: He'll be all right for the short period we're here. Then they'll turn him back on his tummy when we leave.

How I do: how child does = maternal identity

Pt.: I always put my other two on their tummy. They wouldn't sleep any other way and that way, if they spit up, they didn't choke.

N.: That's right.

Baby's active movements surprise her (Other claimants?)

Pt.: My little girl never would lie on her back. She would cry and cry until I turned her over. Oh, look: he's making a face and he's pushing on the side of that (incubator) with his feet. My grandmother would say the devil is after him when he frowns or makes a face like that, and when a baby smiles she says the angels are talking to him. Silly, isn't it?

N.: I've heard other people say that.

Pt.: Oh, there he goes again (making a face and moving legs against Isolette). He must be having a B.M.: he's making such a face and moving his legs around.

Staff nurse was in the nursery trying to quiet another infant by holding and talking to her.

Likes = caring + holding + talking

Pt.: She really likes them, doesn't she?

N.: Yes, she seems to enjoy caring for them.

Recycling identification process.

As she looked at her baby, Joanne's eyes would go from his head to his toes, sometimes moving her head or changing her position to see him better.

More details, completeness

Pt.: I can see his fingernails and toenails today.

N.: Yes, he has them. I'll bet you can't wait to really inspect him. Probably first thing you'll do when you get to hold him is check everything.

She looked up at me and smiled, then looked back at infant.

Pt.: What's that on his heel?   *Intactness*

N.: You may see a Band-aid on his foot every day 'cause they will be doing repeated tests to make sure his blood count is all right.

Pt.: Why do they do so many?   *Intactness*

N.: It's the only way they can keep check. Before he goes home they'll probably put him on some vitamins with iron.

Pt.: He sure looks like my little boy and   *"Like"/claiming*
his face is just like his.

N.: Looks like he has a pug nose the way he's lying there.

Pt.: My Johnny has a pug nose like that.   *"Like"/claiming*
He looks bigger than my Janis did. She was smaller boned than he is, I think. I like the way newborn baby eyes look. See, his eyes are   *Puffiness and discharge*
puffy too. He had some white stuff in them   *(from within?); she can*
yesterday that was coming out. What was that   *ask now that it's gone*
from?

N.: From the eyedrops that were put in at time of delivery. They look clear today. Notice his hands. Such nice long, slender fingers.

Pt.: He has big hands. Just think, they'll   *Big, hard, rough =*
get bigger and some day be hard and rough,   *masculine*
like a man's.

N.: What are you going to name this son of yours?

Pt.: That birth certificate lady was in yesterday and asked me. Had to tell her to come back. My other boy is John Joseph. We're going to name this one Joseph John.

N.: Your husband's name is John, isn't it?

Pt.: Yes, and my little girl's is Janis.

N.: And yours is Joanne. All start with J.

Symmetry (she had a girl's name ready)

Pt.: Yes, that's what we wanted. If it had been a girl, her name was going to be Jill Ann. My husband didn't like that name too much but couldn't find another we liked better that started with a J. Guess next Christmas I can sign the Christmas cards from the five J.H._____, or something like that.

Fantasy: How it will be

N.: That will be cute.

Pt.: Gosh, wish I could just hold him.

N.: You'd really like to, hmm?

Pt.: They said I could before I go home. . . . (She looked at her watch) Time to go back?

N.: When you're ready. We can stay longer, if you like.

Pt.: No, I'll come back this afternoon. . . . Wonder if Mrs. W. (roommate) has gone yet. I forgot to tell her goodbye.

As we arrived back to her room, Mrs. W. was still there. They greeted each other. "When are you going?" "Soon. How was your baby?" "Okay. Still looks small." Roommate's infant was brought in as I left with the wheelchair. When I returned, Joanne was standing by the bed watching the infant being dressed.

N.: Want to get back in bed? You've been up quite awhile.

Pt.: I'll sit here (sat on edge of bed, facing roommate's bed.)

Phone rang. She recounted morning happenings to person on phone (husband), requested him to bring fan and magazines when he came. Told him her mother had returned from vacation and had called and that she would be coming to see her that afternoon, but why didn't he call her? Finished conversation.

Pt.: Do you think they'd move my bed over there by the window after she leaves?

N.: I'll check with the charge nurse at the desk.

When I returned, roommate was leaving, goodbyes said and phone rang again. Patient noted to whoever was on phone the size and looks of infant in relation to other children, noted that she had her own nurse then said, "Not really, she's studying mothers who have premature babies. She takes me to the nursery to see him"; then recounted the labor onset: membranes ruptured at home, pains, and ride to hospital. As she replaced the phone:

Pt.: Did you find out if I could move?

N.: The nurse is checking now.

As I said this the nurse and an L.P.N. came in to move her. As we moved the furniture about, Joanne sat in a chair in the hallway, commenting at times about how much trouble it was, but it was so hot and she felt it would be cooler near the window. Both the L.P.N. and I noted it was all right and not that much trouble and why not be comfortable during her stay. Upon completion of the move, we helped Joanne into her bed.

N.: I'd better be going, Joanne. You'll be having company this afternoon and evening, won't you?

Pt.: Yes.

N.: Well, I'll wait until morning to come back and see you and visit your son.

Pt.: Okay.

N.: Anything I can do for you before I leave?

Pt.: No. Thank you for coming this morning. It gives me something to do when you're here. The time would really go slow if you didn't come. Before, I didn't have time to even read or anything cause they were always bringing the baby in. But this time I don't have anything to do. It's a vacation (said with some feeling of disgust).

N.: Sort of lost without a baby to feed and hold?

Pt.: Uh huh. I wish I could hold him. They did tell me I could before I went home.

N.: That's right. You can go into the nursery and hold him.

Pt.: I wouldn't want to unless Dr. S. says it's all right for me to.

N.: The nursery nurses wouldn't let you unless it was all right for the baby and okayed by the doctor.

The lunch tray was served.

N.: Well, here's a little food for you. Enjoy it and I'll be back tomorrow. Bye, Joanne.

Pt.: Bye and thank you again.

Thursday, July 13th   /   Postpartum Day 3

Joanne's bed was empty as I arrived this morning. New roommate noted she was in the shower and also asked, "Are you her nurse she was telling me about?" As I started to check on Joanne in the shower room, she walked out dressed in yellow gown, her hair damp.

N.: Hot in there, wasn't it?

Pt.: Yes, but it felt good to stand in the shower; my stitches are drawing more today. I've used one box of those tucks already. During the day it's all right. But about 4:00 in the morning they start bothering me. Had to ask for a pill again this morning. They woke us up

(4:00 A.M. is a low point in metabolism.)

Sleep disruption × 2

early, sticking the thermometers in our mouth. That was at 7:00. And then that nurse wanted me to get up so she could make my bed. I just told her I wasn't getting up till after breakfast and then I'd get up and take my shower. I wasn't about to get up then: I had just gotten comfortable and was still sleepy.

Pain and sleep deprivation make her irritable.

She was getting back into bed without any outward sign in facial expression or rate of movement to indicate stitches were bothering her now.

Pt.: I got scared awhile ago: I passed a big blood clot when I went in to take my shower. The nurse was next door and she came in and looked at it and said it was all right. I was really scared: I had never done that before.

"Unlike"/model: self

N.: Had you been having cramps this morning?

Pt.: I have some gas, but no cramps. I hadn't been up since last night and I didn't have any discharge until that clot came. Guess it was blocking it. I never did have anything like that happen to me before.

"Unlike"/self

N.: When you lie down for long periods of time without moving or getting up, you may notice when you do get up that you'll flow more or have a few clots. Let me feel your abdomen and see how and where your uterus is today. (Quite receptive. Abdomen and bladder distended, fundus two finger breadths below umbilicus.) Having any discomfort here (as I was feeling)?

Pt.: No, just some gas.

N.: How about urinating? Been this morning since you got up?

Pt.: Umm . . . No, went right into the shower. Guess I better go now.

She went into the bathroom and as she came out:

N.: Why not try to lie on your tummy awhile? That will help the gas and it will also help get rid of any discharge that might need to come out.

Pt.: I'll get so I can watch Donna (new roommate) feed her baby when it comes (she lay with her head at foot of the bed, on top of covers.) Can you get me a pain pill for these stitches?

N.: Sure, but how about me taking a look and see how they look?

Pt.: Okay.

Stitches inspected with her pointing to area that was drawing. Area clean, slightly edematous.

N.: Looks good. Probably just gets so dry it starts drawing; that's part of the healing process.

Pt.: I try to keep those tucks on, but guess they dry out during the night.

Pain pill given to her. When Joanne had come out of the shower, she had placed a soiled gown and pants in the closet.

N.: Don't you want that gown and pair of pants rinsed out?

(Gas pains, stitch pains, sweaty, tired; but not complaining)

Pt.: Oh, no. My husband can take them home and do it. They don't have any blood on them. Just sweaty.

N.: I'll do them. Won't take a minute, then you'll have a fresh gown if you want it.

As I rinsed them out I could hear some of her conversation with her roommate and that which she directed to me.

Empty time

Pt. You know, today I'm really bored, nothing to do. When I was here before, they were always bringing in the baby to feed and that really makes the day go fast. But this

way, I don't have anything to do. The first day
I didn't care and yesterday I missed my other
children so much. And I felt like I was missing
out: wanted to hold my baby.

Empty room
Empty arms

Roommate: Would you like to hold your
baby?

Pt.: If I could just touch him, then it
would seem more real that I have one. Having
it like this, just looking at him, I don't feel
like I have had a baby.

Roommate's baby was brought it. Joanne
sat up so that she could see infant. Talked to
roommate about how her other babies had
eaten and her care of her other children, once
in awhile bringing up the new infant in comparison with her other children and Roommate's baby. On size: "Yours weighs exactly
two pounds more than mine does. She doesn't
look much bigger, does she? (to me). Hope he
eats as well as the others." Commented on
dressing the infants to go home from the hospital, felt previous roommate had overdressed
infant in relation to the weather and what she
felt was the right kind and amount of clothing
for the infant to wear at home.

Roommate: When will you get to hold
your baby?

Pt.: Before I go home, I'm supposed to
hold him. I keep telling myself that if this
hadn't happened early, I wouldn't have gotten
to hold him for about seven more weeks. So a
couple of weeks shouldn't matter.

N.: Sort of hard to go along with that with
him in the nursery, isn't it?

Pt.: Uh huh. What was he doing this
morning when you went by?

N.: They were doing some blood work and
had the formula out for him to be fed as soon
as they were through. He has lost a little

weight. Here's a weight chart. (Showed her a weight chart noting his birth weight and to-day's weight and told her most infants lose weight before starting to gain.)

"Like"/model, her girl

Pt.: Oh yeah. My little girl lost from 5 pounds 10 ounces to 5 pounds 6 ounces before she started to gain. When we visited last night he looked small still. But when I came back up here, we went to the nursery and those babies look like they should be 8 or 9 months old: they're so big beside mine. Looked at the other babies down there. There are some smaller than mine. There's one colored baby that's so cute. He's about ready to go home, I think. Did you see him?

N.: The one in the next nursery?

Pt.: Yes. Isn't he cute?

N.: Yes.

Pt.: One mother came last night and they had moved her baby from where it usually is and she didn't know it. She really got upset when she couldn't find it. Those twins look smaller than my baby and they were born over a month ago and weigh 4 pounds and 4 ounces.

N.: With smaller infants, four pounds or less, it seems to take a long time for them to hit four pounds. Once they get there, they usually gain quite rapidly.

Pt.: Hope mine does. Think he'll get to come home in a couple of weeks?

N.: Yes, if he eats all right. He has started out eating well. Joanne, was this pregnancy different than the others, do you think?

Pt.: What do you mean?

N.: Did you have any more physical dis-comfort or were you upset more with this one than the others?

Pt.: Well, you know I told you it was always low, lower than my other two, and he didn't move hardly at all, maybe over here (rubbed side). I could feel his hands. I guess it was moving sometimes. My others really moved and way up here. (upper abdomen)

Comparing a 6–7 month pregnancy with two 8–9 month pregnancies

N.: Anything else?

Pt.: I had to take vitamins and calcium with this one and never took them with the others. Once in awhile I would take a vitamin pill but the doctor told me to take them this time. And you know that discharge you have when you are pregnant?

N.: You mean from the vagina?

Pt.: Uh huh. Well before, it was just clear. This time it would be bloody sometimes.

N.: Was there any pain when you noticed the bloody discharge?

Pt.: No. You know, there's been something going on at our house since February. I guess that's why I came early.

N.: Why do you say that?

Pt.: Well, first my dad was sick at home. Then he was in the hospital and died and he had to be buried, you know. All that and I went to see him everyday. Then John's brother had been in Japan for three years and he came home. His family was with him. They have four children and we hadn't seen the youngest child: it was born over there. And they just left from visiting us and I just finally got to relax since February. I guess that's why it came early.

Stress + +, first trimester

Stress ±, second trimester

N.: Sounds like you have been kept busy the last six months or so.

Pt.: You know, we have a dog and she'll be in heat in August. We were kidding the other day, saying that the dog would be in heat and I'd have the baby at the same time.

N.: Did you just get the dog?

Girl puppy for pregnancy

Pt.: No. I got her when I was pregnant with my little girl. She's four years old.

Phone rang. Apparently mother. Excused myself for a break, noting I'd be back in time to take her to the nursery. When I returned with the wheelchair she was combing her hair and putting makeup on.

N.: Getting fixed up for your son?

Pt.: Yeah. (laughed)

N.: Ready?

Pt.: Yes. (seated herself in the wheelchair) Do you think that lady that came around for the birth certificate information will come back today?

N.: I don't know, but she'll get the information before you leave.

Pt.: Can his name be put on his bed like the others?

N.: Sure. We can tell the nurse today. They like to know what the infant's name is so they can start calling him by it instead of some nickname.

As we arrived at the nursery viewing window, her infant was moved over. I can't really remember exactly what she said, but she did comment on how small he looked, something about his being asleep and that they must have just fed him and that she hoped he was that good when she got him home.

(So far she has not missed one visiting time, nor has she stayed beyond the allotted time)

Pt.: Each time I come down it makes me want to hold him that much more. Oh. . . . Guess I ought not to come every time.

N.: Do you really think that would help?

Pt.: No. (smiled up at me) But I can't come over every day when I go home. And it's going to be bad after I've been able to come down here three times every day.

Miss C. (faculty advisor) came out to us at this time and asked Joanne about her baby. In answering, Joanne said something about wanting to just touch or hold him so she'd really know she had a baby.

Miss C.: Would you like to hold him now?

Joanne looked from Miss C. to me and back to the baby, then back to Miss C.

Pt.: Could I? (hushed tone)

Miss C.: If you'd like to you can.

Pt.: Now? (looked at me as she said this, I nodded.)

Miss C.: Want to?

Pt.: Oh, yes.

Prior to this exchange, when Joanne was talking about visiting and holding the infant, her hands had been in her lap but moving: rubbing together or on her thighs or closing and opening. As the talk became more specific about holding and the real possibility of it, she grasped the arms of her wheelchair as though to hold herself.

N.: Well, let's go get a gown on you and go in the nursery so you can, okay?

Pt.: Oh, look my hands are all sweaty. I'm so excited.

In the dressing room she took her own robe off very quickly and inserted her arms into the gown held for her, not hesitating, and quickly washed her hands as instructed. She moved toward the door as I gowned and washed my hands. She made some comment about was I sure this was all right: she didn't want to do

(This was an off-scene arrangement. The hospital has since adopted a more permissive policy.)

anything that would hurt the baby. I reassured her that this was often done for mothers who desired to hold their babies and made it known. By this time we were in the nursery.

Joanne stood and looked through the Isolette for several seconds before taking a seat in the rocking chair provided. She sat on the edge of the chair, leaning toward the Isolette, her hands held tightly together in her lap.

Holding on, for control

Pt.: He looks smaller than from out there. Oh, he's a lot smaller than my Janis was.

Miss C. placed a blanket in her lap, over her hands. Joanne moved back into the chair and unclasped her hands.

Pt.: Oh, he's so small. You sure it's all right to take him out of that incubator?

Throughout the next few minutes she was inspecting her infant and commenting. The first portion of his body she touched was his hand, which he was moving about. She noted, along with Miss C. and myself, the features of his hands and fingers. She inspected his hand quite thoroughly, felt the skin on his arms and commented "how soft." He stretched and she took hold of one of his lower legs and foot, said, "My father would have liked him," then noted how long his foot was. She asked Miss C. how long he really was; that they had told her not quite 18 inches in the delivery room and on the information sheet it said 18 inches. Miss C. left to check and returned saying he was all but 18 inches. Joanne said her Janis was 17 inches but "She sure looked bigger than he does now." His eyes were closed during all of this. She touched his chin. He in turn opened his mouth. Then she touched his cheeks and forehead, commenting on how soft and smooth his skin was and noting that the forceps mark was gone. She asked how the forceps were put on but went on looking quite closely to the left side of his face, apparently where she had seen

Face, hands, feet: the periphery

Mismatch

Bigger ⇄ smaller
Oscillating, locating

the blood on delivery: "There isn't even a scratch here where I thought there was a cut the other night." She touched his ear, commenting on how flat his ears were and that the night before one was turned over like this; she demonstrated and then smoothed his ear back in place.

From here she went to his chest. He was dressed in an undershirt but a portion of his chest could be seen at the neck of the shirt. She asked, "What are those marks?" and pointed to the linen impressions apparently from him being on his abdomen so long. I pulled his shirt up while noting the impressions of the linen for her. She touched the further exposed chest. Cord clamp had been removed and a very short stump remained. She did not touch this part of his body.

Low tolerance for blemishes on baby

She made some comment about the size of the diaper pin and then told us that the first day the diaper pin looked like it went completely across his abdomen but today, it didn't look so big. She then told us that the doctor said he'd circumcise the baby before he came home. I took the diaper pin out and moved the diaper away. The penis looked minute even to me. "Oh, it's so small. . . . My little boy's was much bigger." Miss C. and I both tried to tell her it would be larger even within days, she would be surprised, but she said: "Oh, but it's so small. How will he circumcise him?"

No further touching at this time

She thought he better be put back into the incubator and seemed to hold her trunk back so that I could reach and take him. She got up out of the chair as I took him and watched as I cleaned his buttocks. As I turned him onto his abdomen, he turned his head so that he was facing away from her. When I noted that his eyes were open now, she quickly walked around the incubator to see. She held her hands together against her body. She was smiling broadly and thanking everyone in the nursery for the opportunity to hold her baby, saying

Can't spare any?
Finished identification session

she now felt like she had one. On the way out of
the nursery, while dressing and going back to
her room, she kept repeating, "He's so small, so
much smaller than my Janis, so much smaller
even in my lap than he was in there (Isolette).
No bigger than a baby doll." She also men-
tioned "how kind that lady (Miss C.) was to
take that time and to stay right there."

To her roommate, she said, "He was that
small" (measured about six inches with her
hands). Then she turned to me and said, "I can
still feel him." She was rubbing her hands
lightly together. She smiled as she said this
and looked down at her hands.

Phone rang. As soon as she said the hel-
los, she announced "I held him. . . . Yes, in the
nursery. I got to go in. He's so small, smaller
than he looks from the outside, through the
window."

Pt.: (to me) Can't believe I held him. He's
so small. Skin is so soft (said rather dreamily).
Thank you, this is my day: I really held my
baby.

Birth certificate lady came in, requesting
information. I went to return wheelchair.
When I returned, the transaction was done.

Pt.: I'm glad my children will have an
easy last name to spell when they go to school.
We had a time when we went to school. Ours
was hard. I could never remember the two fs.

N.: What was your maiden name?

Pt.: P_____ff.

N.: What nationality is that?

Pt.: My father was Bulgarian and my
mother is Ukrainian.

She then reviewed her father's illness.
Her roommate asked how old her father was
when he died: 57. He had been home ill for 10
years and had not been able to work since

having surgery on heart, had plastic valve put in then; had had rheumatic fever as a child.

Pt.: There were six of us (children) but mother and father saw we had what was needed and they went without. Since father died, she was lost without father in the house. She had gone to be with my brother for a vacation. That was three days before this happened. My grandmother fussed at her for going off and leaving. Mother was so upset. I've tried to tell her she couldn't tell I was going to deliver early.

Note

N.: Has she been to see you?

Pt.: Yes, came yesterday when she got back from vacation. She came home a day early.

N.: Did she see the baby?

Pt.: Yes, she thinks he looks like my Johnny. She's going to keep my children next week. John's mother has had them this week.

N.: That will be nice; then you won't have the responsibility of keeping up with them. But won't you be lonesome?

Pt.: Oh, they'll come over during the day for a few hours. But they'll spend the night with her and she'll fix their meals. That way I won't be trying to do too much. John will be off next week, too. John is on 3:00 to 11:00 tomorrow and Saturday. Can he come in early to see me?

Organization of household; she has done a lot of arranging

N.: Yes, all we have to do is explain. He'll have to be sure babies aren't out or you two can go to the reception room right down the hall.

Roommate questioned about mother's classes and Joanne noted she'd like to go, too. I didn't know when they were held, so I said I would find out or would ask the teacher to come see them.

Pt.: I went to them when I had my other children. We learned how to do things a new way.

N.: I guess I'd better go: it's getting near lunch time and I have a class at 1:00.

Pt.: When are you coming back this afternoon?

N.: I hadn't planned to unless you won't be having visitors or would like for me to come back. Do you think you'll have some company? Because if not, would be glad to come back this afternoon or evening.

Pt.: No, I will have company this afternoon, I know, and tonight John will be here. Will you be here early tomorrow?

N.: About the same time, okay?

Pt.: Yes, bye and thank you so very much: I can still feel him.

Friday, July 14th / Postpartum Day 4

Joanne was in bed, wearing a pink gown; hair in rollers, without makeup. Breakfast trays were being collected by personnel.

N.: Morning. Looks like you two are ready for the day. How did the night go or shouldn't I ask?

Pt.: Oh, our nurse, you know, the little old lady, she got after us this morning. Neither one of us could sleep so we turned these (overbed) lights on and were reading. And she came down and said it was a hospital rule: no one could have the light on 'til 7:00 in the morning.

Roommate: Isn't that a silly rule?

Pt.: Well, anyway, we turned them out. Then we got up about 6:30 and got our showers and all.

Pt.: I had to ask for another pain pill this morning. I don't think that nurse liked it. She came down here with her flashlight, wanted to know, what did I want now?

4:00 A.M.?

Roommate: You know, last night about 6:30 (P.M.) or so that nurse came and asked if I wanted a pain pill or sleeping pill at bedtime. And I told her I didn't know what I'd want then. She said she had to know 'cause she was setting up her medicines. I told her I'd take a pain pill right then instead of later. (Both women laughed) So, she had to go get it then. Think she was mad but I thought, how do I know what I'll need at bedtime?

Pt.: I didn't have to take anything until 4:00 this morning. Not even a laxative. I had a good B.M. last night and another this morning without taking anything. I'm not going to take anything.

Narcisstic input: functioning okay

N.: Did you get rid of the gas?

Pt.: Oh, yes. I was so embarrassed yesterday when I had company and had gas.

N.: Did you have quite a bit of company?

Pt.: Did I! (Named off 7 to 10 persons)

Celebration; she's loved

N.: Did your husband ask about coming in early today and tomorrow?

Pt.: Yes. He's coming at 11:00. They said he could stay from 11:00 to 2:00.

N.: Good. He'll be here when we go to the nursery this morning.

Pt.: Better get these rollers out now.

Combed hair out and put on eyebrow pencil, lipstick, and powder.

Readying for a larger social sphere

N.: Getting all fixed up for your best beau?

Pt.: He's been taking all my girlfriends home from here, I better get fixed up. (Laughed)

N.: Now Donna and I know who's important. You don't get fixed up for us, but when your best beau is due in, that's when you get busy. (All of us laughed)

Gift shop cart came to room.

Keeping in touch

Pt.: Oh, I want to get something for the children. Each day I've been in here, I have sent something home to them.

Increased activity, almost aggressive

She was out of bed and practically out the door before I caught up with her with her robe. She selected gifts for each child.

Pt.: Been trying to send them something different each day. I don't want them to think I've forgotten them.

N.: Have you been calling them each day?

Pt.: They've called me several times a day, huh Donna?

Roommate: I can tell when it's them on the phone. She always tells them, "Now do what Grandma says."

Pt.: My little boy called the other day to tell me Grandma wouldn't let him play ball. It was that hot day and I knew what she was trying to do, you know: keep him inside until it was cooler out. But he wanted to go out.

N.: Will you have someone help you when you go home?

Pt.: They will stay with my mother next week.

N.: That's right, you did tell me that. And your husband will be off next week. That will be nice to have your husband around when you first go home. He can bring you in to see the baby. What did he say when he heard you had held the baby yesterday?

Pt.: Nothing, just "you did?" Did you see him this morning?

N.: Yes, before I came up here. He was crying and moving around. It was time for him to eat.

Pt.: He was by the window last night. Dr. S. came by last night and said he was doing all right. Dr. B. came by this morning, just before you came, said I was doing all right, too, and that he would discharge me for Sunday when he comes in tomorrow.

Roommate: Is discharge time 11:00 or 12:00?

N.: That's the time they would like patients to leave.

Pt.: He said that if I stayed till 3:00, I'd have to pay the extra day, that the insurance would not pay it. But John is working till 3:00 Sunday and I don't have anyone that can come for me: my father-in-law is working too.

N.: You can go before 11:00 if that would help.

Pt.: Umm. . . . John will have to get someone to relieve him, I guess.

Roommate was through feeding her infant and questioned where the scales were and where she had to go for mother's class.

N.: Oh, the nurse (teacher) came by to talk to you about the classes?

Pt.: Yes and they're held at 11:00 and I'll be downstairs at the nursery, so I won't get to go.   *Priorities*

N.: Would you like to get weighed, too?

Pt.: Yes. I don't think I lost any: I only gained seven pounds.

N.: Okay, we can walk down there and I can show Donna where to go for class at the same time.

They put on their robes and we walked down the corridor to the scale, the women talking together about weight gain.

N.: Joanne, let's see if you've lost or gained eating the food here. 128 pounds.

Pt.: That's five pounds more than when I came in. How come?

N.: Been eating too much since you've been here?

Pt.: No. I think cause I've finally relaxed.

Roommate then weighed and we walked back to the room with them discussing Joanne's weight gain and roommate's weight loss.

N.: It's almost time to go for class and to the nursery. Do you need to go to the rest-room?

Third one?

Pt.: I think I better: feels like I can have another B.M.

While she was in the bathroom, I took her roommate to the classroom and brought back a wheelchair.

N.: Ready?

Pt.: Want to wait for my husband.

Enlarging space

We stood at the door waiting. Joanne walked across corridor to talk with the woman in that room. Then we walked up the corridor to the full-term baby nursery.

1. Introjection, trying on modeled behavior for goodness of fit
2. Projecting or generalizing her feeling: lonesome

Pt.: Why would anyone want to be in a private room? I would be so lonesome. I've been lucky every time I've been in here: had someone who likes to talk. First time, they put a woman in with me that had had five and that was good: she taught me a lot. Do they put mothers up here who lose their babies?

N.: Yes, sometimes. Why?

Pt.: I wouldn't like that. To be where others are getting theirs.

Introject-project (basis of empathy)

N.: You don't mind being here when you can't have yours brought out?

Pt.: That's different. I know mine is downstairs and I can go see him. But if you lose your baby and couldn't see it, it would be awful.

N.: Sometimes we think it might help the mother who loses one to be with other mothers.

Pt.: I guess everybody is different, but I don't think I would.

At 11:05, I suggested we go ahead down to the nursery.

Pt.: No, wait for a few more minutes. He's usually on time. Probably having a time parking. He did yesterday. Had to park at the Gulf station.

At 11:10, she seated herself in the wheelchair.

Pt.: Let's go. He'll know where I am.

As we arrived at the nursery, quite a few personnel and medical staff were in the room observing another infant. Joanne hardly looked at her infant: her eyes were fastened on the personnel and on the infant they were observing. She kept looking back at me.

Model, prematurity?

N.: Joanne, look: he's moving about for you.

Pt.: He is moving around. Must have just eaten: there's a little milk at his mouth. Don't his legs and arms look like they're filling out?

Seeking confirmation of her observations

Her eyes were soon back on the other infant.

Pt.: What's wrong with that other baby?

N.: I don't really know. Looks like he's having trouble breathing.

She got up out of the wheelchair and walked over to where she could see the other baby better.

Pt.: Its chest is up so high, why? What are they getting ready to do?

N.: I don't know, possibly some lab work or give it some medication.

Pt.: Why don't all the babies have shirts on?

N.: When they'd rather not disturb them, they don't dress them. With some of the smallest ones, they even leave the diaper off. Look at Joseph, he's making some faces and opening his eyes.

She came back to where she could see her infant, but her attention was not on him but on the activity going on in the room in relation to the other infant. Miss C. came out, spoke to Joanne. Greeting exchanged.

Pt.: He looks bigger, you know, like his legs aren't as wrinkled as before. Is he eating all right, keeping it down?

Miss C. said she would check to make sure.

Pt.: What did he weigh? The nurse that came by earlier didn't know.

N.: They hadn't weighed him when I was by, either.

Miss C. would check both items for her.

Pt.: Oh, look he's smiling. . . . He's moving his bowels.

Miss C.: Is that what you think is going on?

"Like"/models   **Pt.:** Uh huh. My others did that.

Miss C. left and returned with the information that there was a slight weight gain and that he was eating well and keeping all of it down.

Pt.: Yesterday, she said he weighed 4 pounds, 10 ounces.

N.: Every little bit will help. Won't take long if he keeps eating all right and gaining a little each day.

Pt.: I wonder where my husband is?

She continued to observe the activity in the room and then turned to Miss C.

Pt.: She said I could come back and see him after I leave.

Miss C.: You can call, too, between 1:00 and 2:00 every day.

Pt.: Dr. S. will call me each day, he said. I hope he won't have to stay too long.

N.: I think we better go back, Joanne. They need to do some treatments on that other baby and would like for us to leave. We can come back later.

She thanked Miss C. for finding out about baby and for yesterday: "That was so nice to hold him." As we went back up to the room, she commented on how he looked and "wasn't he filling out?"

Pt.: I wish I could take him home when I go. That's what I hate: going home without.

N.: Will that be hard?

Pt.: Uh huh. I can come back and see him?

N.: Yes. They prefer you come at regular viewing hours, but if you can't, I think they'd let you come at another time. Just ask before coming. Also, you know you can call and I'll be checking on him, too, if you want to call me.

As we got to the room, her husband was sitting, looking out the window.

Pt.: Oh, honey. I thought you'd come down to the nursery. You didn't know where I was?

Husband: I started to, but didn't know if I could: got some looks when I came down here.

Pt.: (To me) Can we go back?

N.: Sure. I think they'll understand.

Pt.: Want to go, honey?

Husband wasn't saying much, seemed more disappointed than angry. Joanne went on to tell him about the baby—weight gain and how he looked like he was filling out. She again asked if he didn't want to go down.

Husband: No. That's all right. (While saying this, he was going toward the door. She followed and got into the wheelchair.)

N.: It's all right if you want to go down for a few minutes. Do you want to go by yourselves or shall I go along in case they say anything?

Husband: (As he was pushing the chair down the hall) Come on, Miss M.

N.: They're doing some treatments on another baby, so we may have to wait a few minutes. But I'll see when we get there.

When we arrived at the nursery, they were indeed still working on the other baby, but we did have an opportunity to view Joseph. I just ignored the staff's motions to leave: we couldn't see what they were doing from where we were. During this time Joanne was *Confirmation of* looking at her baby, relating to husband how *observations* the baby looked to her and didn't he think so?

As we went back upstairs, she asked why he was so late coming and apologized for not waiting for him. He was smiling and joking now. Told about his troubles parking and also about what the children were doing. As we got back to the room and helped her out of the chair, she noticed two paper bags on the overbed table.

Pt.: Did you bring those for us?

Husband: You said you wanted something.

Pt.: He's always bringing me and the kids something everytime he comes home from work.

Husband: Where's Donna? I brought her a milkshake. Miss M. there is plenty there, help yourself.

Declined, thanking him. Joanne was busy investigating the contents of the bags. She showed him what she had bought for the children, and then set out the food that he had brought.

Giving/receiving

N.: I guess I'd better be going since your husband is here to keep you company. I'll come back later this afternoon when you won't have company.

Pt.: You don't have to leave just 'cause he came.

N.: I have some work to do. (I was also tired from the tension of arrangements for her to hold baby again today that had to be canceled.) I'll be back. You and your husband will want to visit. See you later this afternoon. Bye.

—Bye's from both of them. Thank you from Joanne.

Friday, 3:00 P.M.

Joanne was in bed, eating supper, as I arrived. She was dressed in her pink gown, hair combed and makeup on. The TV was on but no one was looking at it.

White noise

Pt.: Hi. I wondered what time you'd come back. I told Donna I bet you'd wait until about visiting hours.

N.: No, I thought I'd come a little earlier than that. Did you have company this afternoon?

Pt.: No. John left about 2:00 and I took a nap. Then the nurse took me down to see the baby. That other baby was still sick. They were still working with it while we were there.

N.: Did Joseph do anything different for you?

Pt.: No, slept the whole time.... I called Dr. B. while John was here to see if I could go home tomorrow. He said yes and that he would be in early tomorrow to discharge me.

N.: Will that make it easier for your husband to come get you?

Note

Fortifying a lesser choice

Pt.: Yes and then we won't have to pay for that extra day they charge you if you stay after 12:00 o'clock. In a way I hate to leave tomorrow. But I will be glad to get home and there is plenty to be done at home instead of me just lying in this bed here doing nothing.

N.: You're supposed to take it easy when you go home.

Fantasy ⇄ planning, "How it will be"

Pt.: Oh, I will. When I say I have plenty to do, I mean like sewing, patching and mending, and there are enough buttons off clothes to keep me busy for weeks. I won't be doing any heavy housework or running after the kids.

Roommate: I'll bet!

N.: You'll probably have a lot of company.

Roommate: Yeah, you'll get on that phone and call all your girlfriends to come see you.

A good way to cope with confinement and isolation

Pt.: No. Not too many will come over. Just the family and the kids will come over for a couple hours each day.

N.: Will visitors come after you get the baby home?

Pt.: Probably, when he's christened. But I'm going to do like I did with Janis: brought her home and put her in her room upstairs and all the company stayed downstairs. When someone asked to see her, I just said she was asleep and they could just go to the door. But I didn't let anyone hold her or get too close to her. And this one will be even smaller than she was, so I'm sure not going to let everyone get around him.

"Like"/model, self

You know, both of my other babies were real good babies. Soon after I brought them home, they slept through the entire night. Didn't have no trouble with them. Johnny had bronchitis and sometimes I had to sit up with him at night, but that would be just a couple of nights, then he'd be all right.

"Real good:" appreciative that they let her sleep

Retrospectively, sleepless nights with the first baby are now almost nothing

N.: What was Johnny's reaction when you brought a new baby home before? He was just a year old then.

Pt.: He didn't seem to be jealous or anything. He'd try to get me to play with him when I was doing something for Janis, but he soon learned that when I was taking care of her, I couldn't play with him. And then when I'd get through, I'd play with him; he'd just sort of wait his turn and now they play real well together.

N.: What do you think his reaction will be when you take the baby home this time?

Note how a woman's
distaste for surprises is
used to advantage in
childrearing

Pt.: I don't know. But Johnny starts kindergarten in September and we've been talking about this. He was real excited about going to school until he was told that we were going to have a new baby and that Janis and I would be home all day with the baby while he went to school. He soon was fussing about not wanting to go to school: he wanted to stay home, too, and play with the baby. But then I told him that Janis and I would have to take a nap when the baby did. That fixed it. He doesn't like to take naps. Neither one of the children likes to; they will lie down and be quiet but won't close their eyes.

She knows her children

N.: Think they'll miss something. Just the rest is usually enough.

Pt.: My kids sleep from about 9:00 at night till 8:00 or 9:00 in the morning. Except when my little boy gets up when John does at 4:30 to go to work. He gives Johnny some milk and cookies while he's eating his breakfast then sends him back to bed.

N.: Do you live close to the school?

*Safe passage; sounds as
though she tried it on in
her own body (introject)
for him (project)*

Pt.: Yes, it's just down the street. No streets for him to cross and when he starts first grade, he won't have to cross streets, either, 'cause he'll be going to parochial school and it's right down the street in the opposite direction and on the same side of the street as our house. We live on a dead end street, too.

N.: That does make it nice for the children. You probably don't have too much traffic.

Pride in organization

She then told about their experience in renting a house and their decision to buy, describing the condition of the house they are buying and what improvements have been made by her husband. She went on to tell of how she has children's play areas arranged and what toys are allowed in the living room and in their bedrooms (only books and small toys) and what is kept in the basement playroom.

Then she and her roommate discussed securing copies of the birth certificate, the merits of various bottles and formula preparation, the various types of diapers and ways to put them on. Joanne related her experiences with her other children and how she is going to do things with this baby. During this conversation, her roommate's baby was brought in and roommate was feeding it. Joanne was watching quite closely. Soon she was off from the sitting position on her bed to stand beside her roommate's bed, looking at the baby.

Planning, organizing

Pt.: Oh, I'd like to hold a baby. I asked the nurse if they had one that needed feeding, that I'd like to, but she said no. (As she said this, she extended her hand as though to touch the infant.)

Roommate: You can touch her if you want.

Joanne touched ever so slightly the infant's foot that was extended toward her then quickly withdrew her hand, turned and walked away, saying, "I better not."

Staff nurse came in to find out what medications they would need at bedtime.

Pt.: I better have a pain pill and a sleeping pill. I know I won't sleep if I don't.

Ensuring sleep

The two women then discussed their stitches, what they found to be the most comfortable sitting position, the medication and/or treatment that brought the best relief, Joanne offering her Americaine spray to her roommate as the best thing she had used so far. They then discussed how they looked at their stitches and what they looked like to each. They then asked that I get them some more pads, that they were about out, and that some nurse had said something about them using too many. Soon Joanne was combing her hair and putting her lipstick on.

N.: Getting ready to go somewhere?

Pt.: (Laughed) Yes. Want to be ready to go downstairs when it's time to go.

N.: Almost time now. I'll get the chair and pads for you.

When I returned, Joanne and roommate were again talking about using the Americaine spray. Joanne questioned me about roommate's using it and would I look at roommate's perineum for her? So after looking at roommate's perineum (clean, intact, some edema), telling her my observations and spraying it for her, found Joanne waiting in the wheelchair.

As we were getting ready to leave, Joanne asked roommate to tell any visitors that she'd be back soon. Just then roommate's husband arrived with greetings for both women plus drinks and food (potato chips, cookies, fruit). Joanne excused herself, noting she was on her way to see the baby.

As we arrived at the nursery, Joanne took a quick look at her infant and then observed the sick infant and the personnel attending it. One nurse soon came to the window, asked who Joanne wanted to see, then went to his Isolette and changed his diaper. Joanne was watching quite closely.

Pt.: Looks like he's bigger down there tonight.

N.: I have to agree with you. His penis does look bigger than when we looked yesterday.

Mimicry/class or generalized other   **Pt.:** Is she supposed to use a diaper to clean him with? I thought you were supposed to use cotton.

N.: There is cotton for her to use but she may feel she needs more than cotton to clean him up with tonight.

Pt.: He doesn't like that, does he? (Infant was flailing arms as he was being cleaned and then as his position was changed, his legs and arms were extended and flailing in the air.)

No contact points

N.: Doesn't seem to.

Pt.: Sure is moving a lot. And it's the first time his eyes have really been open. And my husband isn't here to see. Looks like he can see, but he can't, can he?

N.: Supposedly not. His eyes really don't focus. If you watch real close, you can see.

Pt.: They always cross their eyes. I don't like it when they do that. See, he has his eyes crossed now, ooh.

She walked away and over to where she could see the sick infant. She studied it and then came back to look at hers.

Pt.: I pray every day mine will be all right. He's so small. . . . That baby (sick infant) is lots bigger than mine. He's not a premature, is he?

Like, unlike

N.: Probably not, from his size. This nursery is used for sick, full-term infants as well as prematures.

Pt.: What is that stuff they're giving him in that bottle? What is she doing?

N.: That's probably some water solution and the nurse is making sure the baby is only getting so many drops of it a minute.

Pt.: Oh. . . .

She returned to her own infant, noted his fingers being nice and long, hands filling out, and that he was moving a lot, "Must be hungry, look, his mouth keeps opening."

Getting a personality through behavior

Seeks confirmation in reading the behavior

Pt.: Is he crying? Looks like it but I can't hear anything.

N.: Think he's yawning rather than crying.

Pt.: Think I'm ready to go back. Maybe I have some visitors.

Note

When we returned to the room she did have a visitor. After the introduction I excused myself to return after visiting hours. After visitors left, Joanne recounted her visit to the nursery noting first that his thing (penis) looked bigger and then that he was filling out, that the other infant was still there and that the nurses were really looking after him. Joanne then received a phone call, apparently from her husband, which lasted only a few seconds. She hung up, went to the bathroom and wasn't in there too long when the phone rang again. It was her husband again and he chose to wait on the line for her rather than have her call him back. As Joanne returned and took the phone, I left for supplies: linen, backrub materials, etc. Joanne finished making arrangements with her husband for going home in the morning and soon hung up the phone. Noting my materials and supplies:

Pt.: Do I have time to go back in there? I didn't even take time to clean myself before coming out.

N.: Sure.

Pt.: Why don't you do Donna while I'm in there? Then I'll be ready.

As I was completing Donna's care, Joanne came out and started packing her suitcase and organizing those items that would not fit in the suitcase.

N.: Ready for your backrub, now?

Pt.: Uh, huh. That will really feel good. Haven't had one since you gave me one the other day.

N.: Maybe you'll rest better with a back-rub plus the pain pill and sleeping pill.

Pt.: Oh, that's better. . . . What's your first name?

N.: Barbara.

Pt.: Do you mind if I call you by your first name? It's so hard to remember last names.

N.: Sure, that's fine. I've been using your first name for the last few days, don't see why you can't use mine.

Pt.: What kind of material have you collected from studying me?

N.: How you are reacting to the birth of a premature baby and how you react to holding and not holding your infant.

Pt.: Will you take care of another patient this week?

N.: No, time is running out right now: I have only about two weeks before I go on vacation.

Pt.: When will you be back?

N.: In September.

Pt.: How long is your course?

N.: I'll be here till December.

Pt.: Then what will you do?   *Good interviewer*

N.: Return to Florida. I'm just on leave from my job.

Pt.: Will you be working with mothers who have premature babies?

N.: Not directly, but I'll be working with nurses who do.

The indirect request
Pt.: Oh. . . . Will you be here next week when I come back to see the baby?

N.: I can arrange to be here. Why don't you call me the day before you plan to come and let me know what time you'll be here?

Good control and organization
Pt.: How can I reach you?

N.: I'll give you my phone number and class schedule when I come in tomorrow.

Pt.: Let me have it now. I might forget tomorrow: I'll be so excited. (With this, she produced a piece of paper and a pen.)

N.: I'll keep tabs on your son as I come and go for classes over here. So if you want to call me in addition to the hospital and the doctor, you are welcome to. If you have any questions or just want to talk, pick up the phone and dial me. . . . Well, guess I better leave you girls: it's getting late. Need anything before I go?

Both said no.

Pt.: Thank you. I feel so comfortable and relaxed, don't know if I really need that pain pill and sleeping pill I ordered earlier.

N.: Better take them and be sure to get a good night's rest before going home. Night.

Pt.: Bye. What time will you be here in the morning?

N.: About 9:00, all right?

Pt.: Yes, bye.

Saturday, July 15th / Postpartum Day 5

Joanne was sitting up in bed, eating breakfast, as I arrived this morning. She was dressed in yellow robe, pink gown. Her hair was in rollers, no makeup on as yet. Her suitcase was on the window ledge. Magazines, Kleenex, dusting powder, and plant—items that would not fit in suitcase—were neatly stacked on the chair.

Organized. Under control

N.: Well, looks like I'm in time for breakfast.

Pt.: You got here early.

N.: Sure. Didn't want to miss seeing you off. How was last night? Sleep all the way through it?

Pt.: Sure did. Took the sleeping pill and the pain pill and didn't know nothing till the nurse was waking me up to take my temperature this morning.

Roommate: Yeah, she snored all night.

N.: You stayed awake just to listen, I bet?

All of us laughed.

Pt.: We had the TV on 'til about 11:00 and I just remember Donna turning it off. She went to sleep right away too, she said.

N.: Had your shower already?

Pt.: Yes. Got right up after the nurse took my temperature. Can't get dressed until John brings my clothes. I told him to bring a bag to put all this in, too.

As she finished breakfast, she got up to go to the bathroom. When she came out, she started to put on makeup and take hair down. She and roommate were exchanging comments on breakfast menu and what was on the menu for the next day. Roommate was teasing her about leaving roommate to eat by herself and look what they're having for dinner tomorrow, that if she stayed and ate with her, she might gain a few more pounds, why not stay.

Dr. B. came in and checked her breasts and fundus, questioned how her bottom felt, and told her to be sure to call his office for an appointment in about four weeks. He also reminded her to be sure to sign the circumcision permit so that when the day came it would be signed and said that there were a couple of other forms the nurse needed to have her sign before she and her husband left. As he left, she got up and completed the task of emptying the overbed and bedside tables of her belongings.

N.: What time is John coming for you?

Pt.: 10:00. Can we go see the baby early?

N.: Yes. I stopped by on the way up here and told them you would be going home and asked if it would be all right for you to come by on your way home.

She seeks every possible supplemental bit of news about her baby

Pt.: What was he doing this morning when you were there?

N.: Sleeping. I think he had just been fed before I got there.

Pt.: Was that other baby still there?

N.: Yes, he's still there. And there is a new premature next to Joey, only this one is real tiny. Joey looked real big beside him.

Roommate's baby was brought in for feeding. As she fed her infant, Joanne looked steadily at how roommate was doing the feeding, handling and burping. Joanne turned to me and asked:

Pt.: Do you ever get nervous when you see mothers feeding or holding their babies?

N.: Yes I do, sometimes.

Roommate: Do I make you nervous?

N.: No, you seem to do real well in feeding and holding her.

Roommate (turned to Joanne): Do I make you nervous the way I do it?

Pt.: Not exactly.

N.: You'd just like to be doing it, huh Joanne?

Pt.: Uh huh. Just to hold and feed a baby. I wonder how long Joey will have to stay before I can come and take him home.

1. See, 2. Hold, 3. Feed

N.: I don't know, but my guess is a couple of weeks.

Pt.: I'm glad I got to hold him the other day. Seems like I can still feel him. (She rubbed her arms as she did Thursday when she made the same remark.)

N.: Do you think holding him the other day has helped you to know him a little bit?

Pt.: A little. He was so much smaller than he looked. His skin was so soft. . . . That was the first time you held him, too?

Less weight pull?

N.: Yes. I think I was almost as excited as you were.

Pt.: I thought you were never going to take him out and let me hold him after I got in the chair.

(About five minutes)

N.: You seemed so engrossed in just looking, I didn't want to rush you. Until Miss C. put the receiving blanket on your lap, you were sitting on the edge of the chair, not relaxed.

Pt.: How can some mothers not want to hold their babies or feed them?

(Not clear who she is referring to)

N.: I don't think many are that way. Many mothers are scared they'll do something wrong. If we just let the mother look first, like we did you, then let her touch and hold and eventually feed, she is usually more comfortable and then goes ahead, doing much more in the way of holding and feeding. Didn't you feel a little uncomfortable, anxious, holding Joey for the first time?

Pt.: Uh, huh. But he was so small.... I wonder where John is.

N.: It's only 10:00 o'clock. Maybe he's having trouble parking.

Pt.: He can't come in with Donna's baby here, can he?

N.: That's right. Why don't we walk down to the desk? He may be waiting there since the infants are out to their mothers.

We walked to the nurses' station, noted to the head nurse that we were expecting him and would she let us know when he came since babies were out. We returned past her room and on down the corridor to the full-term nursery. As we passed the mothers' feeding room, Joanne slowed down and looked in. There were about four mothers, their babies, and a nurse.

Pt.: What's that room?

N.: That's what is called the mothers' feeding room. Mothers that feel like it and want to go in there to feed their babies and visit.

Pt.: The chairs look real comfortable. I bought a rocking chair when I had Janis. It doesn't have as high a back, but it's comfortable.

We walked back to her room. Joanne dialed a number, apparently home, and apparently no answer: "He's not at home." She went into the bathroom saying she wanted to spray herself one more time before packing the spray. While she was in the bathroom I went out to the corridor to watch for Mr. H.

He soon came down the corridor with her dress on a hanger and a large bag under his arm. I met him, told him that the baby was still in the room and asked if I could take the clothes for Joanne. He removed a couple of packages from the bag and handed me the dress and the bag. He asked if Joanne could step out into the corridor; he needed to ask her something. I conveyed his message and Joanne soon came out of the bathroom, went out to the corridor, and returned, asking how long it would be before they'd come to pick up the baby.

Pt.: John doesn't want to leave until he can come in and talk with Donna.

We both returned to the corridor. John presented me with a gift and said he had something for Donna's baby, but he wanted to give it to her himself and would like to wait if it wouldn't be too long.

N.: Why not go to the desk now and sign the papers Dr. B. talked about and find out what else we have to do while we wait?

At this they started down the corridor, Joanne and her husband talking about why he was late, where he parked the car, etc. After the papers were signed and we were still at the desk:

Husband: Do you know how much you cost me?

Pt.: No. How much did it cost this time?

Husband: I don't know if you're worth it or not.

Pt.: Come on, how much? Quit teasing.

Husband: I told cashier that if it was over $1.50 to keep you. I couldn't afford any more. Know what she said? "How about stretching that just a little bit more?" I said, "Not much."

Pt.: How much, $2.00?

Husband: $1.60, that's all. And she gave me the bill for the baby up to today and the insurance is going to cover all of it. She said there may be a dollar or two, but not any large amount.

Pt. $1.60, that's not much. About the same as for Janis, huh?

Husband: That was phone calls.

N.: You must have good insurance coverage.

Husband: Should: we pay enough and haven't used it except for her when she's had the children. It's worth it, though.

N.: Why not go to the nursery now? They haven't picked up Donna's baby yet but they will by the time we get back and you can visit with Donna.

Husband: That's a good idea. Can we go before 11:00?

Pt.: Miss M. told them I was going home this morning and they said we could come down before we left. And we have to sign the circumcision permit before we leave the nursery.

I returned with the wheelchair, Joanne got in, and husband pushed her to elevator and to nursery. As we got to the nursery, an L.P.N. was feeding the baby by holding his head with one hand (thumb on one side of his face and finger on other side, holding his head as in a vise). A diaper was draped like a bib practically covering the baby so that only the feet showed.

Some feeders do make one "nervous"

Pt.: Why does she hold him like that?

N.: It must be easier for her to feed babies like that rather than cradling them in her arms, close to her body.

Pt.: That's the way I held mine: close to me.

"Like", "not like"

About this time the infant let the formula run back out of his mouth.

Pt.: Oh. He's spitting it out.

N.: Maybe had enough. He's taken a good bit. That's a two-ounce container she has and he has just about taken all of it.

Joanne walked over to see the other (sick) baby. Husband and I both noted that Joey had his eyes open, and told her she better come look. As she returned:

Event

Pt.: He really had them open last night, didn't he Miss M.?

N.: Yes, he was wide awake when we were down.

Joanne then looked at the new premature next to her infant. Her husband looked, too.

Pt.: How much does that one weigh?

Husband: Two pounds. Is that about right, Miss M.?

N.: I would guess between two and three. Isn't he tiny?

Pt.: Uh huh. Joey looks big beside him.

Husband: How much does one of those things cost?

N.: About $1200; some cost more: it depends on the extras you get. See the one the tiny baby is in has another gadget on it that costs several hundred more.

Pt.: We gave to that research fund each time we've had a baby here. The first time, when our Johnny was in here, he was in some special nursery where they were testing to see whether boys or girls had more germs and they had just six babies in a nursery. One nurse cared for the six babies each shift and the doctors couldn't go in the nursery. They had to take the baby into another room or something when they wanted to examine them.

Husband: We're glad to give them some money if it will help some baby.

The L.P.N. was returning the baby back to the Isolette. As they watched, I went to get today's weight and the circumcision permit. As they completed signing the permit, Joanne abruptly turned away from the window, said, "Better go," and walked out to where the wheelchair had been left and got in it.

When we got back to the room, Mr. H. gave Donna her gift. While husband and roommate were exchanging comments, Joanne was dressing: green shift, hose and girdle, black low-heeled shoes and black sweater over shoulders. We then gathered her belongings and placed what we could in the bag. We helped her into the wheelchair and she and roommate said goodbyes, exchanged phone numbers, invitations to visit, and such. Joanne was quiet as we went down the corridor. As we neared the reception room on the main floor, she turned to look at her husband:

Pt.: Feel like I've forgotten something without a baby this time. Everytime before, had a baby. (Voice cracked.)

Husband said something to the effect that they were still lucky to have one that the doctor said was healthy. "That's what we wanted: a healthy normal baby."

Joanne looked toward me. There were tears in her eyes.

N.: Hard to go home without him, isn't it?

Pt.: Um. . . . (nodded)

N.: It won't be too many days and you will be taking him home.

As we waited for husband to bring the car around to the door, Joanne sat in the wheelchair, hands folded loosely in her lap, then one hand would go to her face then back again to her lap.

Pt.: I wish I'd had him bring the other children.

N.: Do you think it would make it easier?

Pt.: I guess not. I've missed them so much I'd probably cry just seeing them. . . . I just feel like I've forgotten something.

N.: You haven't really forgotten. You're just leaving someone who is very precious to you, to grow a little more, then you can come get him.

She was quiet for quite a few minutes.

Pt.: I have a lot to keep me busy for the next few days and John will be home. I need to get things ready for the baby and have sewing and mending to do for the other children and myself.

Car arrived. Helped her into car, exchanging goodbyes and plans for meeting them when they come to visit the baby next week.

Discussion

There are no typical patients, but this one shows the typical normative postpartal pattern of behavior. The first two days after delivery are in the taking-in mode: taking-in the service of restoration of food (ate everything on her tray), sleep (slept or napped at every opportunity), and contact care that reintegrates body boundaries (bath, perineal care, and back rubs). This is a passive-receptive stage, too tired to be aggressive about anything that is not very important to her. She also takes-in in the service of assimilating the events of the recent labor and delivery. She reviews the events before and during labor, ordering the chaos of the unexpected, and uses as much information as she can obtain from others to form a picture (cognitive map) of the condition, intactness, completeness, and appearance of her baby. Secondary information is not enough, however. She must see, take-in visually, her infant for herself.

On the third day, she is sweaty and tired, her stitches are now painful, the abdominal distension and gas are troublesome. She has no complaints, but has some hostility about less than generous nurses. In the companionship of a roommate and in shared experience, the hostility is resolved in laughter. The hostility about self is manifest in the disparaging comments about being on vacation, an unpleasurable vacation, stuck and trapped. This normally energetic and independent woman does not welcome immobility and dependency. Even though she held her baby, there is fatigue and depression. She could not sleep that night, even with pain relief. As much as she likes to talk, she and her roommate took refuge behind a book with their private thoughts during the remaining night hours.

The bowel movement with the return of normal functioning is a turning point. It's hard to say why, but a woman who has a bowel movement by herself and in copious amount on the third day has a return of pleasure in herself. Joanne had *two* bowel movements. The change is remarkable. The increased mobility (up and down the corridors) and social space (visited with patient across corridor, mentally exploring the experience of other women like but unlike her experience), and the situation of another infant are almost dramatic in change of pace and scope. The change continues and she shows more competence, more control, and more organization skills. This is preceded by a review of how she has organized the household to accommodate the children's need for play materials and the adults' need for a place to live, how she handles a child's desire to go to school but not to miss out on anything at home. Her organization of Miss Moulton into continued attendance was as superb as her acceptance of the disappointment of going home earlier and being ready to go home way before it was necessary. She doesn't keep her husband waiting.

With the experience of multiparity, she has ensured a week of rest for personal recovery. Even though she is not coming home with a baby, her husband will be at home and her children will stay with her mother for a week.

Her twice-stated possible causation of premature delivery should not be ignored. Mourning does not stop with a funeral. It requires time for one's self. Her mother left two or three days before Joanne got the crib downstairs and stopped in the store for a new sanitary belt. Loss and loneliness is a theme throughout, not only for her children but for the woman in a private room and for women in the abstract who have stillborns. She's "lucky" when she is not alone.

Her family and support system at this point in her life:

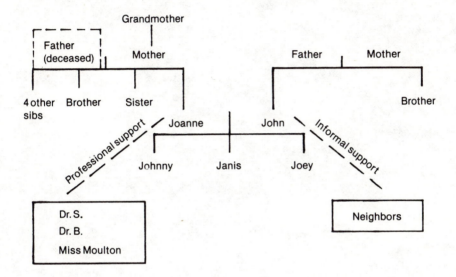

References and Bibliography

Ainsworth, M.D.S., "The Development of Infant-Mother Attachment," in B.M. Cladwell and H.N. Ricciuti, eds., *Review of Child Development Research, III,* Chicago: University of Chicago Press, 1974.

Arieti, S., "The Experiences of Inner Status," in Kaplan and Wapner, eds., *Perspectives in Psychological Theory,* New York: International Universities Press, 1960.

Barnett, C. et al., "Neonatal Separation: The Maternal Side of Interactional Deprivation," *Pediatrics,* 45: 197–205, 1970.

Babcock, C., "Food and Its Emotional Significance," *Journal of the American Dietetic Association,* 24: 390–393, 1948.

Bell S. and Ainsworth, M., "Infant Crying and Maternal Responsiveness," *Child Development,* 43: 1171–1191, 1972.

Bell, N.W. and Vogel, E.F., *A Modern Introduction to the Family,* New York: Free Press, 1976.

Benedek, T., "The Psychosomatic Implications of the Primary Unit: Mother–Child," *American Journal of Orthopsychiatry,* 19: 642–645, 1949.

———, "Psychobiological Aspects of Mothering," *American Journal of Orthopsychiatry,* 26: 272–278, 1956.

———, *Psychosexual Functions in Women,* New York: Ronald Press, 1952.

———, "Parenthood as a Developmental Phase," *Journal of the American Psychoanalytic Association,* 7: 389–417, 1959.

———, "On the Psychic Economy of Developmental Processes," *Archives of General Psychiatry,* 17: 271–276, 1967.

———, "Motherhood and Nurturing," in E.J. Anthony and T. Benedek, eds., *Parenthood: Its Psychology and Psychopathology,* Boston: Little, Brown and Co., 1970.

Benedict, R., "Child Rearing in Certain European Countries," *American Journal of Orthopsychiatry,* 19: 342–348, 1949.

Bibring, G., "Some Considerations of the Psychological Processes in Pregnancy," *Psychoanalytic Study of the Child,* 14: 113–121, 1959.

Bibring, G. et al., "A Study of the Psychological Processes in Pregnancy of the Earliest Mother–Child Relationship," *Psychoanalytic Study of the Child,* 16: 9–72, 1961.

Blake, F., *The Child, His Parents, and the Nurse,* Philadelphia: J. B. Lippincott Co., 1954.

Blos, P., *On Adolescence,* New York: The Free Press of Glencoe, 1962.

———, "Second Individuation Process of Adolescence," *Psychoanalytic Study of the Child,* 22: 162–186, 1967.

Bowlby, John, *Maternal Care and Mental Health and Deprivation of Maternal Care,* New York: Shocken Books, 1966.

———, *Attachment and Loss,* Vols. I, II, New York: Basic Books, Inc., 1969.

———, *Attachment and Loss,* Vol. III: Loss, New York: Basic Books, Inc., 1980.

Brody, S., *Patterns of Mothering,* New York: International Universities Press, 1956.

Bronfenbrenner, U., "Socialization and Social Class Through Time and Space," *Readings in Social Psychology,* T.M. Newcomb and E.H. Hartley, eds., New York: Holt and Co., 400–425, 1958.

Bruner, J. S., Goodnow, J. and Austin, G., *A Study of Thinking,* New York: Science Editors, 1962.

Burlingame, D., "Some Notes on the Development of the Blind," *Psychoanalytic Study of the Child,* XVI: 212–245, 1961.

Bychowski, G., "Disorders in the Body Image," *Journal Nervous and Mental Disorders,* 97: 310–335, 1943.

Caplan, G., "Mental Health Aspects of Social Work in Public Health," University of California: *Proceedings of School of Social Welfare,* 1955.

———, "Psychological Aspects of Maternity Care," *The American Journal of Public Health,* January 1957.

———, "Patterns of Parental Response to the Crisis of Premature Birth," *Psychiatry,* 23: 365–374, 1960.

Chandrabha, V., *Effect of Sleep on the Mood of Postpartum Women,* Unpublished Ph.D. dissertation, University of Pittsburgh, 1975.

Chao, Yu-Mei, "Cognitive Operations During Early Maternal Role Enactment," *Maternal-Child Nursing Journal,* Monograph 8, 1979.

Chertok, L., *Motherhood and Personality,* Philadelphia, J.B. Lippincott Co., 1969.

Coleman, R. et al., "The Study of Variations in Early Parental Attitudes," *Psychoanalytic Study of the Child,* 8: 20–47, 1953.

Colman, A., "Psychological State During First Pregnancy," *American Journal of Orthopsychiatry,* 39: 788–797, 1969.

Committee on Adolescence, Group for the Advancement of Psychiatry, *Normal Adolescence: Its Dynamics and Impact,* New York: Charles Scribner's Sons, 1968.

Coppen, A., "Psychosomatic Aspects of Pre-eclamptic Toxemia," *Journal of Psychosomatic Research,* 2: 241–265, 1958.

Daedalus, Journal of American Academy of Arts and Science, Spring, 1977.

Kagan, J., "The Child and the Family," pp. 35–56.

Hareven, T., "Family Time and Historical Time," pp. 57–70.

Sawhill, I., "Economic Perspectives on the Family," pp. 115–126.

Dement, W. C., "Sleep Deprivation and the Organization of Behavior States," in Clemente, C. D. et al., *Sleep and the Maturing Nervous System,* New York: Academic Press, 1972.

Deutsch, H., "The Significance of Masochism in the Mental Life of Women," *International Journal of Psychoanalysis,* 11: 52, 1930.

———, *Psychology of Women,* Vols. I, II, New York: Grune and Stratton, 1944.

———, "Some Psychoanalytic Observations in Surgery," *Psychosomatic Medicine,* 4: 105–115, 1942.

———, "Selected Problems of Adolescence," *The Psychoanalytic Study of the Child,* Monograph 3, New York: International Universities Press, 1967.

Dunbar, J., "Maternal Contact Behaviors with Newborn Infants," *Maternal-Child Nursing Journal,* Monograph 6, 1977.

Engel, G:, "Grief and Grieving," *American Journal of Nursing,* 64: 93–98, 1964.

Erikson, E., "The Problem of Ego Identity," *Journal of the American Psychoanalytic Association,* 4: 77–88, 1956.

———, "The Problem of Ego Identity," *Psychological Issues,* I, No. 1, Monograph 1: 101–164, 1959.

———, *Childhood and Society,* 2nd edition, New York: W. W. Norton & Co., 1963.

———, *Insight and Responsibility,* New York: W. W. Norton & Co., 1964.

———, "Inner and Outer Space: Reflections of Womanhood," *Daedalus,* Spring 1964, pp. 582–606.

———, *Identity, Youth and Crisis,* New York: W. W. Norton & Co., 1968.

Escalona, S., "The Psychological Situation of Mother and Child Upon Return From the Hospital," in M. Seen, ed., *Problems of Infancy and Childhood: Third Conference,* New York: Josiah Macy, Jr. Foundation, pp. 30–94, 1959.

———, *The Roots of Individuality,* Chicago: Aldine Publishing Co., 1968.

Festinger, L., *A Theory of Cognitive Dissonance,* Chicago: Row, Peterson, 1957.

Fisher, S. and Cleveland, S., "Body Image Boundaries and Sexual Behavior," *The Journal of Psychology,* 45: 207–211, 1958.

Flugel, J., *Psychoanalytic Study of the Family,* London: Hogarth Press, 1950.

———, *The Psychology of Clothes,* New York: International Universities Press, 1969.

Frank, L. K., "Tactile Experiences in Personality Development," *Genetic Psychology Monographs,* 56: 223–265, 1963.

Freud, A. and Burlingame, D., *Young Children in Wartime,* New York: International Universities Press, 1942.

Freud, S., "A Note Upon the Mystic Writing-Pad," in Rapport, D., ed., *Organization and Pathology of Thought,* New York: Columbia University Press, 1951.

————, *The Interpretation of Dreams,* New York: Basic Books, 1956.

Gedo, J. E., "Unmarried Motherhood: A Paradigmatic Single Case Study," *The International Journal of Psychoanalysis,* XLVI: Part 3, 1965.

Gillman, R., "The Dreams of Pregnant Women and Maternal Adaptation," *American Journal of Orthopsychiatry,* 38: 688–692, July 1968.

Greenacre, P., "Early Determinants in the Development of the Sense of Identity," *Journal of the American Psychoanalytic Association,* VI: 612–627, 1958.

————, "Considerations Regarding the Parent-Infant Relationship," *Emotional Growth,* Vol. I, New York: International Universities Press, Chapter 13, 1971.

Grimm, E. and Venet, W., "The Relationship of Emotional Attitudes to the Course and Outcome of Pregnancy," *Psychosomatic Medicine,* 28: 34, 1966.

Grimm, E., "Women's Attitudes and Reactions to Childbearing," in George Goldman and Donald Milman, eds. *Modern Woman: Her Psychology and Sexuality,* Springfield, Ill.: Charles C. Thomas, 1969, pp. 129–151.

Gring, M., "A Multipara's Sustained Belief in her Pseudocyetic Pregnancy," *Maternal-Child Nursing Journal,* 1: 199–230, 1972.

Grubb, C., "Body Image Concerns of a Multipara in the Situation of Intrauterine Fetal Death," *Maternal-Child Nursing Journal,* 5: 93–117, 1976.

————, "Perceptions of Time by Multiparous Women in Relation to Themselves and Others During the First Postpartal Month," *Maternal-Child Nursing Journal,* Monograph 10, 1980.

Goode, W. J., "Industrialization and the Family Structure," in N.W. Bell and E.F. Vogel, eds., *A Modern Introduction to the Family,* New York: Free Press, 113–120, 1960.

Harlow, H. et al., "Manipulatory Motivation in Monkeys," in Kuhlen, R. G. and Thompson, G. C., eds., *Psychological Studies of Human Development,* New York: Appleton-Century-Crofts, 1963.

Hellman, L. and Pritchard, J., *Williams Obstetrics,* 15th edition, New York: Appleton-Century Crofts, 1976.

Hess, E. H., "Imprinting: An Effect of Early Experience," in Kuhlen, R.G. and Thompson, G.C. eds., *Psychological Studies of Human Development,* New York: Appleton-Century-Crofts, 1963.

Hoffer, W., "Development of the Body Ego," *Psychoanalytic Study of the Child,* Vol. 5, New York: International Universities Press, 1950, pp. 18–23.

Horowitz, M. J., "Body Buffer Zone," *Archives of General Psychiatry,* Vol. II, December 1964.

Inhelder, B., "Criteria of the Stages of Mental Development," in Kuhlen, R. G. and Thompson, G. C., eds., *Psychological Studies of Human Development,* New York: Appleton-Century-Crofts, 1963.

Josselyn, I., *Adolescent and His World,* New York: Family Service Association, 1954.

Kestenberg, J., "On the Development of Maternal Feelings in Early Childhood," *Psychoanalytic Study of the Child,* Vol. 11, New York: International Universities Press, 1956, pp. 257–291.

——, "Phases of Adolescence, Part I: Antecedents of Adolescent Organization in Childhood," *Journal of the American Academy of Child Psychiatry,* VI: 426–463, 1967.

Kikuchi, J. F., "Assimilative and Accommodative Responses of Mothers to Their Newborn Infants with Congenital Defects," *Maternal-Child Nursing Journal,* Monograph 9, 1980.

Kirkpatrick, C., *The Family as Process and Institution,* New York: Ronald Press, 1963.

Klaus, M. and Kennel, J., *Maternal-Infant Bonding,* St. Louis: The C. V. Mosby Co., 1976.

Kleitman, N., *Sleep and Wakefulness,* Chicago: University of Chicago Press, 1963.

Langer, J., "Werner's Theory of Development," in Mussen, P., ed., *Carmichael's Manual of Child Psychology,* Vol. 1, New York: John Wiley & Sons, 1970.

Lazarsfeld, P. F. and Rosenberg, M., *Language of Social Research,* New York: The Free Press, 1955.

Levi-Strauss, C., "The Family," in H. L. Shapiro, ed., *Men, Culture, and Society,* New York: Oxford University Press, 1970.

Lewis, M. and Rosenblum, L., eds., *The Effect of the Infant on its Caregiver,* New York: John Wiley & Sons, 1974.

Lewis, Oscar, *Anthropological Essays,* New York: Random House, 1970.

Lindemann, E., "Symptomatology and Management of Acute Grief," *American Journal of Psychiatry,* 101: 141–148, 1944.

Lindzey, G. and Borgatta, E., "Sociometric Measurement," in Lindzey, G., ed., *Handbook of Social Psychology,* Vol. 1, Reading, Mass.: Addison-Wesley, 1954.

Linn, L., "Some Developmental Aspects of the Body Image," *International Journal Psycho-Analysis,* 36: 36–42, 1955.

Linton, R., "The Natural History of the Family," in Anshen, R., ed., *The Family: Its Function and Destiny,* New York: Harper and Bros., 1947.

Magoun, H. W., *The Waking Brain,* Springfield, Ill.: Charles C. Thomas, 1958.

Mahler, Margaret, Pine, Fred and Bergman, Anni, *The Psychological Birth of the Human Infant Symbiosis and Individuation,* New York: Basic Books, 1975.

Mahmoud, A., *Maternal Development of Object Constancy for the Newborn Infant,* unpublished doctoral dissertation, University of Pittsburgh, 1979.

Mason, R. E., *Internal Perception and Bodily Functioning,* New York: International Universities Press, 1961, pp. 57–149, 253–274, 356–399.

May, Robert, *Sex and Fantasy: Patterns of Male and Female Development,* New York: W. W. Norton & Co., 1980.

Mead, G. H., *Mind, Self and Society,* Chicago: University of Chicago Press, 1934.

McConnell, O. and Daston, P., "Body Image Changes in Pregnancy," *Journal of Projective Techniques*, 25: 451–456, 1968.

Melzack, R., "The Perception of Pain," *Psychobiology: The Biological Basis of Behavior*, San Francisco: W. H. Freeman, 1966.

Mercer, R., "Responses of Five Multigravidae to the Event of the Birth of an Infant with a Defect," *Nursing Research*, 23: 133–137, 1974.

———, "Mother's Responses to Their Infants with Defects," *Nursing Research*, 23: 133–137, 1974.

Olmstead, M. S., *The Small Group*, New York: Random House, 1959.

Papez, J. W., "Visceral Brain," *Journal Nervous and Mental Disorders*, 1958.

Parsons, T. and Bales, R. F., *Family, Socialization and Interaction Process*, Glencoe, Ill.: The Free Press, 1955.

Piaget, Jean, *The Language and Thought of the Child*, New York: Harcourt, Brace, 1926.

———, *The Origins of Intelligence in Children*, New York: International Universities Press, 1952.

———, *Genetic Epistemology*, New York: Columbia University Press, 1970.

———, "Piaget's Theory," in Mussen, P., ed., *Carmichael's Manual of Child Psychology*, Vol. 1, New York: John Wiley & Sons, 1970.

———, *The Development of Thought: Equilibration of Cognitive Structures*, New York: The Viking Press, 1977.

———, *The Child and Reality*, New York: Grossman, 1973.

Pribram, K. S., "The New Neurology: Memory, Novelty, Thought and Choice," in Glaser, G. H., ed., *E.E.G. and Behavior*, New York: Basic Books, 1963.

———, "Reinforcement Revisited: A Structural View," in Jones, M., ed., *Nebraska Symposium on Motivation*, Vol. XI, Lincoln: University of Nebraska Press, 1963.

———, "Emotion: Steps Toward a Neuropsychological Theory," in Glass, D. C., ed., *Neurophysiology and Emotion*, New York: Rockefeller University Press, 1967.

Proshansky, H., Ittelson, W. and Rivlin, L., *Environmental Psychology*, New York: Holt, Rinehart and Winston, 1970.

Rapaport, D., *Emotions and Memory*, New York: Science Editions, 1964.

Reid, D. E., Ryan, K. J. and Benirschke, K., *Principles and Management of Human Reproduction*, Philadelphia: W. B. Saunders Co., 1972.

Rich, O. J., "Temporal and Spatial Experience of Multiparous Women During Labor," *Maternal-Child Nursing Journal*, Monograph 2, 1973.

Richardson, P., "Approach and Avoidance Behaviors by Women in Labor Toward Others," *Maternal-Child Nursing Journal*, 8: 1–21, 1979.

———, "Women's Perceptions of Their Important Dyadic Relationships During Pregnancy," *Maternal-Child Nursing Journal*, 10: 159–174, 1981.

Ritvo, S., "Adolescent to Woman," *Journal of the American Psychoanalytic Association*, 24, 5: 127–137, Supplement, 1976.

Rochlin, G., "The Dread of Abandonment: A Contribution to the Etiology of the Loss Complex and to Depression," *Psychoanalytic Study of the Child*, 16: 451–470, 1961.

——, *Grief and Discontent,* Boston: Little, Brown and Co., 1968.

Rubin, R., "Basic Maternal Behavior," *Nursing Outlook,* 9: 683–687, 1961. (a)

——, "Puerperal Change," *Nursing Outlook,* 9: 753–755, December, 1961. (b)

——, "Maternal Touch," *Nursing Outlook,* 11: 828–831, 1963.

——, "Behavioral Definitions in Nursing Therapy," *Conference on Maternal-Child Nursing,* Columbus, Ohio: Ross Laboratories, 1964.

——, "Attainment of the Maternal Role: Part I, Processes," *Nursing Research,* 16, No. 3: 1967. (a)

——, "Attainment of the Maternal Role: Part II, Models and Referrents," *Nursing Research,* 16: 237–245, 1967. (b)

——, "Food and Feeding: A Matrix of Relationships," *Nursing Forum,* 6, No. 2: 195–205, 1967. (c)

——, "The Neomaternal Period," in Bergerson, B., ed., *Current Concepts in Clinical Nursing,* St. Louis: C. V. Mosby, 1967. (d)

——, "A Theory of Clinical Nursing," *Nursing Research* 17, (6), May–June, 1968. (a)

——, "Body Image and Self-esteem," *Nursing Outlook,* 16: 20–23, 1968. (b)

——, "Cognitive Style in Pregnancy," *American Journal of Nursing,* 70, No. 3: 1970.

——, "Fantasy and Object Constancy in Maternal Relations," *Maternal-Child Nursing Journal,* No. 2: 101–111, 1972.

——, "Maternal Tasks in Pregnancy," *Maternal-Child Nursing Journal,* 5, No. 3: 1975.

——, "Binding-in in the Postpartum Period," *Maternal-Child Nursing Journal,* 6: 67–75, 1977.

——, "Two Psychological Aspects of Childbearing," in Lonstegard, et al., eds., *Women's Health,* Vol. 2, New York: Grune and Stratton, 1983.

Rubin, R., and Erickson, F., "Research in Clinical Nursing," *Maternal-Child Nursing Journal,* 6: 151–164, Fall 1977.

Rosenzweig, N., "Affect System: Foresight and Fantasy," *Journal of Nervous and Mental Disorders,* 127: 113–118, 1958.

Santayana, George, *Realms of Being,* New York: Charles Scribner's Sons, 1942.

Sarbin, T. R., "Role Theory," in Lindzey, G., *Handbook of Social Psychology,* Vol. 1, Reading, Mass.: Addison-Wesley, 1954.

Schilder, P., *Brain and Personality,* New York: International Universities Press, 1969.

——, *The Image and Appearance of the Human Body,* New York: International Universities Press, 1970.

Sears, R. R. et al., "The Child Rearing Process," in Kuhlen, R. G. and Thompson, G. C., eds., *Psychological Studies of Human Development,* New York: Appleton-Century-Crofts, 1963.

Senn, M. and Hartford, C., eds., *The Newborn: Experience of Eight American Families,* Cambridge: Harvard University Press, 1968.

Shontz, F. E., *Perceptual and Cognitive Aspects of Body Experience,* New York: Academic Press, Chapters 1, 2, 4, 1969.

Simmel, G., "Dyads and Triad," in *Sociology of George Simmel*, New York: The Free Press of Glencoe, 1950, pp. 122–128, 135–136.

Simmel, M. L., "Developmental Aspects of the Body Schema," *Child Development,* 37: 83–95, 1966.

Spitz, R., "Anaclitic Depression," *Psychoanalytic Study of the Child,* 1, 1945.

Sugar, Max, "Normal Adolescent Mourning," *American Journal of Psychotherapy,* XXII: 258–269, 1968.

Sorensen, Robert C., *Adolescent Sexuality in Contemporary America,* New York: World Publishing Co., 1973, pp. 127–213.

Sullivan, H. S., *Conceptions of Modern Psychiatry,* Washington, D.C.: William A. White Psychiatric Foundation, 1947.

Szasz, T. S., *Pain and Pleasure: A Study of Bodily Feelings,* New York: Basic Books, 1957.

Wapner, S. and Werner, H., *The Body Percept,* New York: Random House, 1965.

Watson, J. M. Sr., *Four Behavioral Patterns of the Ego of Multigravidous Women During Labor,* unpublished doctoral dissertation, University of Pittsburgh, 1971.

Weick, K. E., "Systematic Observational Methods," in Lindzey, G. and Aronson, E., eds., *The Handbook of Social Psychology,* Vol. II, 2nd edition, Reading, Massachusetts: Addison-Wesley, 1968.

Werner, H., *Comparative Psychology of Mental Development,* New York: International Universities Press, 1957.

White, S., "Learning Theory Approach," in Mussen, P., ed., *Carmichael's Manual of Child Psychology,* Vol. 1, New York: John Wiley & Sons, 1970.

Wolff, P., "Mother-Infant Relations at Birth," in Howell, J., ed., *Modern Perspectives in International Child Psychiatry,* 1971, pp. 80–97.

Wright, R. W., "Motivation Reconsidered," *Psychological Review,* Vol. 66, 1959.

Zelditch, M. Jr., "Role Differentiation in the Nuclear Family: A Comparative Study," *A Modern Introduction to the Family,* N. W. Bell and E. F. Vogel, eds., New York: The Free Press, 1960.

Index